A+® Fast Pass

David Groth

Faithe Wempen

San Francisco • London

SYBEX

Associate Publisher: Neil Edde
Acquisitions Editor: Elizabeth Hurley Peterson
Developmental Editor: Colleen Wheeler Strand
Production Editor: Susan Berge
Technical Editor: Craig Vazquez
Copyeditor: Tiffany Taylor
Compositor/Graphic Illustrator: Scott Benoit
CD Coordinator: Dan Mummert
CD Technician: Kevin Ly
Proofreaders: Amey Garber, Eric Lach, Laurie O'Connell, Nancy Riddiough
Indexer: Ted Laux
Book Designer: Bill Gibson
Cover Design and Illustration: Richard Miller, Calyx Design

Library of Congress Card Number: 2003106718

ISBN: 0-7821-4259-1

How to Become CompTIA Certified:

This training material can help you prepare for and pass a related CompTIA certification exam or exams. In order to achieve CompTIA certification, you must register for and pass a CompTIA certification exam or exams.

In order to become CompTIA certified, you must:

(1) Select a certification exam provider. For more information please visit http://www.comptia.org/certification/test_locations.htm.
(2) Register for and schedule a time to take the CompTIA certification exam(s) at a convenient location.
(3) Read and sign the Candidate Agreement, which will be presented at the time of the exam(s). The text of the Candidate Agreement can be found at www.comptia.org/certification
(4) Take and pass the CompTIA certification exam(s).

For more information about CompTIA's certifications, such as their industry acceptance, benefits, or program news, please visit www.comptia.org/certification

CompTIA is a non-profit information technology (IT) trade association. CompTIA's certifications are designed by subject matter experts from across the IT industry. Each CompTIA certification is vendor-neutral, covers multiple technologies, and requires demonstration of skills and knowledge widely sought after by the IT industry.

To contact CompTIA with any questions or comments:
Please call + 1 630 268 1818
questions@comptia.org

Manufactured in the United States of America

10 9 8 7 6 5 4

Software License Agreement: Terms and Conditions

To Margaret, for the usual reasons

Acknowledgments

Many thanks to the Sybex editorial team, one of the best in the business and always a pleasure to work with.

Contents

Introduction

The A+ certification program was developed by the Computer Technology Industry Association (CompTIA) to provide an industry-wide means of certifying the competency of computer service technicians. The A+ certification, which is granted to those who have attained the level of knowledge and troubleshooting skills that are needed to provide capable support in the field of personal computers, is similar to other certifications in the computer industry. For example, Novell offers the Certified NetWare Engineer (CNE) program to provide the same recognition for network professionals who deal with its NetWare products, and Microsoft has its Microsoft Certified Systems Engineer (MCSE) program. The theory behind these certifications is that if you need to have service performed on any of their products, you would sooner call a technician who has been certified in one of the appropriate programs than you would just call the first so-called expert in the phone book.

CompTIA's A+ exam objectives are periodically updated to keep the exam applicable to the most recent hardware and software. This is necessary because a technician must be able to work on the latest equipment. The most recent revisions to the objectives, active as of late 2003, are reflected in this book. The objectives themselves have not been altered dramatically since the last revision in 2001, but the wording has been clarified and the example topics have been updated to include the latest hardware, Windows Millennium Edition (Me), and Windows XP.

This book and the Sybex *A+ Complete Study Guide* are tools to help you prepare for this new exam—and for the new focuses of a modern computer technician's job.

What Is A+ Certification?

The A+ certification program was created to offer a wide-ranging certification, in the sense that it is intended to certify competence with personal computers from many different makers/vendors. You must pass two tests to become A+ certified:

- The A+ Core Hardware Service Technician exam, which covers basic computer concepts, hardware troubleshooting, customer service, and hardware upgrading

- The A+ Operating System Technologies exam, which covers several versions of the Windows operating system

You don't have to take the Core Hardware and Operating System Technologies exams at the same time; you have 90 days from the time you pass one test to pass the second test. The A+ certified "diploma" is not awarded until you've passed both tests. For the latest pricing on the exams and updates to the registration procedures, call Prometric at (866) Prometric (776-6387) or (800) 77-MICRO (776-4276). You can also go to either www.2test.com or www.prometric.com for additional information or to register online. If you have further questions about the scope of the exams or related CompTIA programs, refer to the CompTIA website at www.comptia.org/.

Is This Book for You?

A+ Fast Pass is designed to be a succinct, portable exam review guide that can be used either in conjunction with a more complete study program (book, CBT courseware, classroom/lab environment) or as an exam review for those who don't feel the need for more extensive test preparation. It isn't our goal to give the answers away, but rather to identify those topics on which you can expect to be tested and to provide sufficient coverage of these topics.

Perhaps you've been working with information technologies for years now. The thought of paying lots of money for a specialized IT exam-preparation course probably doesn't sound too appealing. What can they teach you that you don't already know, right? Be careful, though. Many experienced network administrators have walked confidently into the test center only to walk sheepishly out of it after failing an IT exam. After you've finished reading this book, you should have a clear idea of how your understanding of the technologies involved matches up with the expectations of the A+ test makers.

Or perhaps you're relatively new to the world of IT, drawn to it by the promise of challenging work and higher salaries. You've just waded through an 800-page study guide or taken a class at a local training center. Lots of information to keep track of, isn't it? Well, by organizing the *Fast Pass* book according to CompTIA's exam objectives, and by breaking up the information into concise, manageable pieces, we've created what we think is the handiest exam review guide available. Throw it in your briefcase and carry it to work with you. As you read the book, you'll be able to quickly identify those areas you know best and those that require a more in-depth review.

The goal of the *Fast Pass* series is to help A+ candidates brush up on the subjects on which they can expect to be tested in the A+ exams. For complete in-depth coverage of the technologies and topics involved, we recommend the *A+ Complete Study Guide* from Sybex.

How Is This Book Organized?

This book is organized according to the official objectives list prepared by CompTIA for the A+ exam. The chapters correspond with the broad objective groupings, such as Installation and Upgrading, Networks, Configuration, and Diagnosing and Troubleshooting.

Within each chapter, the individual exam objectives are addressed in turn. Each objective's section is further divided into Critical Information, Exam Essentials, and Review Questions:

Critical Information   The Critical Information section presents the greatest level of detail on information that is relevant to the objective. This is the place to start if you're unfamiliar with or uncertain about the technical issues related to the objective.

Exam Essentials   Here you are given a short list of topics that you should explore fully before taking the test. Included in the Exam Essentials areas are notations of the key information you should have taken out of the *A+ Complete Study Guide* or the Critical Information section.

Review Questions   This section ends every chapter and provides 10 questions to help you gauge your mastery of the chapter.

The A+ Core Hardware Service Technician Exam Objectives

The following are the areas (or *domains*, according to CompTIA) in which you must be proficient in order to pass the A+ Core Hardware Service Technician exam:

Domain 1: Installation, Configuration, and Upgrading   This content area deals with the installation, configuration, and upgrading of common computer Field Replaceable Units (FRUs). Most technicians spend a lot of time performing these operations. Toward that end, CompTIA has made sure that questions from this content area make up 35 percent of the exam.

Domain 2: Diagnosing and Troubleshooting   Before a technician can install or upgrade a component, he or she must determine which component needs to be replaced. A technician normally uses the skills addressed by the diagnosing and troubleshooting content areas to make that determination. Questions about these two topics together make up 21 percent of the exam.

Domain 3: PC Preventive Maintenance, Safety, and Environmental Issues   Most people don't think of computer service as a dangerous job. Most often, safety precautions are taken to prevent damage to the computer's components. In actuality, a few components can cause severe injury if improperly handled. This topic also covers maintaining and cleaning computer components. Questions about these topics constitute 5 percent of the exam.

Domain 4: Motherboard/Processors/Memory   Several of the items in this content area give people the most problems (for example, learning the differences between the various types of processors). This content area makes up 11 percent of the exam.

Domain 5: Printers   Although there are only two objectives here and the questions on printers make up 9 percent of the test, printer problems are extremely common and can cause no end of trouble. Therefore, you should be prepared to deal with all facets of troubleshooting printer hardware. Printer software issues are dealt with in the OS exam.

Domain 6: Basic Networking   With the explosion of the Internet into the service world, the line between service technicians and networking technicians has blurred. Frequently, computers that are brought in for service have problems that are related to their networking hardware. An A+ certified technician should know how both the hardware and software components of networking can affect the operation of the computer. CompTIA has put basic networking concepts on the A+ Core Hardware exam, and they make up 19 percent of the total exam questions.

Operating System Technologies Exam Objectives

The following are the areas in which you must be proficient in order to pass the A+ Operating System Technologies exam:

Domain 1: Operating System Fundamentals   This domain requires knowledge of the Windows 95/98/Me, Windows NT 4, Windows 2000, and Windows XP operating systems. You need to know how they work, as well as the components that compose them. You also need to understand topics relating to navigating the operating systems and, in general, how to use them. Operating system fundamentals make up 28 percent of the exam.

Domain 2: Installation, Configuration, and Upgrading   This domain basically tests your knowledge of the day-to-day servicing of operating systems. This includes topics such as installing, configuring, and upgrading the various operating systems. You are also expected to know system boot sequences. These topics make up 31 percent of the exam.

Domain 3: Diagnosing and Troubleshooting   Questions in this domain test your ability to diagnose and troubleshoot Windows 9x/Me/NT/2000/XP systems and make up 25 percent of the test.

Domain 4: Networks   This domain requires knowledge of the network capabilities of Windows 9x/Me/2000/XP and how to connect to networks. It includes the Internet, its capabilities, basic concepts relating to Internet access, and generic procedures for system setup. Network questions make up 16 percent of the exam.

How to Contact the Publisher

Sybex welcomes feedback on all of its titles. Visit the Sybex website at www.sybex.com for book updates and additional certification information. You'll also find forms you can use to submit comments or suggestions regarding this or any other Sybex title.

The A+ Exam Objectives

Throughout this book, we've used abridged versions of the A+ objectives. For easy reference and clarification, the following is a complete listing of both sets of A+ objectives.

Exam objectives are subject to change at any time without prior notice and at CompTIA's sole discretion. Please visit the A+ Certification page of CompTIA's website (www.comptia.org/certification/aplus/index.htm) for the most current listing of exam objectives.

The A+ Core Hardware Service Technician Exam Objectives

The following are the domains in which you must be proficient to pass the A+ Core Module exam:

Domain 1 Installation, Configuration, and Upgrading   The objectives in domain 1 test your knowledge of the basic service practices of installing, configuring, and upgrading computer hardware. You will learn the basic parts of a computer and how they work, as well as how to properly remove, configure, and install the components of a computer. Questions from this domain make up 35 percent of your final exam score:

1.1 Identify the names, purpose, and characteristics of system modules. Recognize these modules by sight or definition.

1.2 Identify basic procedures for adding and removing field-replaceable modules for desktop systems. Given a replacement scenario, choose the appropriate sequences.

1.3 Identify basic procedures for adding and removing field-replaceable modules for portable systems. Given a replacement scenario, choose the appropriate sequences.

1.4 Identify typical IRQs, DMAs, and I/O addresses, and procedures for altering these settings when installing and configuring devices. Choose the appropriate installation or configuration steps in a given scenario.

1.5 Identify the names, purposes, and performance characteristics of standardized/common peripheral ports, associated cabling, and their connectors. Recognize ports, cabling, and connectors by sight.

1.6 Identify proper procedures for installing and configuring common IDE devices. Choose the appropriate installation or configuration sequences in given scenarios. Recognize the associated cables.

1.7 Identify proper procedures for installing and configuring common SCSI devices. Choose the appropriate installation or configuration sequences in given scenarios. Recognize the associated cables.

1.8 Identify proper procedures for installing and configuring common peripheral devices. Choose the appropriate installation or configuration sequences in given scenarios.

1.9 Identify procedures to optimize PC operations in specific situations. Predict the effects of specific procedures under given scenarios.

1.10 Determine the issues that must be considered when upgrading a PC. In a given scenario, determine when and how to upgrade system components.

Domain 2 Diagnosing and Troubleshooting   Questions on the objectives in this domain test your knowledge of troubleshooting. These objectives cover troubleshooting practices, common problems, how to begin troubleshooting, and how to diagnose and fix a problem. Questions from this domain make up 21 percent of your final exam score:

2.1 Recognize common problems associated with each module and their symptoms, and identify steps to isolate and troubleshoot the problems. Given a problem situation, interpret the symptoms and infer the most likely cause.

2.2 Identify basic troubleshooting procedures and tools, and how to elicit problem symptoms from customers. Justify asking particular questions in a given scenario.

Domain 3 PC Preventive Maintenance, Safety, and Environmental Issues   Questions based on the objectives in this domain test your knowledge of various preventive maintenance, safety, and environmental topics. You should know how to perform preventive maintenance tasks on a computer, which products to use and how to use them, how to ensure safety when working on a computer, and how to protect the environment when servicing a computer. Questions from this domain make up 5 percent of your final exam score:

3.1 Identify the various types of preventive maintenance measures, products, and procedures and when and how to use them.

3.2 Identify various safety measures and procedures, and when/how to use them.

3.3 Identify environmental protection measures and procedures, and when/how to use them.

Domain 4 Motherboard/Processors/Memory   In this domain, questions test your knowledge of the details of motherboards, processors, and memory. You should know the specifications of PC CPUs and the differences between them. You should also be familiar with the different types of RAM and what differentiates them from each other. Finally, you should know the different motherboard types, what makes motherboards different from one another, and how they are configured. Questions from this domain make up 11 percent of your final score:

4.1 Distinguish between the popular CPU chips in terms of their basic characteristics.

4.2 Identify the types of RAM (Random Access Memory), form factors, and operational characteristics. Determine banking and speed requirements under given scenarios.

4.3 Identify the most popular types of motherboards, their components, and their architecture (bus structures).

4.4 Identify the purpose of CMOS (Complementary Metal-Oxide Semiconductor) memory, what it contains, and how and when to change its parameters. Given a scenario involving CMOS, choose the appropriate course of action.

Domain 5 Printers   Questions from this domain test your knowledge of the different types of printers, their parts, the problems they have, and how to fix/install/upgrade them. Questions from this domain make up 9 percent of your final exam score:

5.1 Identify printer technologies, interfaces, and options/upgrades.

5.2 Recognize common printer problems and techniques used to resolve them.

Domain 6 Basic Networking   As more computers are networked at home, the networking domain has become increasingly important. Therefore, this domain now counts for 19 percent of your final exam score. Questions from this domain test your knowledge of the physical connections and layout of a network, as well as how networks work and how to connect a PC to the Internet:

6.1 Identify the common types of network cables, their characteristics and connectors.

6.2 Identify basic networking concepts including how a network works.

6.3 Identify common technologies available for establishing Internet connectivity and their characteristics.

The Operating System Technologies Exam Objectives

The following are the areas in which you must be proficient to pass the A+ Operating System Technologies exam.

Domain 1 Operating System Fundamentals   This domain requires knowledge of the Windows 95/98/Me (a.k.a. 9x), Windows NT, Windows 2000, and Windows XP operating systems. You need to know the way they work, as well as the components that compose them. You also need to understand topics relating to navigating the operating systems and, in general, how to use them. Operating system fundamentals make up 28 percent of the exam:

1.1 Identify the major desktop components and interfaces, and their functions. Differentiate the characteristics of Windows 9x/Me, Windows NT 4.0 Workstation, Windows 2000 Professional, and Windows XP.

1.2 Identify the names, locations, purposes, and contents of major system files.

1.3 Demonstrate the ability to use command-line functions and utilities to manage the operating system, including the proper syntax and switches.

1.4 Identify basic concepts and procedures for creating, viewing, and managing disks, directories, and files. This includes procedures for changing file attributes and the ramifications of those changes (for example, security issues).

1.5 Identify the major operating system utilities, their purpose, location, and available switches.

Domain 2 Installation, Configuration, and Upgrading This domain tests your knowledge of the day-to-day servicing of operating systems. This includes topics such as installing, configuring, and upgrading the various operating systems (Windows 9x, NT Workstation, 2000 Professional, and XP Professional). You are also expected to know system boot sequences. These topics make up 31 percent of the exam:

2.1 Identify the procedures for installing Windows 9x/Me, Windows NT 4.0 Workstation, Windows 2000 Professional, and Windows XP, and bringing the operating system to a basic operational level.

2.2 Identify steps to perform an operating system upgrade from Windows 9.x/ME, Windows NT 4.0 Workstation, Windows 2000 Professional, and Windows XP. Given an upgrade scenario, choose the appropriate next steps.

2.3 Identify the basic system boot sequences and boot methods, including the steps to create an emergency boot disk with utilities installed for Windows 9x/Me, Windows NT 4.0 Workstation, Windows 2000 Professional, and Windows XP.

2.4 Identify procedures for installing/adding a device, including loading, adding, and configuring device drivers, and required software.

2.5 Identify procedures necessary to optimize the operating system and major operating system subsystems.

Domain 3 Diagnosing and Troubleshooting Questions in this domain test your ability to diagnose and troubleshoot Windows 9x/NT/2000/XP systems and make up 25 percent of the test:

3.1 Recognize and interpret the meaning of common error codes and startup messages from the boot sequence, and identify steps to correct the problems.

3.2 Recognize when to use common diagnostic utilities and tools. Given a diagnostic scenario involving one of these utilities or tools, select the appropriate steps needed to resolve the problem.

3.3 Recognize common operational and usability problems and determine how to resolve them.

Domain 4 Networks This domain requires knowledge of the networking capabilities of the various versions of Windows and how to connect them to networks. It includes what the Internet is, its capabilities, basic concepts relating to Internet access, and generic procedures for system setup. Network questions make up 16 percent of the exam:

4.1 Identify the networking capabilities of Windows. Given configuration parameters, configure the operating system to connect to a network.

4.2 Identify the basic Internet protocols and terminologies. Identify procedures for establishing Internet connectivity. In a given scenario, configure the operating system to connect to and use Internet resources.

A+: Core Hardware Service Technician Exam

Chapter 1

Domain 1 Installation, Configuration, and Upgrading

COMPTIA A+ EXAM OBJECTIVES COVERED IN THIS CHAPTER:

- ✓ **1.1 Identify the names, purpose, and characteristics of system modules. Recognize these modules by sight or definition.**

- ✓ **1.2 Identify basic procedures for adding and removing field-replaceable modules for desktop systems. Given a replacement scenario, choose the appropriate sequences.**

- ✓ **1.3 Identify basic procedures for adding and removing field-replaceable modules for portable systems. Given a replacement scenario, choose the appropriate sequences.**

- ✓ **1.4 Identify typical IRQs, DMAs, and I/O addresses, and procedures for altering these settings when installing and configuring devices. Choose the appropriate installation or configuration steps in a given scenario.**

- ✓ **1.5 Identify the names, purposes, and performance characteristics of standardized/common peripheral ports, associated cabling, and their connectors. Recognize ports, cabling, and connectors by sight.**

- ✓ **1.6 Identify proper procedures for installing and configuring common IDE devices. Choose the appropriate installation or configuration sequences in given scenarios. Recognize the associated cables.**

- ✓ **1.7 Identify proper procedures for installing and configuring common SCSI devices. Choose the appropriate installation or configuration sequences in given scenarios. Recognize the associated cables.**

✓ **1.8 Identify proper procedures for installing and configuring common peripheral devices. Choose the appropriate installation or configuration sequences in given scenarios**

✓ **1.9 Identify procedures to optimize PC operations in specific situations. Predict the effects of specific procedures under given scenarios.**

✓ **1.10 Determine the issues that must be considered when upgrading a PC. In a given scenario, determine when and how to upgrade system components.**

This chapter dissects the personal computer, identifies its various components, and attempts to explain those components as succinctly and precisely as possible. As a doctor must be intimately acquainted with human anatomy, so a computer technician must understand the physical and functional structure of a personal computer.

Any PC is a complex machine. It could be described as a bit of a "melting pot" of various technologies and products, manufactured by a host of companies in many different countries. This diversity is also a great advantage because it gives the PC all of its versatility. However, these components don't always "melt" together into a unified whole without the help of a technician. These different products—whether they are hard disks, modems, sound cards, or memory boards—must share one processor and one motherboard and therefore must be designed to work in harmony. For this reason, configuration of the computer components is especially emphasized on the A+ Core Hardware exam, and nearly one-third of the exam's question pool pertains to the objectives reviewed in this chapter.

Before sitting for the exam, you will need to have a working knowledge of the components that make up a computer and their function within the system as a whole. The exam will test your knowledge of the types of components and their functions. The objective of this chapter is to review and identify the main components and their functions.

To pass the exam, you must be able to recognize these components and understand their relationship to one another. Figure 1.1 shows a typical PC, its components, and their locations.

FIGURE 1.1 Typical PC components

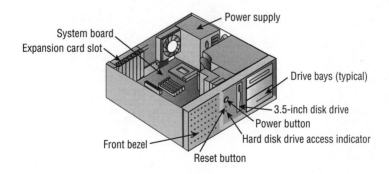

1.1 Identifying System Modules

The function of each of these components is critical to the operation of the computer. The knowledge needed to effectively describe each of these components and their operation is not only key to passing the exam, but is necessary to productively troubleshoot issues that arise in daily PC break-fix repair environments.

Critical Information

The system modules described in this section are either essential computer components or available on the market as optional equipment. Each has a distinct and very practical function.

Concepts and Modules

To troubleshoot and repair computers, you must be familiar with the components and their function when operating. Each component provides a specific function to the operation of the computer.

System Board

The spine of the computer is the *system board*, or *motherboard*. This component is made of green or brown fiberglass and is placed in the bottom or side of the case. It is the most important component in the computer because it connects all the other components of a PC together. Figure 1.2 shows a typical PC system board, as seen from above. On the system board you will find the CPU, underlying circuitry, expansion slots, video components, RAM slots, and a variety of other chips.

FIGURE 1.2   A typical system board

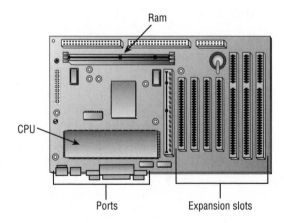

INTEGRATED COMPONENTS

Some motherboards have some of the peripheral devices built in, such as video, sound, and/or networking. These are referred to as *integrated system boards*. Such boards are cost-effective because they do not require a separate video card, sound card, and so on. The built-in components can be disabled through BIOS Setup if they should ever malfunction or need to be replaced by newer models.

SYSTEM BOARD COMPONENTS

Motherboards include components that provide basic functionality to the computer. The following components are found on a typical motherboard:

- Expansion slots
- Memory (RAM) slots
- CPU slot or socket
- Power connector
- Floppy and IDE drive connectors
- Keyboard and mouse connectors
- Peripheral port connectors (COM, LPT, USB)
- BIOS chip
- Battery

Figure 1.3 illustrates many of the components found on a typical motherboard.

FIGURE 1.3   Components on a motherboard

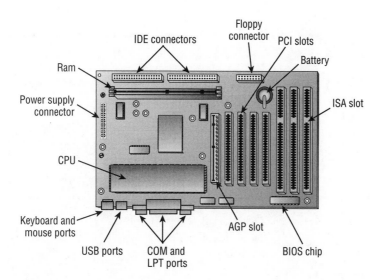

Expansion Slots   Expansion slots are used to install various devices in the computer to expand its capabilities. Some expansion devices that might be installed in these slots include video, network, sound, and disk interface cards.

Expansion slots come in three main types: ISA, PCI, and AGP. Each type is different in appearance and function, which you'll learn more about in future chapters. This chapter shows how to visually identify the different expansion slots on the motherboard.

ISA Expansion Slots   If you are repairing a computer made before 1997, chances are the motherboard in your computer has a few Industry Standard Architecture (ISA) slots. These slots are usually brown and are separated into two unequal lengths. Computers made after 1997 generally include a few ISA slots for backward compatibility with old expansion cards.

PCI Expansion Slots   Most computers made today contain primarily Peripheral Component Interconnect (PCI) slots. They are easily recognizable, because they are short (around 3 inches long) and are usually white. PCI slots can usually be found in any computer that has a Pentium-class processor or higher.

AGP Expansion Slots   Accelerated Graphics Port (AGP) slots are becoming more popular. In the past, if you wanted to use a high-speed, accelerated 3-D graphics video card, you had to install the card into an existing PCI or ISA slot. AGP slots were designed to be a direct connection between the video circuitry and the PC's memory. They are also easily recognizable because they are usually brown and located right next to the PCI slots on the motherboard. Figure 1.4 shows an example of an AGP slot, along with a PCI slot for comparison. Notice the difference in length between the two.

FIGURE 1.4   An AGP slot compared to a PCI slot

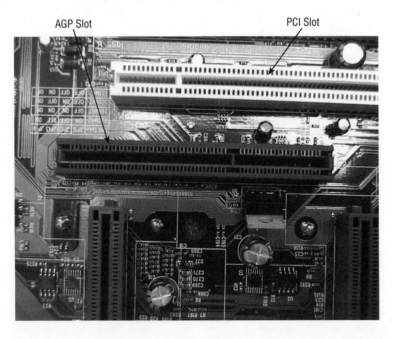

Memory Slots   Memory, or random access memory (RAM), slots contain the actual memory chips. There are many and varied types of memory for PCs today. We'll further discuss the memory itself later in this chapter. PCs use memory chips arranged on a small circuit board. These circuit boards are called *Single Inline Memory Modules* (*SIMMs*) or *Dual Inline Memory Modules* (*DIMMs*). DIMMs utilize memory chips on both sides of the circuit board, whereas SIMMs utilize memory chips on a single side. There is also a high-speed type of RAM called *Rambus Dynamic RAM (RDRAM),* which comes on circuit boards called *RIMMs.*

Along with chip placement, memory modules also differ in the number of conductors, or pins, that the particular module uses. The number of pins used directly affects the overall size of the memory slot. Slot sizes include 30-pin, 72-pin, 168-pin, and 184-pin. Laptop memory comes in smaller form factors known as *Small Outline DIMMs* (*SODIMMs*). Figure 1.5 shows the popular form factors for the most popular memory chips. Notice that they basically look the same, but the memory module sizes are different.

Memory slots are easy to identify on a motherboard. They are usually white and placed very close together. The number of memory slots varies from motherboard to motherboard, but the appearance of the different slots is very similar. Metal pins in the bottom make contact with the soldered tabs on each memory module. Small metal or plastic tabs on each side of the slot keep the memory module securely in its slot.

FIGURE 1.5   Various memory module form factors

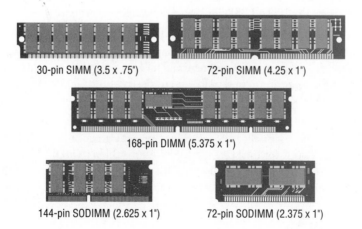

30-pin SIMM (3.5 x .75")   72-pin SIMM (4.25 x 1")

168-pin DIMM (5.375 x 1")

144-pin SODIMM (2.625 x 1")   72-pin SODIMM (2.375 x 1")

FIGURE 1.6 A PGA CPU socket

Central Processing Unit (CPU) and Processor Slots The CPU slot permits the attachment of the CPU to the motherboard, allowing the CPU to use the other components of the system. There are many different types of processors, which means many types of CPU slots. We'll expand on the different types of processors in Chapter 4, "Motherboard/Processors/Memory"; for now we will discuss only the CPU's interface with the motherboard.

The CPU slot can take on several different forms. In the past, the CPU slot was a rectangular box called a Pin Grid Array (PGA) socket, with many small holes to accommodate the pins on the bottom of the chip. With the release of new and more powerful chips, additional holes were added, changing the configuration of the slot and its designator or number. Figure 1.6 shows a typical PGA-type CPU socket.

With the release of the Pentium II, the architecture of the slot went from a rectangle to more of an expansion-slot style of interface called a Single Edge Contact Cartridge (SECC). This style of CPU slot includes Slot 1 and Slot 2 for Intel CPUs, and Slot A for Athlon (AMD) CPUs. This type of slot looks much like an expansion slot, but it is located in a different place on the motherboard than the other expansion slots.

To see which socket type is used for which processors, examine Table 1.1.

TABLE 1.1 Socket Types and the Processors They Support

Connector Type	Processor
Socket 1	486 SX/SX2, 486 DX/DX2, 486 DX4 Overdrive
Socket 2	486 SX/SX2, 486 DX/DX2, 486 DX4 Overdrive, 486 Pentium Overdrive
Socket 3	486 SX/SX2, 486 DX/DX2, 486 DX4 486 Pentium Overdrive
Socket 4	Pentium 60/66, Pentium 60/66 Overdrive
Socket 5	Pentium 75-133, Pentium 75+ Overdrive
Socket 6	DX4, 486 Pentium Overdrive
Socket 7	Pentium 75-200, Pentium 75+ Overdrive
Socket 8	Pentium Pro
Socket 370	Pentium III
Socket 423	Pentium 4
SECC (Type I), Slot 1	Pentium II
SECC2 (Type II), Slot 2	Pentium III
Slot A	Athlon

SYSTEM BOARD FORM FACTORS

Form factor refers to the size and shape of a component. Most system boards today use the ATX form factor. Some of its key features are its orientation of the expansion slots parallel to the narrow edge of the board, a one-piece power connector from the power supply, the built-in I/O ports on the side, and the orientation of the CPU in such a position that the power supply fan helps to cool it. Figure 1.7 shows an example.

FIGURE 1.7   An ATX-style motherboard

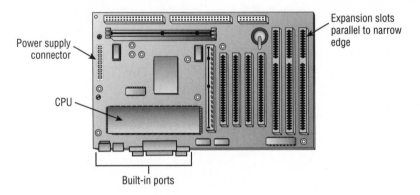

An older, alternative form factor for a system board is the Baby AT style, shown Figure 1.8. This type uses a two-piece power supply connector, uses ribbon cables to connect ports to the board, and orients the expansion slots parallel to the wide edge of the board.

FIGURE 1.8   An AT-style motherboard

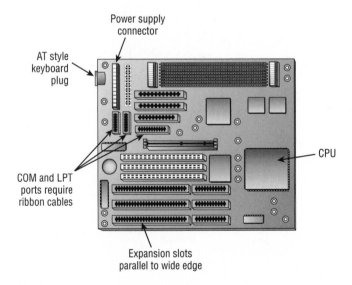

A case is generally designed to hold one or the other of these motherboard form factors, and a power supply is designed to work with one or the other; therefore those three components must be chosen as a group.

Power Connectors   A power connector allows the motherboard to be connected to the power supply. As you saw in Figures 1.7 and 1.8, the power supply connector is different for AT versus ATX systems. On an ATX, there is a single power connector consisting of a block of 20 holes (in two rows). On an AT, there is a block consisting of 12 pins sticking up; these pins are covered by two connectors with six holes each.

Figure 1.9 shows a very versatile motherboard that happens to have both kinds, so you can compare. The upper connector is for ATX, and the lower one is for AT.

FIGURE 1.9   Power connectors on a motherboard

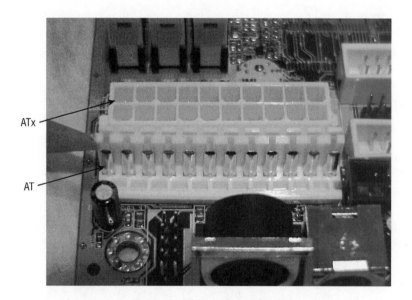

On-Board Floppy and IDE Connectors   With the exception of diskless workstations, every PC made today uses some type of disk drive to store data and programs until they are needed. Disk drives need a connection to the motherboard in order for the computer to utilize the disk drive. These connections are known as *drive interfaces*. There are two primary types: *floppy drive interfaces* and *IDE interfaces*. Floppy disk interfaces allow floppy disk drives to be connected to the motherboard and, similarly, IDE interfaces do the same for hard disks, CD drives, and other IDE-based drives. When you see them on the motherboard, these interfaces are said to be *on board*, as opposed to being on an expansion card, known as *off board*. The interfaces consist of circuitry and a port. A few motherboards also have SCSI interfaces that can be used for connecting drives.

Keyboard and Mouse Connectors Keyboard connectors allow for the direct connection of the keyboard to the motherboard. There are two keyboard connector types: AT and PS/2.

AT connectors are round, about ½ inch in diameter, and have five sockets in the DIN-5 configuration. They are found on AT motherboards. The second style, PS/2 connectors, are smaller and looks just like a PS/2 mouse connector; these are found on ATX motherboards. Mouse connectors are PS/2 style connectors; on an ATX it is built into the side of the motherboard, and on an AT there is a small ribbon cable that connects a back-mountable port to the motherboard.

Peripheral Ports and Connectors PCs were developed to perform calculations on data. In order for the PC to be useful, there must be a way to get the data into and out of the computer. To accomplish this, several ports are available. The four most common types of ports are the serial, parallel, Universal Serial Bus (USB), and game ports. Figure 1.10 shows some typical ports built into an ATX motherboard.

These ports are connected to the motherboard using small ribbon cables on an AT system, or are built directly into the side of the motherboard on an ATX system.

BIOS Chip This special memory chip contains the BIOS software that tells the processor how to interact with the hardware in the computer. The BIOS chip is easily identified. If you have a branded computer (such as Compaq, IBM, or HP), this chip is marked with the name of the manufacturer and usually the word *BIOS*. Clones usually have a sticker or printing on them from one of the three major BIOS manufacturers (AMI, Phoenix, and Award).

The BIOS chip is a ROM chip. ROM stands for Read Only Memory, and refers to the fact that the data on the chip is permanent; it cannot be changed by ordinary PC activities. However, if it is an EEPROM (Electrically Erasable Programmable Read Only Memory) chip, it can be flash-updated with a special utility program downloadable from the PC or motherboard maker.

FIGURE 1.10 Built-in ports on a motherboard

If you can't find the BIOS chip with these guidelines, look for a fairly large chip close to the CPU. It might also have a shiny or hologram sticker on it.

Battery   Your PC has to keep certain settings when it's turned off and its power cord is unplugged. These settings include the date, time, hard drive configuration, and memory.

Your PC stores the settings in a special memory chip called the Complementary Metallic Oxide Semiconductor (CMOS) chip. To retain these settings, the CMOS chip requires power constantly. To prevent the CMOS chip from losing its charge, a small battery is located on the motherboard.

JUMPERS AND DIP SWITCHES

Jumpers and DIP switches are used to configure various hardware options on the motherboard. Processors use different voltages and multipliers to achieve their target voltage and frequency. You must set these parameters on the motherboard by changing the jumper or DIP-switch settings. Figure 1.11 shows a jumper and two types of DIP switches. Individual jumpers are often labeled with the moniker *JP*x (where *x* is the number of the jumper).

FIGURE 1.11   A jumper set and DIP switches

Jumper   "Rocker-type" DIP switch   "Slide-type" DIP switch

Cases

The *case* is the metal or plastic box in which the motherboard, power supply, disk drives, and other internal components are installed. A case is typically—but not always—purchased with a power supply already installed.

Choosing the right case for the motherboard is important. Recall from the preceding sections that motherboards come in two form factors: ATX and AT. Each requires a different style of case and a different type of power supply.

One case may also be distinguished from another in terms of its orientation. A desktop case lies with its widest side flat on the desk; a tower case stands up on end.

Finally, one case differs from another in terms of the number of drive bays it has. For example, within the broad category of *tower* cases are mini-towers (typically with two large and two small drive bays), mid-towers, and full towers (typically with four large and three small drive bays). However there is little standardization of the number of drive bays that constitute a particular size; one manufacturer's full tower might have more or fewer bays than another's.

Although it is not common, you may occasionally encounter a slim-line case, which is a desktop-orientation case that is shorter and thinner than a normal one—so short that normal expansion boards will not fit perpendicular to the motherboard. In such cases a *riser card* is installed, which sits perpendicular to the motherboard and contains expansion slots. The expansion cards can then be oriented parallel to the motherboard when installed.

Power Supply

The device in the computer that provides the power is the *power supply*. A power supply converts 110-volt AC current into the voltages a computer needs to operate. On an AT motherboard, these are +5 volts DC, –5 volts DC, +12 volts DC, and –12 volts DC. Components in modern PCs do not use the negative voltages; they are provided for backward compatibility only. On an ATX motherboard, an additional voltage is provided: +3.3 volts DC.

Power supplies contain transformers and capacitors that carry *lethal* amounts of current. They are not meant to be serviced. *Do not* attempt to open them or do any work on them. Figure 1.12 shows a generic power supply.

FIGURE 1.12   A power supply

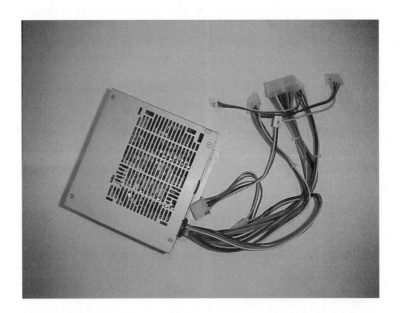

The CPU

The *CPU*, or *central processing unit*, is a processor chip consisting of an array of millions of integrated circuits. Its purpose is to accept, perform calculations on, and eject numeric data. It is considered the "brain" of the computer because it is the part that performs the mathematical operations required for all other activity.

As mentioned earlier, there are two form factors for CPU chips: Pin Grid Array (PGA) and Single Edge Contact Cartridge (SECC). The PGA style is a flat square or rectangular ceramic chip with an array of pins in the bottom. The actual CPU is a tiny silicon wafer embedded inside that ceramic chip. The SECC style is a circuit board with the silicon wafer mounted on it. The circuit board is then surrounded by a plastic cartridge for protection; the circuit board sticks out of the cartridge along one edge. This edge fits into a slot in the motherboard.

All CPUs today require cooling because they generate heat as they operate. The cooling can be either active or passive. A *passive heat sink* is a block of heat-conductive material that sits close to the CPU and wicks away the heat into the air. An *active heat sink* contains a fan that pulls the hot air away from the CPU.

One way to determine which CPU your computer is using is to open the case and view the numbers stamped on the CPU. However, some passive heat sinks are glued to the CPU, so the numbers may not be visible without removing it. Another way to determine a computer's CPU is to save your work, exit any open programs, and restart the computer. Watch closely as the computer returns to its normal state. You should see a notation that tells you what chip you are using. The General tab of the System Properties in Windows 95 and higher may also report the CPU speed.

EXTERNAL SPEED (CLOCK SPEED)

The clock speed, or external speed, is the speed at which the motherboard communicates with the CPU. It is determined by the motherboard, and its cadence is set by a quartz crystal (the system crystal) that generates regular electrical pulses.

INTERNAL SPEED

The internal speed is the maximum speed at which the CPU can perform its internal operations. This may be the same as the motherboard's speed (the external speed), but it is more likely to be a multiple of it. For example, a CPU might have an internal speed of 1.3GHz but an external speed of 133MHz. That means for every tick of the system crystal's clock, the CPU has 10 internal ticks of its own clock.

CACHE MEMORY

A *cache* is an area of extremely fast memory used to store data that is waiting to enter or exit the CPU. The *Level 1* cache, also known as the L1 or front-side cache, holds data that is waiting to enter the CPU. On modern systems, the L1 cache is built into the CPU. The Level 2 cache, also known as the L2 or back-side cache, holds data that is exiting the CPU and is waiting to return to RAM. On modern systems, the L2 cache is in the same packaging as the CPU but on a separate chip. On older systems, the L2 cache was on a separate circuit board installed in the motherboard, and was sometimes called COAST (cache on a stick).

THE BUS

The processor's ability to communicate with the rest of the system's components relies on the supporting circuitry. The system board's underlying circuitry is called the *bus*. The computer's bus moves information into and out of the processor and other devices. A bus allows all devices to communicate with each other. The motherboard has several buses. The *external data bus* carries information to and from the CPU and is the fastest bus on the system. The *address bus* typically runs at the same speed as the external data bus and carries data to and from RAM. The PCI, AGP, and ISA interfaces also have their own buses with their own widths and speeds.

Memory

As the computer's CPU works, it stores information in the computer's memory. The rule of thumb is that the more memory a computer has, the faster it will operate. Let's briefly look at the four major types of computer memory:

Dynamic Random Access Memory (DRAM)   This is actually the "RAM" that most people are talking about when they mention RAM. *Dynamic* refers to the chips' need for a constant update signal (also called a *refresh* signal) in order to keep the information that is written there.

Static Random Access Memory (SRAM)   SRAM doesn't require the refresh signal that DRAM does. The chips are more complex and are thus more expensive. However, they are faster. DRAM access times come in at 80 nanoseconds (ns) or more; SRAM has access times of 15 to 20 ns. SRAM is often used for cache memory.

Read-Only Memory (ROM)   ROM is called *read-only* because it can't be written to. Once the information has been written to the ROM, it can't be changed. ROM is normally used to store the computer's BIOS. The system ROM enables the computer to "pull itself up by its bootstraps," or *boot* (start the operating system).

Complementary Metallic Oxide Semiconductor (CMOS)   CMOS is a special kind of memory that holds the BIOS configuration settings. CMOS memory is powered by a small battery so that the settings are retained when the computer is shut off.

Storage Devices

Storage media hold the data being accessed, as well as the files the system needs to operate and data that needs to be saved. The various types of storage differ in terms of capacity, access time, and the physical type of media being used.

HARD DISK SYSTEMS

Hard disks reside inside the computer (usually) and can hold more information than other forms of storage. The hard disk system contains three critical components: the controller, the hard disk, and the host adapter. The controller controls the drive, the hard disk provides a physical medium to store the data, and the host adapter is the translator.

FLOPPY DRIVES

A floppy disk drive is a magnetic storage medium that uses a floppy disk made of thin plastic enclosed in a protective casing. The floppy disk itself (or *floppy*, as it is often called) enables the information to be transported from one computer to another very easily. The downside of a floppy disk drive is its limited storage capacity. Floppy disks are limited to a maximum capacity of 2.88MB, but the most common type of floppy in use today holds only 1.44MB. Table 1.2 lists the various floppy disks and their capacity. All of these except the 1.44MB capacity model are obsolete.

TABLE 1.2   Floppy Disk Capacities

Floppy Drive Size	Common Designation	Number of Tracks	Capacity
$5\frac{1}{4}''$	Double-sided, Double-density	40	360KB
$5\frac{1}{4}''$	Double-sided, High-density	80	1.2MB
$3\frac{1}{2}''$	Double-sided, Double-density	80	720KB
$3\frac{1}{2}''$	Double-sided, High-density	80	1.44MB
$3\frac{1}{2}''$	Double-sided, Ultra High Density	80	2.88MB

CD-ROM DRIVES

CD-ROM stands for Compact Disc Read-Only Memory. The CD-ROM is used for long-term storage of data. CD-ROMs are read-only, meaning that once information is written to a CD, it can't be erased or changed. Access time for CD-ROMs is considerably slower than for a hard drive. CDs normally hold 650MB of data and use the ISO 9660 standard, which allows them to be used in multiple platforms.

DVD-ROM DRIVES

Because DVD-ROMs use slightly different technology than CD-ROMs, they can store up to 1.6GB of data. This makes them a better choice for distributing large software bundles. Many software packages today are so huge that they take multiple CD-ROMs to hold all the installation and reference files. A single DVD-ROM, in a double-sided, double-layered configuration, can hold as much as 17GB (as much as 26 regular CD-ROMs).

OTHER STORAGE MEDIA

Many additional types of storage are available for PCs today. However, most of them are not covered on the A+ exam, so we'll just discuss them briefly here. Among the other types of storage are Zip drives, tape backup devices, and optical drives.

Zip Drives and Jaz Drives   Iomega's Zip and Jaz drives are detachable, external hard disks that are used to store a large volume (around 100MB for the Zip, 1GB and 2GB for the Jaz) of data on a single, floppy-sized disk. The drives connect to either a parallel port or a special interface card. The major use of Zip and Jaz drives is transporting large amounts of data from place to place. This used to be accomplished with several floppies.

Tape Backup Devices   Another form of storage device is the tape backup. Tape backup devices can be installed internally or externally and use a magnetic tape medium instead of disks for storage. They hold much more data than any other medium but are also much slower. They are primarily used for archival storage.

Optical Drives   Optical drives work by using a laser rather than magnetism to change the characteristics of the storage medium.

Monitors

Display systems convert computer signals into text and pictures and display them on a television-like screen. Several different types of computer displays are used today, including the TV. All of them use either the same *cathode ray tube* (*CRT*) technology found in television sets or the *liquid crystal display* (*LCD*) technology found on all laptop, notebook, and palmtop computers.

As we have already mentioned, a monitor contains a CRT. But how does it work? Basically, a device called an *electron gun* shoots electrons toward the back of the monitor screen (see Figure 1.13). The back of the screen is coated with special chemicals (called *phosphors*) that glow when electrons strike them. This beam of electrons scans the monitor from left to right and top to bottom to create the image.

FIGURE 1.13   How a monitor works

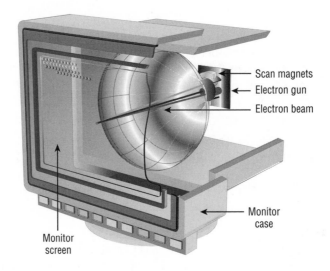

There are two ways of measuring a monitor's image quality: dot pitch and refresh (scan) rate. A monitor's *dot pitch* is the distance between two dots of the same color on the monitor. Usually given in fractions of a millimeter (mm), it tells how sharp the picture is. The lower the number, the closer together the pixels are, and thus the sharper the image. An average dot pitch is 0.28mm.

A monitor's *refresh rate* specifies how many times in one second the scanning beam of electrons redraws the screen. The phosphors stay bright only for a fraction of a second, so they must constantly be hit with electrons to stay lit. Given in draws per second, or hertz (Hz), the refresh rate specifies how much energy is being put into keeping the screen lit. Most people notice a flicker in the display at refresh rates of 75Hz or lower because the phosphors begin to decay to black before they are revived; increasing the refresh rate can help reduce eyestrain by reducing the flickering.

Liquid Crystal Displays

Two major types of LCDs are used in laptops today: *active matrix* screens and *passive matrix* screens. Their main differences lie in the quality of the image. Both types use some kind of lighting behind the LCD panel to make the screen easier to view.

PASSIVE MATRIX

A passive matrix screen uses a row of transistors across the top of the screen and a column of them down the side. It sends pulses to each pixel at the intersections of each row and column combination, telling it what to display.

Passive matrix displays are becoming obsolete because they are less bright and have poorer refresh rates and image quality than active matrix displays. However, they use less power than active matrix displays do.

ACTIVE MATRIX

An active matrix screen uses a separate transistor for each individual pixel in the display, resulting in higher refresh rates and brighter display quality. These screens use more power, however, because of the increased number of transistors that must be powered. Almost all notebook PCs today use active matrix. A variant called Thin Film Transistor (TFT) uses multiple transistors per pixel, resulting in even better display quality.

Adapter Cards

Adapter cards are also known by many other names, including circuit boards/cards and expansion boards/cards. In all cases, adapter cards are circuit boards that fit into expansion slots in the motherboard. They can include modems, network interface cards, sound cards, and many other types of devices.

Adapter cards are purchased to match an available expansion slot in the motherboard. PCI is the most common type of expansion slot for an adapter card in today's PCs. ISA slots are nearly obsolete, and AGP slots are used only for video cards.

Exam Essentials

Know what the BIOS does.   This is a ROM chip on the motherboard. It contains the BIOS software that tells the processor how to interact with the hardware in the computer. The BIOS chip tells the motherboard how to start up, check itself and its components, and pass off control to the operating system.

Know the different types of memory.   DRAM is Dynamic Random Access Memory. SRAM is Static Random Access Memory. ROM stands for Read-Only Memory, and it is normally used to store the computer's BIOS. CMOS is a special kind of memory that holds the BIOS configuration settings.

Know the CPU package types.   Pin Grid Array (PGA) is a square or rectangular ceramic chip with pins in the bottom. Single Edge Contact Cartridge (SECC) is a plastic cartridge that fits into a slot in the motherboard.

1.2 Adding and Removing Field-Replaceable Modules for Desktop Systems

At some point, every computer will need to be upgraded. Upgrading usually means one of two things: replacing old technology with new technology or adding functionality to an existing system. An example of upgrading old technology would be replacing a slower, older modem with a faster, newer one. An example of adding functionality to an existing system would be adding more RAM to increase performance. In either case, upgrading usually involves adding a new component. This process consists of several basic steps, each of which must be carefully followed. In this section, we will cover the following steps:

- Disassembly
- Inspection
- Part Replacement and Reassembly

 As you work inside a PC, be aware of safety hazards both to yourself and to the equipment. These are covered in detail in Objective 3.2, but you may wish to review them earlier than that as well.

Critical Information

When you choose an area in which to work on a computer, pick a workspace that is sturdy enough to support the weight of a computer and any peripherals you are adding to your system. The area must also be well lit, clean, and large enough to hold all the pieces and necessary tools.

Disassembling the Computer

You do not need to disassemble the computer completely to perform most upgrade and repair jobs; part of being a successful technician is to identify what parts must be removed for each job. For example, replacing a motherboard requires almost complete disassembly, but replacing a disk drive does not require any disassembly at all in most cases (except for removing the drive itself).

Preparing Your Work Area

For any work you do on a computer, you must have an adequate workspace. First, the work area must be flat. Second, the area must be sturdy. Make sure the work surface you are using can support the weight of the components. Third, the area must be well lit, clean, and large enough to hold all pieces (assembled and disassembled) and all necessary tools.

Before you begin, make sure all necessary tools are available and in working order. Also make sure that the documentation for the system you are working on is available (including owner's manuals, service manuals, and Internet resources).

The final guideline to preparing your work area is to set aside plenty of time to complete the task. Estimate the time required to complete the entire task (disassembly, installation, reassembly, and testing). Once you've prepared your work area and gathered your tools, you're ready to begin the actual disassembly of the computer. The steps are basically the same for all brands and types of computers.

Disassembly Prerequisites

You need to do several things do before you even move the computer to your work area:

1. Shut down any running programs and turn off the computer.
2. Remove all cables that are attached to the computer.
3. Remove any floppy disks from their drives.
4. Check to see that all the prerequisites have been met, and move the computer to the work surface.

Removing Input Devices

External devices such as the monitor, keyboard, and mouse should be unplugged before you open the case. Although this step is not necessary for every upgrade, it does make it easier to remove the case cover because the cords and connectors are not in the way.

Removing the Case Cover

Now you can unfasten the computer's cover by removing any retaining screws at the back of the computer. Some cases do not have screws; instead they have a sliding bar or latches that release the cover. Many of today's PCs can be completely disassembled without a single tool.

Then remove the cover by sliding or lifting it. The exact procedure varies greatly depending on the case; Figure 1.14 shows an example for a desktop style case.

Don't remove *all* the screws at the back of the computer! Some of these screws hold vital components (such as the power supply) to the case, and removing them will cause those components to drop into the computer.

FIGURE 1.14   Removing the case cover on a desktop case

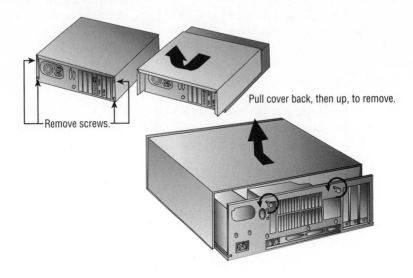

Remove screws.

Pull cover back, then up, to remove.

Removing the Expansion Cards

The next step in disassembly is to put on an antistatic wrist strap, plugging one end into the ground plug of an outlet. Then you can start to remove any *expansion cards*. There are four major steps in removing the expansion cards, as shown in Figure 1.15:

1.   Remove any internal or external cables or connectors.

2.   Remove any mounting screws that are holding the boards in place, and put the screws somewhere where they won't be lost.

3.   Grasp the board by the top edge with both hands and gently rock it front to back (not side to side).

4.   Once the board is out, place it in an antistatic bag to help prevent electrostatic discharge (ESD) damage while the board is out of the computer.

Duplicate this procedure for each card.

Be sure to note the slot from which you remove each card, because some bus types (including PCI) keep track of the slots in which the expansion boards are installed. Reinstalling an expansion card in a different slot later will probably not cause a problem, because the Plug-and-Play BIOS should redetect it, but better safe than sorry.

FIGURE 1.15   Removing an expansion board

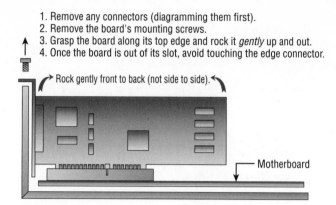

1. Remove any connectors (diagramming them first).
2. Remove the board's mounting screws.
3. Grasp the board along its top edge and rock it *gently* up and out.
4. Once the board is out of its slot, avoid touching the edge connector.

Rock gently front to back (not side to side).

Motherboard

Removing the Power Supply

Before you remove the power supply from the computer, you must do two things: disconnect the power supply connectors from the internal devices, and remove the mounting hardware for the power supply, as shown in Figure 1.16.

FIGURE 1.16   Removing power supply connectors

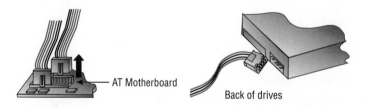

AT Motherboard

Back of drives

Grasp the connector (*not* the wires) and gently wiggle it out of its receptacle. Then, proceed to the next connector. The system board and disk drives both use power connectors. Make sure all of them are removed. AT cases have power leads connected to a switch at the front of the case that will also need to be removed.

An AT PC power supply has two connectors to the motherboard. These plug into receptacles that are side by side. If you get confused about how these connectors attach, the general rule is black-to-black. An ATX power supply has a single 20-wire connector to the motherboard.

Once all the power supply connectors are disconnected from their devices, you can remove the mounting hardware. You can usually detach the power supply from the case by removing four screws. Some power supplies don't need to have screws removed; instead, they are installed on tracks or into slots in the case and need only to be slid out or lifted out.

Removing the Disk Drives

To remove a disk drive, first disconnect it from the power supply (if you have not done so already) and then disconnect the ribbon cable that runs from the drive to the motherboard (or drive controller board). Then, physically remove the drive from its bay. On some cases, drives are secured in the bays with screws in the sides, as in Figure 1.17; on other cases they slide in and out on rails with clips that release and retain them.

FIGURE 1.17   Removing the hard drive

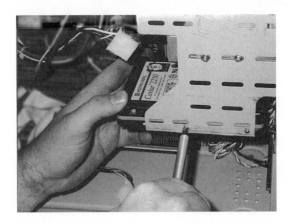

Most servers have hot-pluggable drives, which means they can be added or removed while the computer is running. You remove them by depressing a retaining clip or button. Consult the documentation provided with the machine or drives for the exact details.

Removing the Motherboard

The motherboard is held away from the metal case using brass or plastic spacers called *stand-offs*, and is secured and grounded using mounting screws. To remove the motherboard, you must remove the screws holding the motherboard to the case floor. On an ATX motherboard, you then simply lift the motherboard out of the case. On an AT motherboard, as in Figure 1.18, you must slide the motherboard about 1 inch to one side to release its plastic stand-offs from the mounting holes in the case floor.

Removing the Memory

Memory is held in place by retaining clips at both ends of the module. For a SIMM, the retaining clips are metal. Pull them back, tilt the SIMM back to a 45-degree angle with the motherboard, and then lift it out of the slot. For a DIMM, the retaining clips are plastic. Push them down (away from the DIMM), and the DIMM will pop free from its slot automatically; you can just lift it out. Place the removed memory in an antistatic bag to prevent damage.

FIGURE 1.18   Removing the motherboard

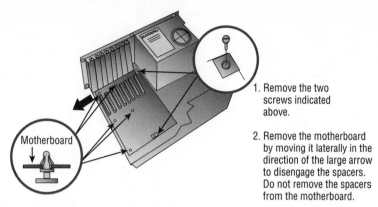

1. Remove the two
   screws indicated
   above.

2. Remove the motherboard
   by moving it laterally in the
   direction of the large arrow
   to disengage the spacers.
   Do not remove the spacers
   from the motherboard.

Motherboard

There are five spacers holding the motherboard off the case.
A spacer is shown above, viewed from its side.

Inspecting the Computer

Inspecting the computer is an important step in the disassembly and reassembly of the system.
You should check the components for any damage and gather any documentation. Damage is
sometimes visible on motherboards. Discolored areas on the board are often caused by power
surges.

After a component is removed, it is a good idea to create a parts list on a notepad and make
sure that you have all of the supporting documentation and device drivers. If you do not have
the supporting documentation and drivers, then it is good practice to download them from the
manufacturer's website or from a multivendor information site.

Part Replacement and Reassembly

The reassembly of the machine is almost an exact reversal of its disassembly. Once you have all
of the necessary documentation and device drivers, the process is quite simple. You reassemble the
computer by replacing the hard-to-reach items first and then attaching the supporting devices.

Installing the System Board

The motherboard attaches to the case by the spacers (stand-offs) that hold it away from the metal
case. There are two kinds. AT systems use plastic stand-offs that fit into holes in the motherboard
and then slide into channels in the case floor. Both AT and ATX systems use brass stand-offs that
attach to the floor of the case and have screw holes in their tops for attaching the motherboard
screws.

Before you reattach the motherboard, it is best to make sure that the memory and the processor are properly secured and seated in the slots. Doing so will help prevent damage to the
chips and protect your hand from cuts, because installing them after the board is secured will

leave you with limited space. After you have snapped the board onto its spacers, one or two retaining screws normally need to be attached. When attaching these screws, be sure not to over-tighten them and damage the board.

Installing the Power Supply

The power supply should be installed next. Attach it with the screws you removed during its disassembly. After it is secure, reattach the power leads to their respective connectors on the motherboard. If it's an AT system, make sure the black wires on the motherboard power connectors (usually labeled P8 and P9) are oriented together on the connector.

Installing Drives

The drives are the next components you attach. The first drive you should attach is the floppy drive. The ribbon cable and the power connector connect to the back of the drive as they were removed. Be sure to check the ribbon cable's attachment, because it is the most commonly reversed item on the PC. The red stripe on the cable indicates 1, which should be oriented closest to the power connector on the drive.

Next, attach the IDE drives, such as hard drives and CD drives. They connect to the motherboard's IDE interface via ribbon cable, and connect to the power supply via a Molex power connector.

Installing PCI, ISA, and AGP Devices

After the drives are attached, add any PCI, ISA, and AGP devices that the system uses, such as a video card, sound card, or modem. If the motherboard has any of these components built in, their ports might be built into the side of the motherboard (typical of an ATX motherboard), or might require you to attach a port to the back of the case and then run a small ribbon cable to connect that port to the motherboard.

Closing the Case

After you install all the components, slide the cover over the metal frame of the case. This may be a challenging part of the repair. Cases are generally designed to be the most inexpensive part of the PC. They are disassembled much more easily than they are reassembled. Tighten the screws on the outside of the case or make sure the case has snapped into the proper position.

Attaching Input Devices

Input devices such as the keyboard and mouse should be attached in the same ports from which they were removed. Be sure the keyboard and mouse are plugged into the correct ports if they both use a PS/2 connector. A good rule of thumb is that the keyboard attaches to the port closest to the outside of the machine.

Exam Essentials

Know when to attach an antistatic wrist strap.   One thing from this chapter that will be on the test is attaching an antistatic wrist strap. You should attach one of these to a ground mat every time you open a computer. More components are damaged from static discharge than from anything else.

Know the "black wires together" rule.   When you're attaching an AT power supply to a motherboard, the connector will be in two pieces, P8 and P9. These must be oriented so the black wires on each connector are near the black wires on the other connector. Otherwise, damage to the motherboard could result.

1.3 Adding and Removing Field-Replaceable Modules for Portable Systems

Fewer technicians work on portable systems than desktop systems, because most portable systems use proprietary parts that can be difficult to obtain unless you are working for an authorized service center. In addition, each portable computer must be opened a slightly different way for service, and some require special tools for entry.

Nevertheless, a professional technician will likely be called upon occasionally to perform basic repairs or maintenance on a notebook computer. The most common tasks are upgrading the RAM and replacing the hard disk, and both of those activities can be performed using widely available parts.

Critical Information

This objective was separated from Objective 1.2 in the latest revision of the A+ objectives, so much of the information contained under Objective 1.2 applies here as well. The following sections provide information specific to portable computers.

Removing and Replacing the Battery

Depending on the notebook model, the battery may be anywhere, but it is usually underneath the keyboard. On some models, you can slide the battery out the side by removing a panel or cover; on other models you must lift the keyboard.

Pull out the battery and insert a fresh battery in the same slot, pressing it firmly into place. Then, replace the cover over the battery's bay.

Batteries are hot-pluggable, so you do not have to shut down in order to remove one. However, unless you have a second battery or are connected to AC power, you will lose power and the PC will shut off when you remove the battery.

Adding and Removing PC Card Devices

PC Card devices are designed to be easily removable and installable. They are approximately the size and shape of a thick credit card, and fit into PC Card (PCMCIA) slots in the side of the notebook PC. PC Card devices can include modems, network interface cards, SCSI adapters, USB adapters, FireWire adapters, and wireless Ethernet cards.

To eject a PC Card device, press the Eject button next to its slot. To insert a PC Card device, press the device into the slot. You can do this while the computer is running. (That's called *hot-plugging* or *hot-swapping*.) However, in Windows it is a good idea to stop the PC Card device first, before ejecting it, to ensure that all operations involving it complete normally. To do so, double-click the Safely Remove Hardware icon in the system tray, click the device, and then click Stop.

Disassembling a Notebook PC

There are many designs of notebook PC cases, and each one disassembles a little differently. The best way to determine the proper disassembly method is to consult documentation from the manufacturer.

Some models of notebook PCs require a special T-8 Torx screwdriver. Most PC toolkits come with a T-8 bit for a screwdriver with interchangeable bits, but you might find that the T-8 screws are countersunk in deep holes so that you cannot fit the screwdriver into them. In such a case you would need to buy a separate T-8 screwdriver, available at most hardware stores or auto-parts stores.

Prepare a clean, well-lit, flat work surface, assemble your tools and manuals, and ensure that you have the correct parts. Shut down the PC, unplug it, and detach any external devices such as an external keyboard, mouse, or monitor.

Removing and Replacing Disk Drives

Accessing the hard disk drive usually involves lifting up the keyboard or removing it entirely. The hard disk typically has a ribbon cable made of thin plastic; be very careful when detaching it so you don't bend or break it. The hard disk also usually has a power supply connector that is smaller than that of a typical hard disk in a desktop PC. After disconnecting the hard disk, remove the screws holding it in place and lift it out.

The procedure for removing the floppy disk and/or CD drive varies widely depending on the model. Some notebook PCs are fully modular, such that the floppy disk and CD drives pop out easily without any tools. On other models, you may find that you need to completely disassemble the PC to access them. Consult the documentation from the manufacturer.

After removing the old drive, insert the new one in the same spot and secure it with screws. Then attach the power supply cable and ribbon cable and reassemble the PC.

Adding Memory

Most notebook PCs have a certain amount of memory hard-wired into them that you cannot remove. They also typically have a memory expansion slot into which you can insert a single circuit board containing additional RAM.

If such an additional memory module has been installed, you can remove it if desired (perhaps to replace it with one that has larger capacity). Most notebook PCs have a panel on the bottom held in place by screws. Remove this panel to expose the memory expansion slot. Then gently pull out the existing RAM module if needed, and insert the new RAM module.

Docking and Undocking

Some notebook PCs have optional accessories called *docking stations* or *port replicators*. These allow quick connect/disconnect with external peripherals and may also provide extra ports the notebook PC does not normally have.

Each docking station works a little differently, but there is usually a button you can press to undock the notebook from the unit. There may also be a manual release lever in case you need to undock when the button is unresponsive.

Because different hardware is available in docked versus undocked configurations, you might want to set up hardware profiles in Windows to account for the differences.

Exam Essentials

Know what devices are hot-pluggable.   PC Card devices are hot-pluggable, meaning you can remove and insert them while the computer is running. So are USB and FireWire devices. However, if you need to remove a drive, add or remove RAM, or connect or disconnect a monitor or a parallel or serial device, you must shut down.

Know where to look for the battery and for RAM expansion slots.   Batteries are usually accessed either from the sides or from under the keyboard. RAM is usually accessed on the bottom of the PC. There will also be some RAM built into the motherboard that is not removable.

1.4 Identify Typical System Resource Assignments and Procedures for Changing Them

Interrupt request lines, direct memory access channels, and input/output addresses are configurable aspects of the communication between the devices inside a PC. *Interrupt request lines (IRQs)* are used to signal that an event has taken place that requires the attention of the CPU. *Input/output (I/O) addresses* refer to the hardware communication lines that carry data between the CPU and the bus slots of the PC. *Direct memory access (DMA) channels* allow a storage device or adapter card to send information directly into memory without passing through the CPU, which results in a faster data transfer rate.

Whenever a new component is installed into a PC, its IRQs, I/O addresses, and DMA channels must be correctly configured or the device will not function correctly. This is the most common problem when installing new circuit boards. For this reason, the A+ Core Hardware exam includes several questions pertaining to the determination and configuration of these resources.

Critical Information

At some point, every computer will require the installation of a new component, whether it's a new sound card, a memory upgrade, or the replacement of a failed device. As a technician, you will be required to perform this task time and time again. You should be well versed in determining the installation configuration and resources.

Understanding Computer Resources

The various tools that you can use to discover the available resources on a PC can make installing new hardware a lot easier. Unfortunately, the tools are of little use unless you understand the information they present. In this section, we discuss the various resources that might be used by PC components and how those resources are used.

In general, there are four main types of PC resources you might need to be aware of when installing a new component: interrupt request (IRQ) lines, memory addresses, direct memory access (DMA) channels, and I/O addresses.

Interrupt Request Lines

IRQs are appropriately named. Interrupts are used by peripherals to interrupt, or stop, the CPU and demand attention. When the CPU receives an interrupt alert, it stops whatever it is doing and handles the request.

Each device is given its own interrupt to use when alerting the CPU. (There are exceptions; some PCI devices can share with one another, for example, and USB devices all use a single interrupt.) AT-based PCs have 16 interrupts available. Given the limited number of available interrupts, it is critical that you assign them wisely! Table 1.3 lists the standard use and other uses associated with each interrupt.

TABLE 1.3   AT Interrupts

Interrupt	Most Common Use	Other Common Uses
0	System timer	None
1	Keyboard	None
2	None; this interrupt is used to cascade to the upper eight interrupts (see note following this table)	None
3	COM2	COM4
4	COM1	COM3
5	Sound card	LPT2
6	Floppy disk controller	Tape controllers

TABLE 1.3   AT Interrupts *(continued)*

Interrupt	Most Common Use	Other Common Uses
7	LPT1	Any device
8	Real-time clock	None
9	None	Any device
10	None	Any device
11	None	Any device
12	PS/2-style mouse	Any device
13	Floating-point coprocessor	None
14	Primary IDE channel	SCSI controllers
15	Secondary IDE channel	SCSI controllers and network adapters

Interrupt 2 is a special case. Earlier (XT-based) PCs had only eight interrupts because those computers used an 8-bit bus. With the development of the AT, eight more interrupts were created (to match the 16-bit bus), but no mechanism was available to use them. Rather than redesign the entire interrupt process, AT designers decided to use interrupt 2 as a gateway, or *cascade*, to interrupts 9–15. In reality, interrupt 2 is the same as interrupt 9. You should never configure your system so that both interrupt 2 and 9 are used.

Most experienced field technicians have the standards (as listed in Table 1.3) memorized. In studying for the A+ exam, make sure you know all the default assignments, as well as the assignments for COM1–COM4 and LPT1–LPT2.

Memory Addresses

Many components use blocks of memory as part of their normal functioning. Network interface cards often buffer incoming data in a block of memory until it can be processed. Doing so prevents the card from being overloaded if a burst of data is received from the network.

When the device driver loads, it lets the CPU know which block of memory should be set aside for the exclusive use of the component. This prevents other devices from overwriting the information stored there. Certain system components also need a memory address. Memory addresses are usually expressed in a hexadecimal range with eight digits, such as 00F0000–000FFFFF.

Direct Memory Access

Direct memory access (DMA) allows a device to bypass the CPU and place data directly into RAM. To accomplish this, the device must have a DMA channel devoted to its use.

All DMA transfers use a special area of memory set aside to receive data from the expansion card (or CPU, if the transfer is going the other direction) known as a *buffer*. The basic architecture of the PC DMA buffers is limited in size and memory location.

No DMA channel can be used by more than one device. If you accidentally choose a DMA channel that another card is using, the usual symptom is that no DMA transfers occur and the device is unavailable.

Certain DMA channels are assigned to standard AT devices. DMA is no longer as popular as it once was, because of advances in hardware technology, but it is still used by floppy drives and some keyboards and sound cards. The floppy disk controller typically uses DMA channel 2. A modern system is not likely to run short on DMA channels because so few devices use them anymore.

I/O Addresses

I/O (input/output) addresses, also known as *port addresses*, are a specific area of memory that a component uses to communicate with the system. Although they sound quite a bit like memory addresses, the major difference is that memory addresses are used to store information that will be used by the device itself. I/O addresses are used to store information that will be used by the system. An I/O address is typically expressed using only the last four digits of the full address, such as 03E8. I/O addresses are usually expressed as a range such as 03E8-03EF. The exam asks about a few I/O addresses; Table 1.4 provides a list of a few that you should know.

T A B L E   1 . 4   I/O Addresses

Port	I/O Address
COM1	03F8–03FF
COM2	02F8–02FF
COM3	03E8–03EF
COM4	02E8–02EF
LPT1	0378–037F
LPT2	0278–027F
Primary IDE	01F0–01F7
Secondary IDE	0170–0177

Determining Available Resources

The best way to determine the PC's available resources is by using hardware-configuration-discovery utilities. These software programs talk to the PC's BIOS as well as the various pieces of hardware in the computer and display which IRQ, DMA, and memory addresses are being used. Most operating systems include some way of determining this information. MS-DOS, Windows 3.x, and Windows 95 included a tool named MSD.EXE. Windows 95 and higher have a graphical utility called Device Manager. Windows NT includes a program known as NT Diagnostics.

Let's look at Device Manager in Windows. To display it in Windows 9x, right-click My Computer and choose Properties, and then click the Device Manager tab. To display it in Windows 2000 and XP, right-click My Computer and choose Properties, then click the Hardware tab, and then click Device Manager.

To display a device's resources, open the category by clicking the plus sign next to it and double-clicking the device name. Then, look in the Resources tab for that device. (See Figure 1.19.)

FIGURE 1.19   Device Manager under Windows XP

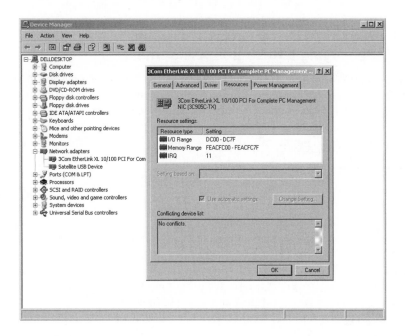

You can also get this same information through the System Information utility, available in Windows 98 and higher. To run it, choose Start ➤ (All) Programs ➤ Accessories ➤ System Tools ➤ System Information. Then, click one of the categories in the left pane to see the information in the right pane. (See Figure 1.20.)

FIGURE 1.20 System Information under Windows XP

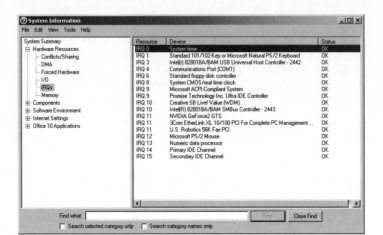

Manually Specifying a Resource Assignment

In Windows' Device Manager, you can manually specify the resources for a device to solve a problem with a *resource conflict*—that is, a situation in which two or more devices lay claim to the same resource. A resource conflict usually appears as a yellow exclamation point next to a device's name in Device Manager. Double-clicking the device opens its Properties box, and on the Resources tab you will find an explanation of the problem in the Conflicting Device List.

To change a device's resource assignments, clear the Use Automatic Settings check box and select a different configuration from the Settings Based On list. (See Figure 1.21.) If none of the alternate configurations resolves the conflict, you can double-click a specific resource on the Resource Type list and enter a manual setting for it.

Most modern computers use a power management and configuration method called ACPI (Advanced Configuration and Power Management), which helps prevent resource conflicts but which also limits the amount of tinkering you can do with manual resource assignments. If you get a message that a particular resource cannot be changed, or if the Use Automatic Settings check box is unavailable, it is probably because of ACPI.

If the device is not Plug-and-Play compatible, it may have jumpers for hard-setting the resources assigned to it. If that's the case, Windows will not be able to change these assignments; it will use the assignments the device requires.

FIGURE 1.21   Manually changing a resource assignment.

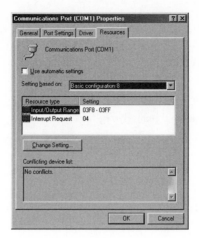

Exam Essentials

Know the default IRQs for COM ports and common devices.   Know the default IRQs for COM ports and common devices such as modems, sound cards, disk drives, and so on.

Be familiar with Device Manager.   Device Manager can display information about the computer's memory, I/O ports, IRQs being used, and many other PC resources.

Know what MSD is.   MSD.EXE was the MS-DOS equivalent of Device Manager. It was included in both MS-DOS and in Windows 95.

Understand how manual resource assignments are set.   Manual resource assignments for Plug-and-Play devices are set on the Resources tab of the device's Properties box. For a non-PnP device, resource assignments are controlled by jumpers on the device itself.

1.5 Identifying Peripheral Ports, Cables, and Connectors

A computer's peripheral ports are the physical connectors found outside the computer. Cables of various types are designed to plug into these ports and create a connection between the PC and the external devices that may be attached to it. A successful IT technician should have an in-depth knowledge of ports and cables.

Critical Information

Because the peripheral components need to be upgraded frequently, either to keep pace with technological change or simply to replace broken devices, the test requires a well-rounded familiarity with the ports and their associated cabling.

Unless a peripheral device connects directly to the motherboard, it must use a port. Ports can be distinguished from one another by three factors:

Bits of Data Simultaneously Conveyed   A *serial cable* carries only one bit at a time. A *parallel cable* carries multiple bits at a time (usually eight).

Data Transmission Speed   This is expressed in kilobits or megabits per second, and refers to the overall data throughput.

Type of Connector   A wide variety of connectors are used in PCs today, including the DB-style (as with legacy parallel and serial ports and VGA monitors), Centronics style (as with printers and some SCSI devices), and USB.

Parallel vs. Serial

A cable (and its port) can be either parallel or serial, and it is not always immediately obvious from looking which is which. For example, both parallel and serial cables can both use the DB-25 style of connector.

Both parallel and serial cables have multiple wires inside them, but they use them for different purposes. A parallel cable uses eight wires to carry bits of data in each direction, plus extra wires for signaling and traffic control. A serial cable uses only one wire to carry data in each direction; all the rest of its wires are for signaling and traffic control.

Transmission Speed

Neither parallel nor serial is intrinsically faster than the other. There are both fast and slow parallel and serial connections. For example, a legacy serial port such as for an external modem carries data fairly slowly (about 115Kbps), but a USB cable (also serial) carries data very quickly (up to 12Mbps for USB 1.1, and even faster for USB 2.0).

Connector Types

The following are common connector types:

DB   A D-shaped connector with a metal ring around a set of pins. Named for the number of pins/holes used: DB-25, DB-9, DB-15, and so on. Can be either parallel or serial. Common uses: VGA video, legacy serial devices such as external modems, and parallel printer cables (the connector on the PC only; the printer end uses Centronics).

RJ   A plastic plug with small metal tabs, like a telephone cord plug. Named for the number of metal tabs in the connector: RJ-11 has two, and RJ-14 has four. Both are used for telephone systems. RJ-45 has eight, and is used for Ethernet 10/100BaseT networking. Always serial.

BNC   Stands for Bayonett-Neill Connector or British Naval Connector. A metal wire surrounded by shielding, like a cable television connector. Used for 10Base2 Ethernet networking. Always serial.

Centronics   A plastic block with metal tabs flat against it, surrounded by a D-shaped metal ring. Used to connect a parallel printer cable to the printer, and also for some SCSI devices. Always parallel.

Ribbon Connector   A rectangular block consisting of a set of square holes that connect to pins on a circuit board. Used to connect floppy drives, IDE drives, and some SCSI devices to their controllers. Always parallel.

PS/2 (Mini-DIN)   A round connector with six small pins inside, commonly used to connect keyboards on ATX motherboards or PS/2 style mice.

DIN   A larger round connector with five rather large pins inside, used for connecting the keyboard on an AT motherboard.

USB   A flat rectangular connector, used with USB interfaces.

Cabling

Cables are used to connect two or more entities together. They are usually constructed of several wires encased in a rubberized outer coating. The wires are soldered to modular connectors at both ends. These connectors allow the cables to be quickly attached to the devices they connect.

Cables may be either shielded or unshielded. This refers to shielding against electromagnetic interference (EMI); it has nothing to do with whether the cable is shielded against dirt or water.

A list of common cable types used in PCs, their descriptions, their maximum effective lengths, and their most common uses is given in Table 1.5. The F or M in a connector's designation is for Female (holes) or Male (pins).

TABLE 1.5   Common PC Cable Descriptions

Application	1st Connector	2nd Connector	Max. Length
Null modem	DB-9F	DB-9F	25 feet
Null modem	DB-25F	DB-25F	25 feet
RS-232 (modem cable)	DB-9F	DB-25M	25 feet
RS-232 (modem cable)	DB-25F	DB-25M	25 feet
Parallel printer	DB-25M	Centronics 36M	10 feet
External SCSI cable	Centronics 50M	Centronics 50M	10 feet (total SCSI bus length)

TABLE 1.5   Common PC Cable Descriptions *(continued)*

Application	1st Connector	2nd Connector	Max. Length
VGA extension cable	DB-15M	DB-15M	3 feet
UTP Ethernet cable	RJ-45M	RJ-45M	100 meters
Thinnet Ethernet cable	BNC-M	BNC-M	100 meters
Telephone wall cable	RJ-11M or RJ-14M	RJ-11M or RJ-14M	N/A

One cable that deserves special mention is the null modem cable. It allows two computers to communicate with each other without using a modem. This cable has its transmit and receive wires crossed at both ends, so when one entity transmits on its TD line, the other entity receives it on its RD line.

UTP (unshielded twisted pair) is the most common type of cable used for network cabling. There are various categories of network cabling; the category required for 10/100BaseT networking is Category 5, often shortened to Cat5. There is also a Cat5e cable type, which is used for higher-speed Ethernet such as gigabit Ethernet.

Exam Essentials

Know what RJ-45 connectors are used for.   You are likely to be asked what type of connector would be used to attach a network connector to a wall jack.

Know what PS2/Mini-DIN connectors are used for.   You are likely to be asked what type of connector would be used to connect a keyboard or mouse to the back of a PC.

Know what RJ-11 connectors are used for.   You are likely to be asked what type of connector would be used to connect a modem to a telephone jack.

Understand parallel versus serial.   Parallel cables carry data eight bits at a time; serial cables carry it one bit at a time.

1.6 Installing and Configuring Common IDE Devices

IDE drives are the most common type of hard drive found in computers. But IDE is much more than a hard drive interface; it is also a popular interface for many other drive types, including CD-ROM, DVD, and Zip. This objective tests your knowledge of the IDE interface and its relationship to drives.

Critical Information

IDE drives are the most prevalent in the industry today. IDE drives are easy to install and configure, and they provide acceptable performance for most applications. Their ease of use relates to their most identifiable feature—the controller is located on the drive itself.

IDE Technologies

The design of the IDE is simple: Put the controller right on the drive and use a relatively short ribbon cable to connect the drive/controller to the IDE interface. This offers the benefits of decreasing signal loss (thus increasing reliability) and making the drive easier to install. The IDE interface can be an expansion board, or it can be built into the motherboard, as is the case on almost all systems today.

IDE generically refers to any drive that has a built-in controller. The IDE we know today is more properly called AT IDE; two previous types of IDE (MCA IDE and XT IDE) are obsolete and incompatible with it.

There have been many revisions of the IDE standard over the years, and each one is designated with a certain ATA number—ATA-1 through ATA-6. Drives that support ATA-2 and higher are generically referred to as Enhanced IDE (EIDE).

With ATA-3, a technology called ATAPI (ATA Packet Interface) was introduced to help deal with IDE devices other than hard disks. ATAPI enables the BIOS to recognize an IDE CD-ROM drive, for example, or a tape backup or Zip drive.

Starting with ATA-4, a new technology was introduced called UltraDMA, supporting transfer modes of up to 33MBps.

ATA-5 supported UltraDMA/66, with transfer modes of up to 66MBps. To achieve this high rate, the drive must have a special 80-wire ribbon cable, and the motherboard or IDE controller card must support ATA-5.

ATA-6 supported UltraDMA/100, with transfer modes of up to 100MBps.

If an ATA-5 or ATA-6 drive is used with a normal 40-wire cable or is used on a system that does not support the higher modes, it reverts to the ATA-4 performance level.

IDE Pros and Cons

The primary benefit of IDE is that it is nearly universally supported. Almost every motherboard has IDE connectors. In addition, IDE devices are typically the cheapest and most readily available type.

A typical motherboard has two IDE connectors, and each connector can support up to two drives on the same cable. That means you are limited to four IDE devices per system unless you add an expansion board containing another IDE interface. In contrast, with SCSI you can have up to seven drives per interface (or even more on some types of SCSI).

Performance also may suffer when IDE devices share an interface. When you're burning CDs, for example, if the reading and writing CD drives are both on the same cable, errors may occur. SCSI drives share an interface much more gracefully.

RAID

RAID stands for Redundant Array of Inexpensive Drives. It is a way of combining the storage power of more than one hard disk for a special purpose such as increased performance or fault-tolerance. RAID is more commonly done with SCSI drives, but it can be done with IDE drives.

There are several types of RAID:

RAID 0   Also known as *disk striping*. This is technically not RAID, because it does not provide fault tolerance. Data is written across multiple drives, so one drive can be reading or writing while the next drive's read-write head is moving. This makes for faster data access. However, if any one of the drives fails, all content is lost.

RAID 1   Also known as *disk mirroring*. This is a method of producing fault tolerance by writing all data simultaneously to two separate drives. If one drive fails, the other contains all the data and can be switched to. However, disk mirroring does not help access speed, and the cost is double that of a single drive.

RAID 5   Combines the benefits of both RAID 0 and RAID 1. It uses a parity block distributed across all the drives in the array, in addition to striping the data across them. That way, if one drive fails, the parity information can be used to recover what was on the failed drive. A minimum of three drives is required.

Installation and Configuration

To install an IDE drive, do the following:

1. Set the master/slave jumper on the drive.
2. Install the drive in the drive bay.
3. Connect the power supply cable.
4. Connect the ribbon cable to the drive and to the motherboard or IDE expansion board.
5. Configure the drive in BIOS Setup if it is not automatically detected.
6. Partition and format the drive using the operating system.

Each IDE interface can have only one *master* drive on it. If there are two drives on a single cable, one of them must be the *slave* drive. This setting is accomplished via a jumper on the drive. Some drives have a separate setting for Single (that is, master with no slave) and Master (that is, master with a slave); others use the Master setting generically to refer to either case. Figure 1.22 shows a typical master/slave jumper scenario, but different drives may have different jumper positions to represent each state.

FIGURE 1.22   Master/slave jumpers

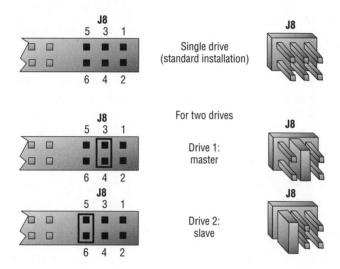

Most BIOS Setup programs today support Plug and Play, so they will detect the new drive automatically at startup. If this does not work, the drive might not be installed correctly, the jumper settings might be wrong, or the BIOS Setup might have the IDE interface set to None rather than Auto. Enter BIOS Setup and find out. Setting the IDE interface to Auto and then allowing the BIOS to detect the drive is usually all that is required.

In BIOS Setup for the drive, you might have the option of selecting a DMA (Direct Memory Access) or PIO (Programmed Input/Output) setting for the drive. For modern drives that support UltraDMA, neither of these settings is necessary or desirable. Both are methods for improving drive performance by allowing the drive to write directly to RAM, bypassing the CPU when possible.

Now that your drive is installed, you can proceed to partition and format it for the operating system you have chosen. Then, finally, you can install your operating system of choice.

For a Windows 9x or MS-DOS system, use the FDISK utility to partition the disk. Then, format the partition(s) using the FORMAT command.

For a Windows 2000 or XP system, allow the Windows Setup program to partition and format the drive, or use the Disk Management utility within Windows to perform that tasks. To access Disk Management, from the Control Panel choose Administrative Tools and then choose Computer Management.

Exam Essentials

Know how many pins an IDE cable has.   An IDE cable has 40 pins. You are likely to be asked to choose a cable in a scenario question simply by knowing how many pins the drive requires.

Know how a controller works in a master/slave environment.   When you have a master and a slave, only one of the two controllers controls data transfers. You are likely to be asked a scenario question that relates to this environment.

Know what other devices besides hard drives use IDE interfaces.   With the popularity of IDE technology, manufacturers have introduced tape drives and CD-ROMs that use IDE interfaces.

Understand RAID levels.   Know that RAID 0 is performance enhancement with no fault tolerance, RAID 1 is fault tolerance with no performance enhancement, and RAID 5 is both.

1.7 Installing and Configuring Common SCSI Devices

The *small computer systems interface (SCSI)* is a type of subsystem that is both highly flexible and robust. The range of devices that can use SCSI technology includes hard disk drives, scanners, tape drives, and CD-ROM drives. This is why it's so flexible, but also why its standards are so complex. In this section, we will review the different types of SCSI, and we'll discuss configuration and installation issues.

Critical Information

SCSI (pronounced "scuzzy") is a technology developed and standardized by the American National Standards Institute (ANSI). The standard specifies a universal, parallel, system-level interface for connecting up to eight devices (including the controller) on a single shared cable, called the *SCSI bus*. One of the many benefits of SCSI is that it is a very fast, flexible interface. You can buy a SCSI disk and install it in a Mac, a PC, or virtually any computer if a SCSI adapter is available.

SCSI is used for more than just drives. There are also SCSI scanners, tape backup units, and even printers.

SCSI Connectors

SCSI devices can be either internal or external to the computer. Eight-bit SCSI-1 and SCSI-2 internal devices use a SCSI A cable, a 50-pin ribbon cable similar to that of an IDE drive. Sixteen-bit

SCSI uses a SCSI P cable, with 68 wires and a DB-style connector. There is also an 80-pin internal connector called SCA used for some high-end SCSI devices.

External SCSI connectors depend on the type. SCSI-1 uses a 50-pin Centronics connector, as with a parallel printer. SCSI-2 uses a 25-, 50-, or 68-pin female DB-style connector. SCSI-3 uses a 68- or 80-pin female DB-style connector.

IDs and Termination

To configure SCSI, you must assign a unique device number (often called a *SCSI address*) to each device on the SCSI bus. These numbers are configured through either jumpers or DIP switches. When the computer needs to send data to the device, it sends a signal on the wire addressed to that number.

A device called a *terminator* (technically a *terminating resistor pack*) must be installed at both ends of the bus to keep the signals "on the bus." The device then responds with a signal that contains the device number that sent the information and the data itself. The terminator can be built into the device and activated/deactivated with a jumper, or it can be a separate block or connector hooked onto the device when termination is required.

Termination can be either active or passive. A *passive terminator* works with resistors driven by the small amount of electricity that travels through the SCSI bus. *Active termination* uses voltage regulators inside the terminator. Active termination is much better, and you should use it whenever you have fast, wide, or Ultra SCSI devices on the chain and/or more than two SCSI devices on the chain. It might not be obvious from looking at a terminator whether it is active or passive.

Types of SCSI

The original implementation of SCSI was just called "SCSI" at its inception. However, as new implementations came out, the original was referred to as *SCSI-1*. This implementation is characterized by its 5Mbps transfer rate, its Centronics 50 or DB-25 female connectors, and its 8-bit bus width. SCSI-1 had some problems, however. Some devices wouldn't operate correctly when they were on the same SCSI bus as other devices. The main problem was that the ANSI SCSI standard was so new, vendors chose to implement it differently. These differences were the primary source of conflicts.

The first improvement that was designed into *SCSI-2* was a wider bus. The new specification specified both 8-bit and 16-bit buses. The larger of the two specifications is known as *Wide SCSI-2*. It improved data throughput for large data transfers. Another important change was to improve upon the now-limiting 5Mbps transfer rate. The *Fast SCSI-2* specification allowed for a 10Mbps transfer rate, thus allowing transfers twice as fast as SCSI-1. So, Wide SCSI-2 transfers data 16 bits at a time, and Fast SCSI transfers data 8 bits at a time but twice as fast (at 10Mbps).

SCSI-3, also known as Ultra SCSI, comes in two widths: 8-bit (narrow) and 16-bit (wide), and three speeds: 20Mbps, 40Mbps, and 80Mbps. See Table 1.6.

TABLE 1.6 SCSI 3 Speeds

SCSI 3 Type	Narrow (8-Bit)	Wide (16-Bit)
Ultra 1	20MBps	40MBps
Ultra 2	40MBps	80MBps
Ultra 3	80MBps	160MBps

SCSI-3 also provides ways to increase the maximum distance for the chain. Standard SCSI is also known as Single Ended (SE) SCSI, and it can go about 10 feet. Low-Voltage Differential (LVD) SCSI is a variant with higher speeds and longer maximum distances, up to 39 feet. LVD and SE can work together on the same chain, but all will revert to SE limitations in that case.

High-Voltage Differential (HVD) is a special type of SCSI incompatible with the other two types. It has a maximum distance of 82 feet and must have a special HVD terminator.

SCSI Device Installation and Configuration

Installing SCSI devices is more complex than installing an IDE drive. The main issues with installing SCSI devices are cabling, termination, and addressing.

We'll discuss termination and cabling together because they are very closely tied. There are two types of cabling:

- *Internal cabling* uses a 50-wire ribbon cable with several keyed connectors on them. These connectors are attached to the devices in the computer (the order is unimportant), with one connector connecting to the adapter.

- *External cabling* uses thick, shielded cables that run from adapter to device to device in a fashion known as *daisy-chaining*. Each device has two ports on it (most of the time). When hooking up external SCSI devices, you run a cable from the adapter to the first device. Then you run a cable from the first device to the second device, from the second to the third, and so on.

Because there are two types of cabling devices, you have three ways to connect them. The methods differ by where the devices are located and whether the adapter has the terminator installed. The guide to remember here is that *both ends* of the bus must be terminated. Let's look briefly at the three connection methods:

Internal Devices Only   When you have only internal SCSI devices, you connect the cable to the adapter and to every SCSI device in the computer. You then install the terminating resistors on the adapter and terminate the last drive in the chain. All other devices are unterminated. This is demonstrated in Figure 1.23.

FIGURE 1.23   Cabling internal SCSI devices only

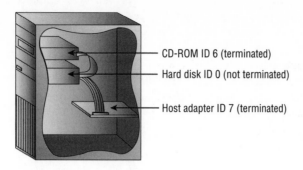

CD-ROM ID 6 (terminated)
Hard disk ID 0 (not terminated)
Host adapter ID 7 (terminated)

 Some devices and adapters don't use terminating resistor packs; instead you use a jumper or DIP switch to activate or deactivate SCSI termination on such devices. (Where do you find out what type your device uses? In the documentation, of course.)

External Devices Only   In the next situation, you have external devices only, as shown in Figure 1.24. By external devices, we mean that each has its own power supply. You connect the devices in the same manner in which you connected internal devices, but in this method you use several very short (less than 0.5 meters) *stub* cables to run between the devices in a daisy chain (rather than one long cable with several connectors). The effect is the same. The adapter and the last device in the chain (which has only one stub cable attached to it) must be terminated.

FIGURE 1.24   Cabling external SCSI devices only

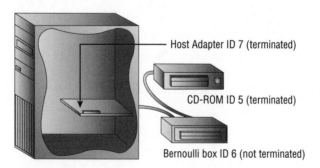

Host Adapter ID 7 (terminated)

CD-ROM ID 5 (terminated)

Bernoulli box ID 6 (not terminated)

Both Internal and External Devices   Finally, there's the hybrid situation in which you have both internal and external devices (Figure 1.25). Most adapters have connectors for both internal and external SCSI devices—if yours doesn't have both, you'll need to see if anybody makes one that will work with your devices. For adapters that do have both types of connectors, you connect your internal devices to the ribbon cable and attach the cable to the adapter. Then, you daisy-chain your external devices off the external port. Finally, you terminate the last device on each chain, leaving the adapter unterminated.

FIGURE 1.25   Cabling internal and external SCSI devices together

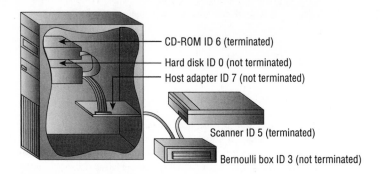

CD-ROM ID 6 (terminated)
Hard disk ID 0 (not terminated)
Host adapter ID 7 (not terminated)

Scanner ID 5 (terminated)

Bernoulli box ID 3 (not terminated)

 Even though the third technique described is the technically correct way to install termination for the hybrid situation (in which you have both internal and external devices), some adapter cards still need to have terminators installed.

Each device must also have a unique SCSI ID number. This number can be assigned by the jumper (with internal devices) or with a rotary switch (on external devices). You start by assigning your adapter an address. This can be any number from 0 to 7 on an 8-bit bus, 0 to 15 on a 16-bit bus, and 0 to 31 on a 32-bit bus, as long as no other device is using that ID.

Here are some recommendations that are commonly accepted by the PC community. Remember that these are guidelines, not rules:

- Generally speaking, give slower devices higher priority so they can access the bus whenever they need it. Higher numbers are higher priority.

- Set the bootable (or first) hard disk to ID 0.

- Set the CD-ROM to ID 3.

After the devices are cabled and terminated, you have to get the PC to recognize the SCSI adapter and its devices. The SCSI adapter manages all SCSI device resource allocation, so generally all that is required is to make sure the operating system is able to see the SCSI adapter. This involves installing a Windows driver for the adapter in Windows, for example, or a real-mode driver in CONFIG.SYS for MS-DOS.

However, if you want to boot from a SCSI drive, the system must be able to read from that drive in order to load the operating system; you must enable the SCSI adapter's own BIOS extension so that the PC can read from it at startup without a driver. Check the documentation for the adapter; sometimes the BIOS Setup program for the SCSI adapter is activated via a function key at startup.

Once the drive is installed and talking to the computer, you can high-level-format the media and install the operating system.

If there are problems, double-check the termination and ID numbers. If everything looks correct, try changing the ID numbers one at a time. SCSI addressing is a gray area where many problems arise.

RAID

RAID works the same with SCSI as it does with IDE drives; see the RAID section under Objective 1.7 for details.

Exam Essentials

Know the transfer rates of the different types of SCSI architectures.   The different types of SCSI controllers and their supporting devices support throughput ranging from 5Mbps to 160Mbps. You should be familiar with these types and their throughput.

Understand SCSI IDs.   SCSI IDs are a critical concept to understand. This information is not only necessary for the exam, but you must be able configure SCSI ID numbers in order to install a SCSI device.

Understand termination.   You must not only understand what termination does, but also know how to implement it for the exam and to install a SCSI device.

Know the difference among SE, LVD, and HVD.   Make sure you know which will coexist (SE and LVD) and what benefits LVD and HVD offer over SE.

1.8 Installing and Configuring Common Peripheral Devices

Peripheral devices are devices that are not built into the PC. They can include monitors, printers, scanners, network hubs, digital cameras, and external modems and transceivers (such as DSL or cable modems).

Critical Information

A PC technician must know how peripheral devices work, how to install them, and how to configure them. These devices are the focus of several test questions.

Procedures for Installing and Configuring Peripherals

Most peripherals connect easily to a port on the main system unit. Some of them then require setup through the operating system.

Monitors

Before connecting or disconnecting a monitor, ensure that the power to both the PC and the monitor is off. Then connect a VGA (DB-15) cable from the monitor to the PC's video card, and connect the monitor's power cord to an AC outlet.

Modems

There are two types of modems: internal and external. Internal modems are installed as expansion cards inside a computer, as described under Objective 1.2. External modems have their own power supplies and connect to an external COM port with an RS-232 cable or to a USB port.

Internal modems are usually smaller and cheaper than their external counterparts. However, they are more difficult to configure, especially if they are not Plug and Play. You need to configure them to use an unused COM port. Non-PnP internal modems have jumpers on them for setting the resources to use. Table 1.7 lists the IRQ and I/O port addresses of the standard COM ports installed. A PnP modem is usually assigned an appropriate COM port and associated resources automatically through the operating system.

TABLE 1.7   Standard COM Port IRQ and I/O Addresses

COM Port	IRQ Address	I/O Address
COM1	4	3F8–3FF
COM2	3	2F8–2FF
COM3	4	3E8–3EF
COM4	3	2E8–2EF

External modems use an existing serial port (legacy serial port or USB), so they don't have the configuration problem with IRQs and I/O addresses. A legacy serial external modem must be connected with the power off for both the PC and the modem. A USB modem can be connected or disconnected to the computer at any time. External modems have their own power supplies that connect to an AC outlet.

Terminal Adapters

Non–dial-up Internet connections such as cable and DSL typically use external *terminal adapters* to make the connection. There are two ways this can work. Some terminal adapters connect to the PC via a USB interface, and the PC sees the terminal adapter as a network device. The device shows up in the Network section of Device Manager. To connect such a terminal adapter, simply plug it into the PC's USB port at any time. The PC can be either on or off. The terminal adapter then connects either to a phone line (for DSL) or a cable line (for cable).

Other terminal adapters interface with the PC via a 10/100BaseT network interface card (NIC). You install the internal NIC in the PC, as described under Objective 1.2, and then connect the terminal adapter to the NIC using Cat5 network cabling (RJ-45 connectors).

Digital Cameras

Most digital cameras connect to a PC via a USB interface. When the camera is connected, the camera appears as a removable drive in My Computer, and you can browse its contents to examine the pictures. You can then copy the pictures to the PC's hard disk with drag-and-drop through a regular file-management interface.

PDAs

A PDA typically connects to a PC via a docking cradle, which may have either a legacy serial or USB interface. When you're initially installing a PDA docking cradle, it may be necessary to run some setup software to connect the PDA's synchronization software to your preferred personal information management program.

Wireless Access Points, Hubs, and Routers

A wireless access point is like a network hub. It works independently of any network node and continues to function even when the PCs are turned off. However, you can configure it by entering its IP address into a web browser interface. Check the documentation to find out the IP address to use and the username and password required for access to it.

Infrared Devices

Infrared ports are most often associated with notebook PCs, although any PC may have one installed as an add-on. An infrared device is automatically recognized through the operating system whenever it comes into range of the PC, and it's available through the infrared port. For example, when an infrared printer comes into range, the printer is detectable.

Printers

Almost all printers are Plug and Play, such that Windows can automatically detect them and either install a driver automatically or prompt you for a Setup disk. To set up a printer, use the Add Printer Wizard through the Printers applet in the Windows Control Panel.

Some printers have their own special queue software. If possible, run the Setup utility that comes with the printer.

A printer may have either a legacy parallel or USB interface. If it's legacy parallel, both the printer and the PC must be powered off to make the connection; if it's USB, the connection can be made at any time.

UPSs and Surge Suppressors

A *surge suppressor* is just a power strip with electrical protection; it has no direct interactivity with the computer.

An uninterruptible power supply (UPS) is like a surge suppressor, but with battery backup capability. However, some UPS devices include a serial or USB connector for communication with the PC. On such systems, you can connect the PC to the UPS and then use utility software that comes with the UPS to monitor battery life and power quality.

As with other devices, if you're using a legacy serial interface, the power must be shut off to the PC before attaching or detaching it. A USB interface may be connected at any time.

Exam Essentials

Most of the information in this section seems very basic. Remember to use the principles set forth in Objective 1.2, "Identify basic procedures for adding and removing field-replaceable modules for desktop systems," earlier in this chapter.

Know which interfaces can be hot-plugged.   USB and FireWire devices can be connected while the PC is running; legacy parallel and serial devices and monitors cannot.

Know how to access a network hub, router, or access point.   You can communicate with one of these devices through a web browser by entering its IP address as the URL.

Know how to install a broadband Internet terminal adapter.   Some are USB; others connect to a network card in the PC.

1.9 Optimizing PC Operations

Upgrades are a part of any technician's job description. Upgrades present their own set of challenges that can range from compatibility to space requirements. This section describes some hardware upgrades that can enhance system performance.

Critical Information

The most common need for an upgrade is to increase system performance. Over time, a computer's performance will decrease as newer software is added. In most cases, newer versions of software require additional resources that are not available. The PC was originally configured to run at certain performance levels that considered the applications and peripherals available when it was produced. Upgrades will increase the system's performance to accommodate newer software and peripheral devices.

Toward the end of the life expectancy of the system, it may become necessary to upgrade the system for required programs or for new hardware to function. If the system is too antiquated, it may be more cost efficient to replace the entire computer. However, in many cases, the system's performance can be enhanced to acceptable levels by adding resources.

Memory

As we mentioned earlier in this chapter, RAM is used to store data temporarily while the PC is operating. The operating system and applications utilize RAM, so if the amount of available RAM is insufficient, the operating system will utilize hard disk space to store some of the data. Because the speed at which the data stored on a hard drive is considerably lower than the speed at which data can be accessed in RAM, the performance of the system will degrade as more and more information is stored on the hard drive.

In such a case, adding RAM can have a significant effect on the system's performance. To fully understand the effect that the amount of RAM can have on a system, consider the memory requirements of past and present operating systems shown in Table 1.8. Refer to Objectives 1.10 and 4.2 for specifics on installing RAM and for help selecting the appropriate RAM type for a system.

TABLE 1.8   RAM Requirements for Operating Systems

Operating System	RAM Requirement
MS-DOS	1MB
Windows 3.1	4MB (8MB recommended)
Windows NT Workstation 4.0	16MB (32MB recommended)
Windows 95	4MB (8MB recommended)
Windows 98	16MB (24MB recommended)
Windows 2000 Professional	64MB
Windows Me	32MB
Windows XP	64MB (128MB recommended)

Disk Subsystem

The disk subsystem consists of the hard drives, the controllers, and the cables used to connect them.

Hard Drives

Hard drives are most commonly replaced because the system runs out of space to store data and program files. A small hard drive is replaced with one of larger capacity, or an additional hard disk is added.

Another reason to upgrade a hard drive is to increase the speed at which data can be written to or read from the drive. For example, replacing an old hard disk that conforms to ATA-3 standards with a newer one that conforms to ATA-6 (UltraATA/100) would result in a disk that had a much faster access time and data transfer rate (provided that the IDE controller and the cable were of the correct type to support it).

There are two common ways to replace a disk drive in a computer: adding a drive or completely replacing the disk. Each approach has benefits and drawbacks.

COMPLETE REPLACEMENT

If you need additional hard disk capacity and do not have the physical room for a second drive inside the computer's case, or you do not want to manage two drives, complete replacement is necessary. Complete replacement requires reinstalling or restoring the operating system, program files, and data on the new drive. Because this is a considerable undertaking, drive-image tools have been developed to aid in this process. A drive-image tool takes a snapshot of the drive and allows you to create an image that can be expanded on the larger drive, avoiding reinstallation.

These images are normally compressed and require less space than the actual contents of the drive, allowing the images to be placed on a CD-ROM or other storage media. Some examples of this type of data transfer programs are Norton Ghost and Seagate Power Quest Drive Image. Larger corporations use these tools to create a basic image of the operating system and commonly used programs to decrease downtime and lower upgrade and repair costs.

ADDING DRIVES

The simplest way to increase hard drive capacity is to add another drive. Most desktop PCs have IDE controllers built into the motherboard. These controllers allow for two devices to be connected to both the primary and secondary controller. With this type of architecture, four IDE devices can be installed in a PC if space permits.

After adding the drive, you can place data and programs on it. This type of installation does not require the reinstallation or restoration of the operating system and program files on the new drive.

Controller Card

If the motherboard is more than a few years old, its IDE interface may not support the latest, fastest UltraATA standards. To get the highest performance out of a new hard drive, you may want to install an IDE controller card that supports the same standard as the new drive (for example, UltraATA/100 or ATA-6).

Cable

UltraATA/66 and UltraATA/100 work only with a special 80-wire ribbon cable; when installing such drives on an existing IDE interface you will probably also want to replace the 40-wire cable with an 80-wire one. Most new hard disks come with the 80-wire cable.

CPU Upgrade

The frequency at which the processor operates, or MHz, determines the speed at which data passes through the processor. Upgrading the processor to a higher frequency will provide a dramatic improvement in the system's overall performance.

It is important to remember that replacing a processor requires some research. Most motherboards support a certain class of processor; they do not have the capacity to upgrade to a different class of chip. For example, it is not possible to upgrade a Pentium-class chip to a Pentium II–class chip. This relates not only to the processor slots, but also to the power requirements of the chip. You must consider the additional cooling requirements of the new chip as well. In most cases, processor upgrades are accomplished by replacing the motherboard and processor using a special overdrive chip. Overdrive chips will be discussed further in Chapter 4.

Some motherboards support the use of multiple CPUs, and in such motherboards additional CPUs can improve overall system performance. Although the system does not run at a faster speed (in terms of MHz), an additional CPU makes the system able to process more operations per second.

Upgrading the BIOS

When the BIOS no longer supports all of the devices that need to be connected to the PC, an upgrade is needed. There are two ways to upgrade the BIOS chip: by manually replacing the chip or by using special flash software.

Manual Chip Replacement

Manual chip replacement requires a technician to remove the old chip and replace it with a new chip provided by the motherboard manufacturer. Manual replacement is not an option in today's PCs.

Flash BIOS Replacement

Flash BIOS is the modern way of upgrading a computer's BIOS. By placing the BIOS update disk in the floppy drive and booting the machine, a technician can reprogram the system's BIOS to handle new hardware devices that the manufacturer has included.

This works because the BIOS in modern systems is written in an Electrically Erasable Programmable ROM (EEPROM) chip. This chip is normally read-only, but when it receives a stronger-than-normal voltage of electricity, it can temporarily become rewriteable. The utility for updating the BIOS includes instructions to the motherboard to deliver this extra-strong electricity prior to the new BIOS update being sent to the chip.

Manufacturers periodically post the flash upgrades on their websites for technicians to download. Be aware that you must take care in this process because the BIOS could be disabled and require the motherboard to be shipped back to the manufacturer. In most cases, the flash program will give the technician the opportunity to save the current software and settings to a restore disk that can reverse the changes if necessary.

Upgrading the Cooling System

The cooling system consists of the fan in the power supply, the fan or heat sink on the CPU, and any additional heat sinks or fans in the case. If a system is inadequately cooled, lockups and spontaneous reboots may occur.

Liquid-cooled cases are now available that use circulating water rather than fans to keep components cool. These cases are typically more expensive than standard ones and may be more difficult to work on for an untrained technician, but they result in an almost completely silent system.

Air cooling is the most common cooling method used in PCs. CPUs typically have active heat sinks, which are heat sinks that include an electric fan that constantly channels heat away. A CPU that is running too hot might benefit from a better cooling fan. The heat sink portion is a block of spikes that channel heat away from the CPU.

Most passive heat sinks (that is, heat sinks that do not include a fan) are attached to the CPU using a glue-like thermal compound. This makes the connection between the heat sink and the CPU more seamless and direct. Thermal compound can be used on active heat sinks too, but generally it is not because of the possibility that the fan might stop working and need to be replaced.

In addition to the main fan in the power supply, you can also install additional cooling fans in a case that help circulate air through the case.

Upgrading to a Faster NIC

The typical speed for an Ethernet network today is 100BaseT, or 100MBps. This speed requires a 100BaseT network card. 10BaseT network cards can coexist on a 100BaseT network but will send and receive data at only 10MBps. Upgrading to a higher-speed network card can improve network performance in such a case.

In addition, new Ethernet technologies such as gigabit Ethernet are becoming popular; they push the speed beyond 100MBps. Upgrading to a NIC that supports these even faster speeds may be advantageous if the PC is on a network that supports them.

Specialized Video Cards

A standard 2-D video card is adequate for business use, but for the serious graphic artist or gamer, a 3-D video card with acceleration features can provide much better performance. These video cards include extra RAM buffers for holding video data, better on-board processing assistance for motion video, and support for the *APIs* (application programming interfaces) that the popular applications and games are written for, such as DirectX.

Exam Essentials

Know what performance enhancements are achieved by upgrading memory.   Upgrading the amount of RAM a computer has will increase the speed of the machine by preventing the use of the hard drive to store data that is being accessed.

Know what performance enhancements are achieved by upgrading the hard drive, the IDE controller, and the IDE ribbon cable.   Replacing the hard drive can allow you to add to the overall storage capacity of the machine. In some cases, read/write performance can be improved by upgrading. Understand the UltraATA/66 and UltraATA/100 requirements.

Know what performance enhancements are achieved by updating the BIOS.   Replacing the BIOS can increase the number of supported devices.

Understand the benefits of improving system cooling.   Make sure you know what symptoms are produced by inadequate cooling and what options are available for upgrading the cooling system.

1.10 Upgrading a PC

When you're planning and executing system upgrades, it is important to know not only how to physically perform the upgrade, but also what effect the upgrade will have and what potential problems may be anticipated. This is a newly added A+ exam objective in the 2003 revision, and it emphasizes critical thinking as it pertains to upgrades.

Critical Information

Although almost any technical information about components may be useful in planning an upgrade, the A+ exam objectives provide a list of example issues for this objective; the most critical of these are summarized in the following sections.

Drivers for Legacy Devices

A *legacy device* is one that is based on old technology. Examples might include an ISA expansion card or a device that connects to a COM or LPT port rather than using the newer USB port. The term *legacy* can also refer to a piece of used hardware that is based on older technology internally.

Windows supports a wide variety of legacy devices with its own native drivers, but it may sometimes be necessary to seek out a driver for a legacy device to run under a particular operating system version. The best source is the website of the device manufacturer. Other sources are also available, such as driver repositories on the Web.

Bus Types and Characteristics

When you're selecting upgrade devices, you may have a choice of bus types to which to connect the new device. It is important to understand the benefits of the various buses so you can choose wisely.

For example, you might have a choice of an ISA or PCI internal modem, or a COM port or USB external modem. Or you might need to choose between an AGP and a PCI video card.

For external ports, USB is better and faster than both COM (legacy serial) and LPT (legacy parallel), and is further advantageous because of its seamless Plug-and-Play integration and its hot-plugging ability.

For internal buses, AGP is the fastest and best, but it is only for video cards. PCI is the next most desirable. ISA is old technology and nearly obsolete, and you should avoid it whenever possible. One exception might be an internal modem. Because an internal modem operates at a maximum of only 56Kbps, it would be least affected by being relegated to the ISA bus. In contrast, a video card would suffer greatly on ISA.

Table 1.9 describes the speeds and characteristics of internal expansion buses.

TABLE 1.9   Comparison of ISA, PCI, and AGP Buses

Bus	Width	Speed	Uses
ISA	8-bit or 16-bit	8MHz	Avoid if possible, or use for slow devices like modems
PCI	32-bit	33MHz	All nonvideo internal expansion boards
AGP	64-bit	66MHz to 133MHz	The primary video card in the system

Memory Capacity and Characteristics

When you're selecting RAM for a memory upgrade, it is important to buy the right kind. On a modern system, you must match the RAM to the motherboard's needs in the following areas:

Physical Size   168-pin or 184-DIMMs or 184-pin RIMMs.

Type   SDRAM, Double Data Rate (DDR) SDRAM, or Rambus RAM.

Speed   PC100, PC133, and up. Faster RAM will work than is required, but not slower.

Capacity   64MB, 128MB, and up. Older systems may use SIMMs (Single Inline Memory Modules), which have somewhat more complex shopping issues:

> **Physical Size**   30-pin (8-bit) or 72-pin (32-bit)
>
> **Speed**   Measured in nanoseconds of delay; for example, 60ns. Lower is better. Faster RAM will work than is required, but not slower. All RAM in the system should be the same speed.
>
> **Parity**   Some SIMMs have an extra chip for parity checking. Some motherboards require parity RAM; others make it optional or forbid it.
>
> **Refresh Technology**   Some SIMMs are Extended Data Out (EDO), allowing for better performance through less frequent refreshing. Some motherboards require it; others make it optional or forbid it.

Capacity   Varies greatly, from 256KB up to 64MB or more.

When you're shopping for RAM for a system that uses SIMMs, it's important to consult the motherboard manual to find out any special rules for installation. Some motherboards have complex charts showing the combinations and positions of the SIMMs that it will allow.

Motherboards may combine one or more RAM slots into a single logical bank, and all the RAM installed in that set of slots must be completely identical in every way. Check the motherboard documentation. On systems that use 30-pin SIMMs, four slots typically combine to create a single bank. On 486 systems that use 72-pin SIMMs, each SIMM slot is a separate bank. On Pentium systems that use 72-pin SIMMs, two SIMM slots together form a bank.

System/Firmware Limitations

One of the most common problems in upgrading to a larger hard disk is the BIOS's inability to support the larger disk size. In the original IDE specification, the size limit was 540MB. This limitation was upped to 8GB with the introduction of *Logical Block Addressing (LBA)* in 1996, which the BIOS must support. A BIOS update may be available for the motherboard to enable LBA if needed.

The 8GB limitation can be broken if the BIOS supports Enhanced BIOS Services for Disk Drives, a 1998 update. Again, a BIOS update for the motherboard may enable this support if it is lacking.

If no BIOS update is available, the choices are to replace the motherboard, to use the drive at the BIOS's maximum size it can recognize, or to install a utility program (usually provided with the hard disk) that extends the BIOS to recognize the new drive. Such utilities are very useful but can introduce some quirks in the system that cannot be easily undone, so their usage is not recommended except where no other alternative exists.

Power Supply Output Capacity

A power supply has a rated output capacity in watts, and when you fill a system with power-hungry devices, you must make sure that that maximum capacity is not exceeded. Otherwise problems with power can occur, creating lockups or spontaneous reboots.

To determine the wattage a device draws, multiply voltage by current. For example, if a device uses 5 amps of +3.3v and 0.7 amps of +12v, a total of 25 watts is consumed. Do this calculation for every device installed. Most devices have labels on them that state their power requirements.

Some devices do not have power labels; for such devices, use the numbers in Table 1.8 for estimations.

TABLE 1.10   Estimating Power Consumption

Component	Watts Consumed, for Estimating Purposes
Motherboard	20–30 watts
CPU	30–70 watts (faster CPU, more watts)
AGP video card	20–50 watts
PCI circuit boards	5 watts each
ISA circuit boards	10 watts each
Floppy drive	5 watts
CD drive	10–25 watts
RAM	8 watts per 128MB
IDE hard drive	5–15 watts
SCSI hard drive	10–40 watts

Selecting a CPU for a Motherboard

The CPU must be compatible with the motherboard in the following ways:

Physical Connectivity   The CPU must be in the right kind of package to fit into the motherboard.

Speed   The motherboard's chipset dictates its external data-bus speed; the CPU must be capable of operating at that external speed.

Instruction Set   The motherboard's chipset contains an instruction set for communicating with the CPU; the CPU must understand the commands in that set. For example, a motherboard designed for an AMD Athlon CPU cannot accept an Intel Pentium CPU, because the instruction set is different.

Voltage   The CPU requires a certain voltage of power to be supplied to it via the motherboard's interface. This can be anywhere from +5v for a very old CPU down to around +2.1v for a modern one. The wrong voltage can ruin the CPU.

Selecting a Notebook Battery

When you're shopping for notebook batteries, be aware not only of the physical size and shape (which vary depending on the notebook manufacturer's specifications), but also of the battery technology:

Nickel Cadmium (NiCad)   The least preferable. Must be recharged every 3 to 4 hours. A full recharge can take as long as 12 hours. Tend to lose their ability to hold a charge unless they are fully discharged each time before being recharged. Thus, leaving the notebook PC plugged in all the time and using the battery only occasionally for short periods of time can actually ruin the battery over time.

Nickel-Metal Hydride (NiMH)   Better than NiCad because they do not use heavy metals with great toxicity. They can also store up to 50 percent more power and do not suffer loss of functionality from partial draining and recharging.

Lithium Ion (LIon)   Lightweight and have a long life, plus they are not subject to problems with partial draining and recharging. They tend to be more expensive than NiCad or NiMH, however.

Fuel Cell   Casio recently announced plans to produce a hydrogen fuel cell battery for notebook computers that promises to last 20 hours or more on a single charge. By the time you read this, it may be available, offering greatly increased performance at a much higher price than normal notebook batteries.

Selecting a PCMCIA Card

PCMCIA cards are the expansion cards for notebook PCs. Most notebook PCs have a PCMCIA bay that can accept one Type III device or two Type I or Type II devices:

Type I   Up to 3.3mm thick. Used mostly for memory.

Type II   The most common type. Up to 5.5mm thick. Used for devices that would typically be expansion boards in a desktop PC, such as network interface cards.

Type III   Up to 10.5mm thick. Used for drives. Not common.

In addition to these types based on thickness, there are also types based on technology. The PCMCIA (PC Card) standard has recently been updated to a new standard called CardBus; look for CardBus in the specification whenever you're buying PC Card devices. CardBus devices are backward compatible with older PCMCIA slots.

Exam Essentials

Understand the differences among PCI, ISA, and AGP.   Know the bus widths and speeds and be able to select the best bus type for a given device.

Know what factors go into making memory compatible with a PC.   These factors can include physical size, capacity, technology, speed, and compatibility with existing RAM in the system.

Understand why updating the BIOS makes it possible to support larger hard disks.   Know the 8GB limit of LBA-supported systems, and how it can be overcome with Enhanced BIOS Services for Disk Drives with a BIOS update.

Be able to calculate the wattage requirements of power supplies.   Given the voltage and amperage draws for a group of devices, determine the wattage of a power supply required to support them.

Review Questions

1. What two types of expansion slots are found on all modern motherboards? What is a third, older type that might or might not also be present?

2. Name three features that distinguish an ATX motherboard from an AT motherboard.

3. What are PGA and SECC? Which of those types is the Socket 423 used with the Pentium 4?

4. What voltages does a typical power supply provide to the motherboard?

5. What is the purpose of an antistatic wrist strap, and when should it be worn?

6. Name two ports/interfaces on a notebook PC that are hot-pluggable, and two more that are not.

7. Name the default IRQs for COM1 and COM2.

8. In what Windows utility would you manually change a hardware resource assignment?

9. What is RAID 5, and what advantages does it provide?

10. Which type of SCSI is incompatible with all other types?

Answers to Review Questions

1. PCI and AGP. The third type is ISA.

2. Possible answers include: (1) position of CPU, (2) expansion slot orientation, (3) built-in ports on the side, (4) one-piece power supply connector, (5) physical size and shape of the motherboard, and (6) type of keyboard connector

3. They are the two types of slots/sockets for CPUs in motherboards. PGA is the type with a grid of holes into which pins fit on a flat chip. SECC is the type that accepts a circuit board surrounded by a cartridge. Whenever you see *socket* in the name, it's always a PGA type. SECC types have *slot* in the name.

4. +5v, -5v, +12v, and -12v for all power supplies, plus +3.3v for an ATX power supply.

5. Its purpose is to prevent electrostatic discharge (ESD, or static electricity) from damaging components. It should be worn whenever you're working inside a PC case.

6. Hot-pluggable ports/interfaces include PC Card (PCMICIA) and USB. Non hot-pluggable ports include legacy parallel, legacy serial, and VGA.

7. COM1 is usually IRQ4, and COM2 is usually IRQ3.

8. Device Manager.

9. RAID 5 uses a parity block when striping data across three or more drives, improving performance and providing fault tolerance.

10. High Voltage Differential (HVD) is incompatible with standard Single End (SE) and Low Voltage Differential (LVD).

Chapter

2

Domain 2 Diagnosing and Troubleshooting

COMPTIA A+ EXAM OBJECTIVES COVERED IN THIS CHAPTER:

- ✓ 2.1 Recognize common problems associated with each module and their symptoms, and identify steps to isolate and troubleshoot the problems. Given a problem situation, interpret the symptoms and infer the most likely cause.

- ✓ 2.2 Identify basic troubleshooting procedures and tools, and how to elicit problem symptoms from customers. Justify asking particular questions in a given scenario.

When you're troubleshooting hardware, there are a few common problems that any experienced technician should know about. These common issues usually have simple solutions. Knowing these problems and their solutions will make you a more efficient troubleshooter.

2.1 Recognizing, Isolating, and Troubleshooting Common Problems

Most computer technicians spend a great deal of time troubleshooting and repairing systems, and Domain 2.1 of the exam tests your knowledge of basic troubleshooting procedures. To study for it, you'll need to familiarize yourself with common problems and solutions related to motherboards, hard disks, RAM, cooling, and the other major system components.

Critical Information

Your value as a technician increases as you gain experience, because of the reduced time it takes you to accomplish common repairs. Your ability to troubleshoot by past experiences and gut feelings will make you more efficient and more valuable, which in turn will allow you to advance and earn a better income. This chapter will give you some guidelines you can use to evaluate common hardware issues that you are sure to face.

POST Routines

Every computer has a diagnostic program built into its BIOS called the *power on self-test* (*POST*). When you turn on the computer, it executes this set of diagnostics. Many steps are involved the POST, but they happen very quickly, they are invisible to the user, and they vary among BIOS versions. The steps include checking the CPU, checking the RAM, checking for the presence of a video card, and so on. The main reason to be aware of the POST's existence is that if it encounters a problem, the boot process stops. Being able to determine at what point the problem occurred can help you troubleshoot.

One way to determine the source of a problem is to listen for a *beep code*. This is a series of beeps from the computer's speaker. The number, duration, and pattern of the beeps can sometimes tell you what component is causing the problem. However, the beeps differ depending on the BIOS manufacturer and version, so you must look up the beep code in a chart for your particular BIOS. Different BIOS manufacturers use the beeping differently. AMI BIOS, for example, relies on a raw number of beeps, but uses patterns of short and long beeps.

Another way to determine a problem during the POST routine is to use a *POST card*. This is a circuit board that fits into an ISA or PCI expansion slot in the motherboard and reports numeric codes as the boot process progresses. Each of those codes corresponds to a particular component being checked. If the POST card stops at a certain number, you can look up that number in the manual that came with the card to determine the problem.

BIOS Central is a website containing charts detailing the beep codes and POST error codes for many different BIOS manufacturers: `www.bioscentral.com/`.

Motherboard and CPU Problems

Most motherboard and CPU problems manifest themselves by the system appearing completely dead. However, "completely dead" can be a symptom of a wide variety of problems, not only with the CPU or motherboard but also with the RAM or the power supply. So, a POST card (described in the preceding section) may be helpful in narrowing down the exact component that is faulty.

When a motherboard fails, it is usually because it has been damaged. Most technicians cannot repair motherboard damage; the motherboard must be replaced. Motherboards can become damaged due to physical trauma, exposure to electrostatic discharge (ESD), or short-circuiting. To minimize the risk of these damages, observe the following rules:

- Handle a motherboard as little as possible, and keep it in an antistatic bag whenever it is removed from the PC case.

- Keep all liquids well away from the motherboard, because water can cause a short circuit.

- Wear an antistatic wrist strap when handling or touching a motherboard.

- When installing a motherboard in a case, make sure you use brass stand-offs with paper washers to prevent any stray solder around the screw holes from causing a short circuit with the metal of the screw.

A CPU may fail because of physical trauma or short-circuiting, but the most common cause for a CPU not to work is failure to install it properly. With a PGA-style CPU, ensure that the CPU is oriented correctly in the socket. With an SECC-style CPU, make sure the CPU is completely inserted into its slot.

I/O Ports and Cables

I/O ports include legacy parallel and serial, USB, and FireWire ports, all of which are used to connect external peripherals to the motherboard. When a port does not appear to be functioning, check the following:

- Cables are snugly connected.

- The port has not been disabled in BIOS Setup.

- The port has not been disabled in Device Manager in Windows.

- No pins are broken or bent on the male end of the port or cable being plugged into it.

If you suspect that the cable, rather than the port, may be the problem, swap out the cable with a known-good one. If you do not have an extra cable, you can test the existing cable with a multimeter by setting it to ohms and checking the resistance between one end of the cable and the other.

Use a pin-out diagram, if available, to determine which pin matches up to which at the other end. There is often—but not always—an inverse relationship between the ends. In other words, at one end pin 1 is at the left, and at the other end it is at the right on the same row of pins.

Cooling Issues

A PC that works for a few minutes and then locks up is probably experiencing overheating due to a heat sink or fan not functioning properly. To troubleshoot overheating, first check all fans inside the PC to ensure they are operating, and make sure that any heat sinks are firmly attached to their chips.

In a properly designed, properly assembled PC case, air flows in a specific path from the power supply fan through the vent holes. Cases are designed to cool by making the air flow in a certain way. Therefore, operating a PC with the cover removed can actually make a PC more susceptible to overheating, even though it is "getting more air."

Similarly, operating a PC with empty expansion slot backplates removed can inhibit a PC's ability to cool itself properly because the extra holes change the airflow pattern from what was intended by its design.

Although CPUs are the most common component to overheat, occasionally chips on other devices, particularly video cards, may also overheat. Extra heat sinks or fans may be installed to cool these chips.

Case Issues

A PC case holds the drives in its bays, holds the power supply, and has lights and buttons on the front. For the first two of those functions, simply make sure that the drives and the power supply are tightly fastened in the case with screws.

If one of the lights or buttons on the front of the PC is not functioning, remove the cover and check the wires that run from the back of that button/light to the motherboard. If the wire has become detached, reattach it. Refer to the motherboard manual or the writing on the motherboard itself to determine what goes where.

Hard Disk System Problems

Hard disk system problems usually stem from one of three causes:

- The adapter (that is, the IDE or SCSI interface) is bad.
- The disk is bad.
- The adapter and disk are connected incorrectly.

The first and last causes are easy to identify, because in either case the symptom will be obvious: The drive won't work. You simply won't be able to get the computer to communicate with the disk drive.

However, if the problem is a bad disk drive, the symptoms aren't as obvious. As long as the BIOS POST routines can communicate with the disk drive, they are usually satisfied. But the POST routines may not uncover problems related to storing information. Even with healthy POST results, you may find that you're permitted to save information to a bad disk, but when you try to read it back you get errors. Or the computer may not boot as quickly as it used to, because the disk drive can't read the boot information successfully every time.

In some cases, reformatting the drive can solve the problems described in the preceding paragraph. In other cases, reformatting brings the drive back to life only for a short while. The bottom line is that read and write problems usually indicate that the drive is malfunctioning and should be replaced soon.

WARNING Never low-level format IDE or SCSI drives! They are low-level formatted from the factory, and you may cause problems by using low-level utilities on these types of drives.

Modem Problems

The most common peripheral problems are those related to modem communications. The symptoms of these problems include the following:

- The modem won't dial.
- The modem keeps hanging up in the middle of the communications session.
- The modem spits out strange characters to the terminal screen.

If the modem won't dial, first check that it has been configured correctly in Windows, including its resource assignments.

Some modems work only under Windows because some of their functions rely on Windows software; these are called *Winmodems* or *software modems*. If such a modem does not work immediately upon installation, try running the Setup software that came with the modem.

If the configuration is correct, and Windows recognizes the modem, it should work for dial-up networking connections.

AT Commands

When you're using a terminal application such as HyperTerminal, it is important to use the correct initialization commands. These are the commands sent to the modem by the communications program to initialize it. These commands tell the modem such things as how many rings to wait before answering, how long to wait after the last keystroke was detected for it to disconnect, and at what speed to communicate.

Modem initialization commands are known as the *Hayes command set* or the *AT command set*, because each Hayes modem command started with the letters AT (presumably calling the modem to ATtention).

Each AT command does something different. The letters AT by themselves ask the modem if it's ready to receive commands. If it returns *OK*, the modem is ready to communicate. If you receive *Error*, there is an internal modem problem that may need to be resolved before communication can take place.

Table 2.1 lists a few of the most common AT commands, their functions, and the problems they can solve. You can send these commands to the modem by opening a terminal program like Windows Terminal or HyperTerminal and typing them in. All commands should return *OK* if they were successful.

TABLE 2.1   Common AT Commands

Command	Function	Usage
AT	Tells the modem that what follows the letters AT is a command that should be interpreted	Used to precede most commands.
ATDT *nnnnnnn*	Dials the number *nnnnnnn* as a tone-dialed number	Used to dial the number of another modem if the phone line is set up for tone dialing.
ATDP *nnnnnnn*	Dials the number *nnnnnnn* as a pulse-dialed number	Used to dial the number of another modem if the phone line is set up for rotary dialing.
ATA	Answers an incoming call manually	Places the line off-hook and starts to negotiate communication with the modem on the other end.
ATH0 (or +++ and then ATH0)	Tells the modem to hang up immediately	Places the line on-hook and stops communication. (Note: The 0 in this command is a zero, not the letter *O*.)
AT&F	Resets the modem to factory default settings	This setting works as the initialization string when others don't. If you have problems with modems hanging up in the middle of a session or failing to establish connections, use this string by itself to initialize the modem.
ATZ	Resets the modem to power-up defaults	Almost as good as AT&F, but may not work if power-up defaults have been changed with S-registers.
ATS0-*n*	Waits *n* rings before answering a call	Sets the default number of rings that the modem will detect before taking the modem off-hook and negotiating a connection. (Note: The 0 in this command is a zero, not the letter *O*.)

TABLE 2.1   Common AT Commands *(continued)*

Command	Function	Usage
ATS6-*n*	Waits *n* seconds for a dial tone before dialing	If the phone line is slow to give a dial tone, you may have to set this register to a number higher than 2.
,	Pauses briefly	When placed in a string of AT commands, the comma will cause a pause to occur. Used to separate the number for an outside line (many businesses use 9 to connect to an outside line) and the real phone number (for example, 9,555-1234).
*70 or 1170	Turns off call waiting	The click you hear when you have call waiting (a feature offered by the phone company) will interrupt modem communication and cause the connection to be lost. To disable call waiting for a modem call, place these commands in the dialing string like so: *70,555-1234. Call waiting will resume after the call is hung up.
CONNECT	Displays when a successful connection has been made	You may have to wait some time before this message is displayed. If this message is not displayed, the modem couldn't negotiate a connection with the modem on the other end of the line, possibly due to line noise.
BUSY	Displays when the number dialed is busy	If this message is displayed, some programs will wait a certain amount of time and try again to dial.
RING	Displays when the modem has detected a ringing line	When someone is calling your modem, the modem will display this message in the communications program. You type **ATA** to answer the call.

If two computers can connect, but they both receive garbage on their screens, there's a good chance that the computers don't agree on the communications settings. Settings such as data bits, parity, stop bits, and compression must all agree in order for communication to take place.

Keyboard and Mouse Problems

Usually, keyboard problems are environmental. Keyboards get dirty, and the keys start to stick.

> If a keyboard is actually malfunctioning (for example, sending the wrong characters to the display), it is most cost effective to replace it rather than spend hours attempting to fix it, because keyboards are fairly inexpensive.

One way to clean a keyboard is with the keyboard cleaner sold by electronics supply stores. This cleaner foams up quickly and doesn't leave a residue behind. Spray it liberally on the keyboard and keys. Work the cleaner in between the keys with a stiff toothbrush. Blow away the excess with a strong blast of compressed air. Repeat until the keyboard functions properly. If you have to clean a keyboard that's had a soft drink spilled on it, remove the key caps before you perform the cleaning procedure; doing so makes it easier to reach the sticky plungers.

> Remember that most of the dollars spent on systems are for labor. If you spend an hour cleaning a $12.00 keyboard, then you have probably just cost your company $20.00. Knowing how to fix certain things doesn't necessarily mean that you *should* fix them. Always evaluate your workload, the cost of replacement, and the estimated cost of the repair before deciding on a course of action.

Similarly, most mouse problems, such as the pointer failing to move in one direction or the other, or the pointer jumping around onscreen, are due to dirt building up inside the mouse. To clean a standard mouse, remove the plate on the bottom of the mouse that holds the ball in place; then remove the ball and clean the inside chamber with an alcohol-dipped cotton swab. Clean the ball itself with mild soap and water. Do not use alcohol on the ball, because it tends to dry out the rubber.

Display System Problems

There are two types of video problems: no video and bad video. *No video* means no image appears on the screen when the computer is powered up. *Bad video* means the quality is substandard for the type of display system being used.

No Video

Any number of things can cause a blank screen. The first three are the most common: the power is off, the monitor's cable is unplugged, or the contrast or brightness is turned down.

If you've checked the power as well as the brightness and contrast settings, then the problem could be a bad video card or a bad monitor. Most monitors these days display a *Working* message briefly when you turn them on, so you can ascertain that the monitor is working and that an amber light appears on the front. When the PC starts up, the light on the front of the monitor changes from amber to green, indicating that the monitor is receiving a signal.

If the monitor is working but not receiving a signal from the PC, the video card may be bad. However, no video can also mean a problem with the motherboard, RAM, or CPU, so it is not a given that the video card is at fault when no video appears.

Malfunctioning monitors are usually not worth fixing, because the cost of the labor involved exceeds the cost of a brand-new monitor. In addition, it may be difficult to find a technician to work on a monitor, because it is not part of most standard PC technician training programs (due to the risk of electric shock from the high-voltage capacitor inside the monitor).

Bad Video

A monitor that does not display one of the three basic colors (red, green, or blue) probably has a bad cable, a bent or broken pin, or a loose connection at either the PC or the monitor. This is the case because different pins on the connectors—and wires in the cable—control different colors.

Color problems may also result from the monitor being out of adjustment. With most new monitors, this is an easy problem to fix. Old monitors had to be partially disassembled to change these settings. New monitors have push-button control panels for changing these settings.

Exposure to a magnetic field can cause swirls and fuzziness even in high-quality monitors. The Earth itself generates magnetic fields, as do unshielded speakers and power surges. Most monitors have metal shields that can protect against magnetic fields. But eventually these shields can get polluted by taking on the same magnetic field as the Earth, so they becomes useless. To solve this problem, these monitors have a built-in feature known as *Degauss*. This feature removes the effects of the magnetic field by creating a stronger magnetic field with opposite polarity that gradually fades to a field of zero. A special Degauss button or feature in the monitor's on-screen software activates it. You need only press it when the picture starts to deteriorate. The image will shake momentarily during the Degauss cycle, and then return to normal.

If you have a monitor that shows bad distortion, and changing the settings or Degaussing has no effect, then look for magnetic interference caused by nearby florescent lights or large power sources.

Floppy and Other Removable Disk Drive Problems

Most floppy-drive problems result from bad media. Your first troubleshooting technique with floppy-drive issues should be to try a new disk.

One of the most common problems that develops with floppy drives is misaligned read/write heads. The symptoms are fairly easy to recognize—you can read and write to a floppy on one machine but not on any others. This is normally caused by the mechanical arm in the floppy drive becoming misaligned. When the disk was formatted, it was not properly positioned on the drive, thus preventing other floppy drives from reading it.

Numerous commercial tools are available to realign floppy drive read/write heads. They use a floppy drive that has been preformatted to reposition the mechanical arm. In most cases, though, this fix is temporary—the arm will move out of place again fairly soon. Given the inexpensive nature of the problem, the best solution is to spent a few dollars and replace the drive.

Another problem you may encounter is a phantom directory listing. For example, suppose you display the contents of a floppy disk, and then you swap to another floppy disk but the listing stays the same. This is almost always a result of a faulty ribbon cable; a particular wire in the ribbon cable signals when a disk swap has taken place, and when that wire breaks, this error occurs.

Sound Card Problems

Sound cards are traditionally one of the most problem-ridden components in a PC. They demand a lot of PC resources and are notorious for being very inflexible in their configuration. The most common problems related to sound cards involve resource conflicts (IRQ, DMA, or I/O address). The problem is much less pronounced on PCI than on ISA cards.

Luckily, most sound-card vendors are quite aware of the problems and ship very good diagnostic utilities to help resolve them. Use your PC troubleshooting skills to determine the conflict, and then reconfigure until you find an acceptable set of resources that are not in use.

Some sound cards are not completely Plug-and-Play compatible. Windows might detect that new hardware has been installed, but be unable to identify the new hardware as a working sound card. To fix this problem, run the Setup software that came with the sound card.

CD-ROM/DVD Issues

CD-ROM and DVD problems are normally media related. Although compact disc technology is much more reliable than floppy disks, it is still not perfect. Another factor to consider is the cleanliness of the disc. On many occasions, if a disc is unreadable, simply cleaning it with an approved cleaner and a lint-free cleaning towel will fix the problem.

If the operating system does not see the drive, start troubleshooting by determining whether the drive is receiving power. If the tray will eject, you can assume there is power to it. Next, check BIOS Setup (for IDE drives) to make sure the drive has been detected. If not, check the Master/Slave jumper on the drive and make sure that the IDE adapter is set to Auto, CD-ROM, or ATAPI in BIOS Setup.

In order to play movies, a DVD drive must have MPEG decoding capability. This is usually accomplished via an expansion board, but it may be built into the video card or sound card, or it may be a software decoder. If DVD data discs will play but not movies, suspect a problem with the MPEG decoding.

If a CD-RW or DVD drive works normally as a regular CD-ROM drive but does not perform its special capability (does not read DVD discs, or does not write to blank CDs), perhaps software needs to be installed to work with it. For example, with CD-RW drives, unless you are using an operating system such as Windows XP that supports CD writing, you must install CD writing software in order to write to CDs.

Network Interface Card

In general, network interface cards (NICs) are added to a PC via an expansion slot. The most common issue that prevents network connectivity is a bad or unplugged patch cable.

Cleaning crews and the rollers on the bottoms of chairs are the most common threats to a patch cable. In most cases, wall jacks are placed 4 to 10 feet away from the desktop. The patch cables are normally lying exposed under the user's desk, and from time to time damage is done to the cable or it is inadvertently snagged and unplugged. When you troubleshoot a network adapter, start with the most rudimentary explanations first. Make sure the patch cable is tightly plugged in, and then look at the card and see if any lights are on. If there are lights on, use the NIC's documentation to help troubleshoot. More often than not, simply shutting down the machine, unplugging the patch and power cables for a moment, and then reattaching them and rebooting the PC will fix an unresponsive NIC.

Although this is not on the test, it's useful information: Wake On LAN cards have more problems than standard network cards. In my opinion, this is because they are always on. In some cases, you will be unable to get the card working again unless you unplug the PC's power supply and reset the card.

BIOS Issues

Computer BIOSes don't really go bad; they just become out-of-date. This is not necessary a critical issue—they will continue to support the hardware that came with the box. It *does*, however, become an issue when the BIOS doesn't support some component that you would like to install—a larger hard drive, for instance.

Most of today's BIOSes are written to an EEPROM and can be updated through the use of software. Each manufacturer has its own method for accomplishing this. Check out the documentation for complete details.

If you make a mistake in the upgrade process, the computer can become unbootable. If this happens, your only option may be to ship the box to a manufacturer-approved service center. Be careful!

Power Supply Problems

Power supply problems are usually easy to troubleshoot. The system does not respond in any way when the power is turned on. When this happens, open the case, remove the power supply, and replace it with a new one.

Be aware that different cases have different types of on/off switches. The process of replacing a power supply is a lot easier if you purchase a replacement with the same mechanism. Even so, remember to document exactly how the power supply was connected to the on/off switch before you remove it.

Problems with Notebook PCs

Notebook PCs have many of the same problems and solutions as desktop PCs. Most of their unique problems have to do with power.

When a battery does not hold a charge well, it is probably a Nickel Cadmium (NiCad) battery. This type of battery has a memory, so if it is not fully discharged before recharging, it fails to hold as much of a charge the next time. The solution is to replace it with a different type of battery, such as Lithium Ion, or to replace it with the same type of battery and then be careful to let it discharge each time.

When a notebook computer will not enter Standby or Hibernate mode, or will not wake up from it, suspect a conflict between the BIOS's power management and Windows'. Disable one or the other to prevent the conflict.

An older BIOS may support the older Advanced Power Management (APM) standard rather than the newer Advanced Configuration and Power Interface (ACPI) power management. Updating the BIOS may provide the support needed for ACPI, which is more trouble-free.

In the short term, to wake up a PC that is stuck in Hibernate or Standby, try pressing and holding the Power button for 5 to 10 seconds. If this does not work, try unplugging the PC from the AC outlet and removing the batteries. Then replace the battery and turn it back on.

Sometimes an outdated video driver can cause power-management problems; updating the video driver may solve the problem.

Miscellaneous Problems

Some common problems do not fit well into categories. This section lists some common hardware issues you will be faced with.

Dislodged Chips and Cards

The inside of a computer is a harsh environment. The temperature inside the case of some Pentium computers is well over 100° F! When you turn on your computer, it heats up. Turn it off, and it cools down. After several hundred such cycles, some components can't handle the stress and begin to move out of their sockets. This phenomenon is known as *chip creep,* and it can be really frustrating.

Chip creep can affect any socketed device, including ICs, RAM chips, and expansion cards. The solution to chip creep is simple: Open the case and reseat the devices. It's surprising how often this is the solution to phantom problems of all sorts.

Another important item worth mentioning is an unresponsive but freshly unboxed PC. With the introduction of the Type II and Type II-style of processors, the number of dead boxes increased dramatically. In fact, at that time I was leading a 2,000-unit migration for a large financial institution. As with any large migration, time and manpower were in short supply. The average dead PC ratio was about 1 out of every 20. When about 10 DOAs had stacked up, I stayed after work one night to assess the problem. After checking the power supply, RAM, and cables on these integrated systems, an examination of the chip provided me with the fix. These large, top-heavy processors can become dislodged during shipment. Shortly after, manufacturers began using a heavier attachment point for the slot style of processor, which has helped tremendously.

Environmental Problems

Computers are like human beings. They have similar tolerances to heat and cold. In general, anything comfortable to us is comfortable to computers. They need lots of clean, moving air to keep them functioning.

Dirt, grime, paint, smoke, and other airborne particles can become caked on the inside of the components. This is most common in automotive and manufacturing environments. The contaminants create a film that coats the components, causing them to overheat and/or conduct electricity on their surface. Simply blowing out these exposed systems with a can of condensed air from time to time can prevent damage to the components. While you are cleaning the components, be sure to clean any cooling fans in the power supply or on the heat sink.

To clean the power supply fan, blow the air from the inside of the case. When you do this, the fan will blow the contaminants out the cooling vents. If you spray from the vents toward the inside of the box, you will be blowing the dust and grime inside the case or back into the fan motor.

One way to ensure that the environment has the least possible effect on your computer is to always leave the *blanks* in the empty slots on the back of your box. These pieces of metal are designed to keep dirt, dust, and other foreign matter from the inside of the computer. They also maintain proper airflow within the case to ensure that the computer does not overheat.

Exam Essentials

Be familiar with the purpose of POST routines.   The POST routines perform entry-level hardware troubleshooting as a PC starts. Be familiar with the abilities of the POST and its use.

Be able to diagnose port problems.   When a port is not functioning, make sure you know the steps to take to ensure that it is physically connected, enabled in BIOS, and recognized in Windows.

Know how to troubleshoot hard-disk system problems.   Be aware of the common causes of hard-disk problems, including improper jumper configuration, BIOS Setup, and formatting/partitioning issues.

Identify problems that can result from overheating.   Overheating can cause spontaneous rebooting or shutdown, and is often caused by nonfunctioning cooling fans or improper airflow through the PC.

Be able to determine display system problems.   The most common display problems relate to power, brightness, or contrast. Simply adjusting the monitor controls should be your first step when troubleshooting.

Recognize the symptoms of floppy-drive problems.   Most floppy-drive problems result from bad media. Your first troubleshooting technique with floppy-drive issues should be to try a new disk.

Know how to troubleshoot sound-card problems.   Sound cards demand a lot of PC resources and are notorious for being very inflexible in their configuration. The most common problems related to sound cards involve resource conflicts (IRQ, DMA, or I/O address).

Learn to identify BIOS issues.   BIOS issues are related to the inability to support hardware. In most cases, a program or flash upgrade is available to update the BIOS so that components can be supported.

Recognize power supply problems.   Become familiar with the symptoms of a dead, failing, or overloaded power supply.

Know the symptoms of dislodged chips and cards.   Dislodged components are the most common issues you will face. Become familiar with the symptoms and their fixes.

2.2 Basic Troubleshooting Procedures and Tools

Just as all artists have their own style, all technicians have their own way to troubleshoot. Some people use their instincts; others rely on advice from other people. The most common trouble-shooting tips can be condensed into a step-by-step process. You try each step, in order. If the first step doesn't narrow down the problem, you move on to the next step.

Critical Information

In this section we'll look at each step in the troubleshooting process.

Step 1: Define the Problem

If you can't define the problem, you can't begin to solve it. You can define the problem by asking questions of the user. Here are a few questions to ask the user to aid in determining what the problem is, exactly:

Can you show me the problem?   This question is one of the best. It allows the user to show you exactly where and when they experience the problem.

How often does this happen?   This question establishes whether this problem is a one-time occurrence that can be solved with a reboot, or whether a specific sequence of events causes the problem to happen. The latter usually indicates a more serious problem that may require soft-ware installation or hardware replacement.

Has any new hardware been installed recently?   New hardware can mean compatibility prob-lems with existing devices. Some Plug-and-Play devices install with the same resource settings as an existing device. This can cause both devices to become disabled.

Have any other changes been made to the computer recently?   If the answer is "Yes," ask if the user can remember approximately when the change was made. Then ask them approxi-mately when the problem started. If the two dates seem related, then there's a good chance that the problem is related to the change. If it's a new hardware component, check to see that the hardware component was installed correctly.

Step 2: Check the Simple Stuff First

This step is the one that most experienced technicians overlook. Often, computer problems are the result of something simple. Technicians overlook these problems because they're so simple that the technicians assume they *couldn't* be the problem. Some examples of simple problems are shown here:

Is it plugged in?   And plugged in on both ends? Cables must be plugged in on *both ends* in order to function correctly. Cables can be easily tripped over and inadvertently pulled from their sockets.

Is it turned on?   This one seems the most obvious, but we've all fallen victim to it at one point or another. Computers and their peripherals must be turned on in order to function. Most have power switches with LEDs that glow when the power is turned on.

Is the system ready?   Computers must be ready before they can be used. *Ready* means the system is ready to accept commands from the user. An indication that a computer is ready is when the operating system screens come up and the computer presents you with a menu or a command prompt. If that computer uses a graphical interface, the computer is ready when the mouse pointer appears. Printers are ready when the On Line or Ready light on the front panel is lit.

Do the chips and cables need to be reseated?   You can solve some of the strangest problems (random hang-ups or errors) by opening the case and pressing down on each socketed chip. This remedies the chip-creep problem mentioned earlier in this chapter. In addition, you should reseat any cables to make sure that they are making good contact.

Step 3: Check to See If It's User Error

This error is common but preventable. The indication that a problem is due to user error is when a user says they can't perform some very common computer task, such as printing or saving a file. As soon you hear these words, you should begin asking questions to determine if it is simply a matter of teaching the user the correct procedure. A good question to ask following their statement of the problem would be, "Were you *ever* able to perform that task?" If they answer "No" to this question, it means they are probably doing the procedure wrong. If they answer "Yes," you must move on to another set of questions.

The Social Side of Troubleshooting

When you're looking for clues as to the nature of a problem, no one can give you more information than the person who was there when it happened. They can tell you what led up to the problem, what software was running, and the exact nature of the problem ("It happened when I tried to print"), and they can help you re-create the problem, if possible.

Use questioning techniques that are neutral in nature. Instead of saying, "What were you doing when it broke?" be more compassionate and say, "What was going on when the computer decided not to work?" It sounds silly, but these types of changes can make your job a lot easier!

Step 4: Reboot the Computer

It is amazing how often a simple computer reboot can solve a problem. Rebooting the computer clears the memory and starts the computer with a clean slate. Whenever I perform phone support, I always ask the customer to reboot the computer and try again. If rebooting doesn't work, try powering down the system completely and then powering it up again. More often than not, that will solve the problem.

Step 5: Determine If the Problem Is Hardware- or Software-Related

This step is important because it determines what part of the computer you should focus your troubleshooting skills on. Each part requires different skills and different tools.

To determine if a problem is hardware- or software-related, you can do a few things to narrow down the issue. For instance, does the problem manifest itself when you use a particular piece of hardware (a modem, for example)? If it does, the problem is more than likely hardware-related.

This step relies on personal experience more than any of the other steps do. You will without a doubt run into strange software problems. Each one has a particular solution. Some may even require reinstallation of the software or the entire operating system.

Step 6: If the Problem Is Hardware-Related, Determine Which Component Is Failing

Hardware problems are pretty easy to figure out. If the modem doesn't work, and you know it isn't a software problem, the modem is probably the piece of hardware that needs to be replaced.

With some of the newer computers, several components are integrated into the motherboard. If you troubleshoot the computer and find a hardware component to be bad, there's a good chance that the bad component is integrated into the motherboard (for example, the parallel port circuitry) and the whole motherboard must be replaced—an expensive proposition, to be sure.

Step 7: Check Service Information Sources

As you may (or may not) have figured out by now, I'm fond of old sayings. There's another old saying that applies here: "If all else fails, read the instructions." The service manuals are your instructions for troubleshooting and service information. Almost every computer and peripheral made today has service documentation in the form of books, service CD-ROMs, and websites. The latter of the three is growing in popularity as more and more service centers get connections to the Internet.

Step 8: If It Ain't Broke...

When doctors take the Hippocratic oath, they promise to not make their patients any sicker than they already were. Technicians should take a similar oath. It all boils down to, "If it ain't broke, don't fix it." When you troubleshoot, make one change at a time. If the change doesn't solve the problem, revert the computer to its previous state before making a different change.

Step 9: Ask for Help

If you don't know the answer, ask one of your fellow technicians. They may have run across the problem you are having and know the solution.

This solution does involve a little humility. You must admit that you don't know the answer. It is said that the beginning of wisdom is "I don't know." If you ask questions, you will get answers, and you will learn from the answers. Making mistakes is valuable as well, as long as you learn from them.

Throughout my career in the computer business, the reluctance to share information has been the thing that most concerns me about this industry. As computer professionals, we are valued due to the extent of our knowledge. Some of us intend to keep our value high by limiting the flow of knowledge to others. My position is different than that of those tight-lipped people. I like to help and to teach. This factor has been my best asset as I climbed from the help desk to become an IS manager. The most amusing thing is that despite my impressive title, many certifications, and two published technical books, I still ask for advice and help on a daily basis. If I don't know the answer, I ask, and it doesn't bother me a bit. If I know and I'm asked, I share and try to bring the other person to the understanding that I have of that particular subject. One of the greatest assets you can have is another opinion or another person to bounce ideas off.

Exam Essentials

Know the basic steps of troubleshooting.   Troubleshooting is a process of trial and error. For the exam and your career, use this system to diagnose and repair hardware-related issues.

Check your information sources.   Service manuals are your instructions for troubleshooting and service information. Almost every computer and peripheral made today has service documentation in the form of books, service CD-ROMs, and websites.

Ask for help.   If you don't know the answer, ask one of your fellow technicians. They may have run across the problem you are having and know the solution. This is one thing I feel very strongly about. Don't be embarrassed to ask, and don't be too tight-lipped to help others.

Review Questions

1. Would the POST test identify a problem with RAM?

2. If a legacy serial port is physically fine but does not show up in Windows' Device Manager, how might you enable it?

3. When testing a cable for broken wires, what type of measurement should the multimeter be set up to register?

4. If an IDE drive's Master/Slave jumper was set incorrectly, and therefore the drive did not appear in Windows, would the drive appear in BIOS Setup?

5. What AT command resets the modem?

6. If the mouse pointer is jumping around erratically on-screen, how can you fix the problem?

7. If a peripheral device such as a sound card shows up in Device Manager as an Unknown Device after being detected by Plug and Play, how can you get it to be recognized fully?

8. If a notebook PC will not wake up from Standby mode, how can you force it to start up?

9. A client calls you, saying his PC will power up, but not boot. What are some questions you would ask to help narrow down the problem?

10. True or false: The best way to clean a mouse's ball is with alcohol.

Answers to Review Questions

1. Yes. One of the components the POST checks is the RAM.

2. It may be disabled in BIOS Setup; try enabling it there.

3. Ohms (resistance).

4. No.

5. ATZ.

6. Clean the mouse.

7. Run the Setup software that came with it.

8. Remove all power from the PC, including removing the battery.

9. Yours may vary, but here are some possible questions: (1) Have you installed any new hardware recently? (2) Have you installed any new software? (3) What were you doing when the problem occurred? (4) Will the PC boot into safe mode? (5) Will the PC boot from a floppy? (6) Does the problem happen every time you try to boot, or only sporadically?

10. False. Alcohol dries out the rubber. The mouse ball is one of the few computer components that should be cleaned with soap and water.

Chapter

3

Domain 3 Preventive Maintenance

COMPTIA A+ EXAM OBJECTIVES COVERED IN THIS CHAPTER:

- ✓ 3.1 Identify the various types of preventive maintenance measures, products and procedures and when and how to use them.

- ✓ 3.2 Identify various safety measures and procedures, and when/how to use them.

- ✓ 3.3 Identify environmental protection measures and procedures, and when/how to use them.

The A+ exam will contain a few questions on preventive maintenance, although the bulk of the questions will relate to troubleshooting and general knowledge. As a certified technician, you can use preventive maintenance to reduce your workload. Simple procedures can be implemented by both the IS department or the users to reduce the number of failed components.

The exam may also include questions about computer safety. You will need to know how to keep people safe, how to make sure equipment does not get damaged, and how to protect the environment from hazardous chemicals and equipment.

3.1 Performing Preventive Maintenance

This section outlines some preventive maintenance products and procedures. Preventive maintenance is one of the most overlooked ways to reduce the cost of ownership in any environment.

Critical Information

Cleaning a computer system is the most important part of maintaining it. Computer components get dirty. Dirt reduces their operating efficiency and, ultimately, their life. Cleaning them is definitely important. But cleaning them with the right cleaning compounds is equally important. Using the wrong compounds can leave residue behind that is more harmful than the dirt you are trying to remove!

Most computer cases and monitor cases can be cleaned using mild soap and water on a clean, lint-free cloth. Make sure the power is off before you put anything wet near a computer. Dampen (not soak) a cloth with a mild soap solution and wipe the dirt and dust from the case. Then wipe the moisture from the case with a dry, lint-free cloth. Anything with a plastic or metal case can be cleaned in this manner.

Don't drip liquid into any vent holes on equipment. CRTs in particular have vent holes in the top.

To clean a monitor screen, use glass cleaner designed specifically for monitors, and a soft cloth. Do not use commercial window cleaner, because the chemicals in it can ruin the antiglare coating on some monitors.

To clean a keyboard, use canned air to blow debris out from under keys, and use towelettes designed for use with computers to keep the key tops clean. If you spill anything on a keyboard, you can clean it by soaking it in distilled, *demineralized water*. The minerals and impurities have been removed from this type of water, so it will not leave any traces of residue that might interfere with the proper operation of the keyboard after cleaning. Make sure you let the keyboard dry for at least 48 hours before using it.

The electronic connectors of computer equipment, on the other hand, should never touch water. Instead, use a swab moistened in distilled, *denatured isopropyl alcohol* (also known as electronics cleaner and found in electronics stores) to clean contacts. Doing so will take the oxidation off the copper contacts.

A good way to remove dust and dirt from the inside of the computer is to use compressed air. Simply blow the dust from inside the computer using a stream of compressed air. However, be sure you do this outdoors, so you don't blow dust all over your work area or yourself. You can also use a vacuum, but it must be designed specifically for electronics—such models do not generate electrostatic discharge (ESD) and have a finer filter on them than normal.

To prevent a computer from becoming dirty in the first place, control its environment. Make sure there is adequate ventilation in the work area and that the dust level is not excessive. To avoid ESD, you should maintain 50- to 80-percent humidity in the room where the computer is operating.

One unique challenge when cleaning printers is spilled toner. It sticks to everything and should not be breathed. Use a vacuum designed specifically for electronics. A normal vacuum's filter is not fine enough to catch all the particles, so the toner may be circulated into the air. A normal vacuum also may generate ESD.

 If you get toner on your clothes, use a magnet to get it out (toner is half iron).

Removable media devices such as floppy and CD drives do not usually need to be cleaned during preventive maintenance. Clean one only if you are experiencing problems with it. Cleaning kits sold in computer stores provide the needed supplies. Usually, cleaning a floppy drive involves a dummy floppy disk made of semi-abrasive material. When you insert the disk in the drive, the drive spins it, and the abrasive action on the read-write head removes any debris.

An uninterruptible power supply (UPS) should be checked periodically as part of the preventive maintenance routine to make sure that its battery is operational. Most UPSs have a Test button you can press to simulate a power outage.

Remember, preventive maintenance is more than just manipulating hardware; it also encompasses running software utilities on a regular basis to keep the filesystem fit. These utilities can include Disk Defragmenter, ScanDisk, Check Disk, and Disk Cleanup.

Exam Essentials

Know what can be used to clean computer components.   Many types of cleaning solutions can be used to perform these procedures. Be familiar with which option is best for each component. Which ones can be cleaned with water? Which ones require alcohol? Which ones need canned air?

Know why the proper cleaning solutions should be used.   Using the wrong cleaning solution can damage components. Along with choosing the right cleaning solution, understand why the unchosen solutions are inappropriate for a particular component.

3.2 Observing Safety Measures

This objective deals with potential hazards, both to you and to the computer system. It focuses on protecting humans from harm due to electricity, heat, and other hazards, and on protecting computer components from harm due to electrostatic discharge (ESD).

Critical Information

As a provider of a hands-on service, you need to be aware of some general safety tips, because if you are not careful, you could harm yourself or the equipment.

Preventing Harm to Humans

Computers, display monitors, and printers can be dangerous if not handled properly. Computers not only use electricity, but they store electrical charge after they're turned off, in components called *capacitors*. The monitor and the power supply have large capacitors, capable of delivering significant shock, so they should not be disassembled except by a trained electrical repairperson.

In addition, various parts of the printer run at extremely high temperatures, and you can get burned if you try to handle them immediately after they've been in operation. Two examples are the CPU chip and the fusing unit inside a laser printer.

Extinguishing Electrical Fires

Repairing a computer is not often the cause of an electrical fire. However, you should know how to extinguish such a fire properly. Three major classes of fire extinguishers are available, one for each type of flammable substance: A for wood and paper fires, B for flammable liquids, and C for electrical fires. The most popular type of fire extinguisher today is the multipurpose, or ABC-rated, extinguisher. It contains a dry chemical powder that smothers the fire and cools it at the same time. For electrical fires (which may be related to a shorted-out wire in a power supply), make sure the fire extinguisher will work for class C fires. If you don't have an extinguisher that is specifically rated for electrical fires (type C), you can use an ABC-rated extinguisher.

Power Supply Safety

Although it is possible to work on a power supply, doing so is *not* recommended. Power supplies contain several capacitors that can hold *lethal* charges *long after they have been unplugged!* It is extremely dangerous to open the case of a power supply. Besides, power supplies are inexpensive, so it would probably cost less to replace one than to try to fix it, and it would be much safer.

The number of volts in a power source represents its potential to do work, but volts don't do anything by themselves. Current (amperage, or amps) is the actual force behind the work being done by electricity. Here's an analogy to help explain this concept. Say you have two boulders; one weighs 10 pounds, the other 100 pounds, and each is 100 feet off the ground. If you drop them, which one will do more work? The obvious answer is the 100-pound boulder. They both have the same potential to do work (100 feet of travel), but the 100-pound boulder has more mass, and thus more force. Voltage is analogous to the distance the boulder is from the ground, and amperage is analogous to the mass of the boulder.

This is why we can produce static electricity on the order of 50,000 volts and not electrocute ourselves. Even though this electricity has a great *potential* for work, it does very little work because the amperage is so low. This also explains why we can weld metal with only 110 volts. Welders use only 110 (sometimes 220) volts, but they also use anywhere from 50 to 200 amps!

Printer Safety

Printer repair has hazards and pitfalls. Some of them are shown here:

- When handling a toner cartridge from a laser printer or page printer, do not shake the cartridge or turn it upside down. You will find yourself spending more time cleaning the printer and the surrounding area than you would have spent to fix the printer.

- Do not put any objects into the feeding system (in an attempt to clear the path) while the printer is running.

- Laser printers generate a laser that is hazardous to your eyes. Do not look directly into the source of the laser.

- If it's an ink-jet printer, do not try to blow into the ink cartridge to clear a clogged opening—that is, unless you like the taste of ink.

- Some parts of a laser printer (such as the EP cartridge) will be damaged if touched. Your skin produces oils and has a small surface layer of dead skin cells. These substances can collect on the delicate surface of the EP cartridge and cause malfunctions. Bottom line: Keep your fingers out of where they don't belong!

Monitor Safety

Other than the power supply, one of the most dangerous components to try to repair is the monitor, or cathode ray tube (CRT). We recommend that you *not* try to repair monitors. To avoid the extremely hazardous environment contained inside the monitor—it can retain a high-voltage charge for hours after it's been turned off—take it to a certified monitor technician or television repair shop. The repair shop or certified technician will know and understand the proper procedures to discharge the monitor, which involves attaching a resistor to the flyback transformer's charging capacitor to release the high-voltage electrical charge that builds up during use. They will also be able to determine whether the monitor can be repaired or needs to be replaced. Remember, the monitor works in its own extremely protective environment (the monitor case) and may not respond well to your desire to try to open it. The CRT is vacuum-sealed. Be extremely careful when handling it—if you break the glass, the CRT will implode, which can send glass in any direction.

Even though we recommend not repairing monitors, the A+ exam does test your knowledge of the safety practices to use when you need to do so. If you have to open a monitor, you must first discharge the high-voltage charge on it using a high-voltage probe. This probe has a very large needle, a gauge that indicates volts, and a wire with an alligator clip. Attach the alligator clip to a ground (usually the round pin on the power cord). Slip the probe needle under the high-voltage cup on the monitor. You will see the gauge spike to around 15,000 volts and slowly reduce to zero. When it reaches zero, you may remove the high-voltage probe and service the high-voltage components of the monitor.

Minimizing Electrostatic Discharge (ESD)

Electrostatic discharge (ESD) happens when two objects of dissimilar charge come in contact with one another, such as your body and a computer component. The two objects exchange electrons in order to standardize the electrostatic charge between them, with the object of higher charge (the human) passing voltage to the object of lower charge (the component). This charge can, and often does, damage electronic components.

The likelihood that a component will be damaged increases with the increasing use of Complementary Metallic Oxide Semiconductor (CMOS) chips, because these chips contain a thin metal oxide layer that is hypersensitive to ESD. The previous generation's Transistor-Transistor Logic (TTL) chips are more robust than the newer CMOS chips because they don't contain this metal oxide layer. Most of today's ICs are CMOS chips, so ESD is more of a concern lately.

When you shuffle your feet across the floor and shock your best friend on the ear, you are discharging static electricity into the ear of your friend. The lowest static voltage transfer that you can feel is around 3,000 volts (it doesn't electrocute you because there is extremely little current). A static transfer that you can *see* is at least 10,000 volts! Just by sitting in a chair, you can generate around 100 volts of static electricity. Walking around wearing synthetic materials can generate around 1,000 volts. You can easily generate around 20,000 volts simply by dragging your smooth-soled shoes across a shag carpet in the winter. (Actually, it doesn't have to be winter to run this danger; it can occur in any room with very low humidity. It's just that heated rooms in wintertime generally have very low humidity.)

It would make sense that these thousands of volts would damage computer components. However, a component can be damaged with as little as 80 volts. That means if your body has a small charge built up in it, you could damage a component without even realizing it.

Antistatic Wrist Strap

There are measures you can implement to help contain the effects of ESD. The easiest one to implement is the *antistatic wrist strap*, also referred to as an ESD strap. You attach one end of the ESD strap to an earth ground (typically the ground pin on an extension cord) and wrap the other end around your wrist. This strap grounds your body and keeps it at a zero charge. Figure 3.1 shows the proper way to attach an antistatic strap.

FIGURE 3.1   Proper ESD strap connection

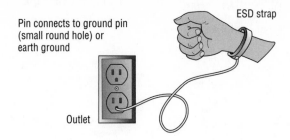

Pin connects to ground pin
(small round hole) or
earth ground

ESD strap

Outlet

If you do not have a grounded outlet available, you can achieve partial benefit simply by attaching the strap to the metal frame of the PC case. Doing so keeps the charge equalized between your body and the case, so that there is no electrostatic discharge when you touch components inside the case.

An ESD strap is a specially designed device to bleed electrical charges away *safely*. It uses a 1-megaohm resistor to bleed the charge away slowly. A simple wire wrapped around your wrist will not work correctly and could electrocute you!

Do not wear the antistatic wrist strap when there is the potential to encounter a high-voltage capacitor, such as when working on the inside of a monitor or power supply. The strap could channel that voltage through your body.

Antistatic Bags for Parts

Antistatic bags protect sensitive electronic devices from stray static charges. The bags are designed so that static charges collect on the outside of the bags rather than on the electronic components. You can obtain these bags from several sources. The most direct way to acquire antistatic bags is to go to an electronics supply store and purchase them in bulk. Most supply stores have several sizes available. Perhaps the easiest way to obtain them, however, is to hold onto the ones that come your way. That is, when you purchase any new component, it usually comes in an antistatic bag. Once you have installed the component, keep the bag. It may take you a while to gather a sizable collection of bags if you take this approach, but eventually you will have a fairly large assortment.

ESD Static Mats

It is possible to damage a device simply by laying it on a bench top. For this reason, you should have an ESD mat in addition to an ESD strap. This mat drains excess charge away from any item coming in contact with it (see Figure 3.2). ESD mats are also sold as mouse/keyboard pads to prevent ESD charges from interfering with the operation of the computer.

FIGURE 3.2   Proper use of an ESD mat

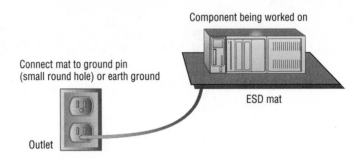

Vendors have methods of protecting components in transit from manufacture to installation. They press the pins of ICs into antistatic foam to keep all the pins at the same potential, and circuit boards are shipped in antistatic bags, discussed earlier. However, keep in mind that unlike antistatic mats, antistatic bags do not drain the charges away—they should never be used in place of antistatic mats.

Modifying the Relative Humidity

Another preventive measure you can take is to maintain the relative humidity at around 50 percent. Be careful not to increase the humidity too far—to the point where moisture starts to condense on the equipment! Also, use antistatic spray, which is available commercially, to reduce static buildup on clothing and carpets. In a pinch, a solution of diluted fabric softener sprayed on these items will do the same thing.

At the very least, you can be mindful of the dangers of ESD and take steps to reduce its effects. Beyond that, you should educate yourself about those effects so you know when ESD is becoming a major problem.

Exam Essentials

Know the fire extinguisher types.   Class C is the type of fire extinguisher needed for electrical fires.

Know that a monitor stores high voltage.   Monitors and power supplies carry the greatest potential for human harm. This is due to their capacitors, which store high-voltage electrical charges. A monitor in particular can store thousands of volts of charge for weeks after it has been unplugged.

Understand ESD.   Electrostatic discharge occurs when two objects of unequal electrical potential meet. The object of higher potential transfers some charge to the other one, just as water flows into an area that has a lower water level.

Understand the antistatic wrist strap.   The antistatic wrist strap is also referred to as an ESD strap. To use the ESD strap, you attach one end to an earth ground (typically the ground pin on an extension cord) and wrap the other end around your wrist. This strap grounds your body and keeps it at a zero charge, preventing discharges from damaging the components of a PC.

3.3 Employing Environmental Protection Measures and Procedures

This objective is new to the 2003 revision; formerly it was part of objective 3.2. It deals with protecting the environment from the potentially hazardous equipment and chemicals involved with personal computers.

Critical Information

It is estimated that more than 25 percent of all the lead in landfills today comes from consumer electronics components. Because consumer electronics contain hazardous substances, many states require that they be disposed of as hazardous waste. Computers are no exception. Monitors contain several carcinogens and phosphors, as well as mercury and lead. The computer itself may contain several lubricants and chemicals as well as lead. Printers contain plastics and chemicals such as toners and inks that are also hazardous. All of these items should be disposed of properly.

Each type of equipment or supply that has a potential environmental risk associated with it has a *Material Safety Data Sheet (MSDS)*, available from the manufacturer or from the Environmental Protection Agency (www.epa.gov). This document details the proper handling and disposal of the item.

Recycling Computers

We recycle cans, plastic, and newspaper, so why not recycle computer equipment? The problem is that most computers contain small amounts of hazardous substances. Some countries are exploring the option of recycling electrical machines, but most have not enacted appropriate measures to enforce their proper disposal. However, we can do a few things as consumers and environmentalists to promote the proper disposal of computer equipment:

- Check with the manufacturer. Some manufacturers will take back outdated equipment for parts.

- Disassemble the machine and reuse the parts that are good.

- Check out businesses that can melt down the components for the lead or gold plating.

- Contact the Environmental Protection Agency (EPA) for a list of local or regional waste disposal sites that will accept used computer equipment.

- Check with local nonprofit or education organizations interested in using the equipment.
- Check out the Internet for possible waste disposal sites. Table 3.1 gives a few websites we came across that deal with disposal of used computer equipment.

TABLE 3.1   Computer Recycling Websites

Site Name	Web Address
Computer Recycle Center	`www.recycles.com/`
PC Disposal	`www.pcdisposal.com`
Re-PC	`www.repc.com/`

Disposing of Batteries

In particular, you should make a special effort to recycle batteries. Batteries contain several chemicals that are harmful to our environment, such as nickel and lead, and won't degrade safely. Batteries should not be thrown away; they should be recycled according to your local laws. Check with your local authorities to find out how batteries should be recycled.

Disposing of CRTs

A CRT contains phosphors on the inside of the screen that can harm the environment if placed in a landfill. The large boxy shell of the CRT also takes up a lot of space in a landfill. Dispose of a monitor at your local hazardous-waste recycling center.

Disposing of Circuit Boards

Circuit boards contain lead in their soldering, so they should not be put in the regular trash. Take them to the local hazardous-waste disposal site, or contract with a company that handles them.

Disposing of Ink and Toner Cartridges

Ink and toner cartridges should be taken to recycling centers for proper disposal. It may also be possible to sell them to companies that refill and reuse them, but some people feel that this is not a good idea. Those re-manufactured cartridges sometimes do not work very well, and can damage the printers they are installed in, and by selling such companies your "empties" you are encouraging that industry.

Disposing of Cleaning Chemicals

The most common cleaning chemicals used for computers are alcohol and water, neither of which are particularly hazardous to the environment. However, if you use other chemical products, consult an MSDS for the product or consult the manufacturer to find out whether any special disposal is required.

Exam Essentials

Know what an MSDS is.   An MSDS is a Material Safety Data Sheet containing instructions for handling an item. It can be acquired from the manufacturer or from the EPA.

Know what components are not suitable for a landfill.   Batteries, CRTs, and circuit boards are all examples of items that should not be thrown away normally because of the elements used in them. Batteries contain metals such as lead and nickel, circuit boards contain lead solder, and CRTs contain phosphors.

Review Questions

1. What is the appropriate cleaning solution to use for monitor screens?

2. When cleaning components with alcohol, what type of alcohol should you use?

3. Why should an ordinary household vacuum cleaner not be used for cleaning the inside of a PC?

4. What is the danger to humans when disassembling and working on a monitor?

5. What type of fire extinguisher is appropriate for electrical fires?

6. True or false: ESD occurs when two objects of unequal electrical charge touch, with the object of higher charge passing some of its voltage to the object of lower charge.

7. Given that static electricity can exceed 10,000 volts, why does it not electrocute you?

8. As room humidity goes up, what happens to the potential for ESD damage?

9. True or false: A CRT should not be thrown in a landfill because it contains lead and nickel.

10. What is the name of the document that contains information about handling and disposal of a potentially hazardous item?

Answers to Review Questions

1. Use a glass cleaner designed specifically for computer monitors. Do not use regular glass cleaner, because it can harm the antiglare coating.

2. Denatured isopropyl alcohol.

3. It can generate ESD. Also acceptable as an answer: Because its filter is not fine enough to catch toner particles and avoid recirculating them into the air.

4. A high-voltage capacitor inside the monitor retains a charge even long after the monitor has been unplugged.

5. Class C.

6. True.

7. Low current (amps).

8. It decreases.

9. False. A CRT is not landfill-safe, but not because of nickel or lead. Instead, it's due to the phosphors on the glass and the CRT's large size and hollow center.

10. Material Safety Data Sheet (MSDS).

Chapter

4

Domain 4
Motherboard/
Processors/Memory

COMPTIA A+ EXAM OBJECTIVES COVERED IN THIS CHAPTER:

- ✓ 4.1 Distinguish between the popular CPU chips in terms of their basic characteristics.

- ✓ 4.2 Identify the types of RAM (Random Access Memory), form factors, and operational characteristics. Determine banking and speed requirements under given scenarios.

- ✓ 4.3 Identify the most popular types of motherboards, their components, and their architecture (bus structures).

- ✓ 4.4 Identify the purpose of CMOS (Complementary Metal-Oxide Semiconductor) memory, what it contains, and how and when to change its parameters. Given a scenario involving CMOS, choose the appropriate course of action.

Domain 4 of the exam covers the four major components of the processing subsystem: CPUs, RAM, motherboards, and CMOS. Whereas earlier objectives touched on these subjects in a general way (Domain 1, for example), or covered specifics about installing and troubleshooting them, this domain checks your knowledge of their technical specifications.

4.1 Distinguishing CPU Chips

Objective 4.1 ensures that you are familiar with the basic characteristics of a vast array of processors, beginning with the Pentium. Although it is helpful to study earlier CPUs for a complete understanding of how a CPU works in general, for study purposes you may confine your examination to Intel Pentium and higher CPUs and their competitors.

Critical Information

There are several ways of differentiating one CPU from another. The following sections explain specifications according to type, speed, voltage, and cache memory.

CPU Speed

The CPU's speed is the frequency at which it executes instructions. This frequency is measured in millions of cycles per second, or megahertz (MHz); or billions of cycles per second, or gigahertz (GHz).

The CPU has an internal and an external speed. The *external speed* corresponds with the motherboard's speed, based on its system crystal. The system crystal pulses, generating a cadence at which operations occur on the motherboard. Each pulse is called a *clock tick*. The CPU's *internal speed* is usually a multiple of that, so that multiple operations occur internally per clock tick. A CPU's speed as described in its specifications is its internal speed.

CPU Cache

Each CPU has at least two caches: L1 and L2. The *L1 cache* is built into the CPU on modern systems. It is the *front-side cache*, where data waits to enter the CPU. The *L2 cache*, or *back-side cache*, is where data exiting the CPU waits. On modern systems, the L2 cache is within the CPU's packaging but not integrated into the CPU's die. On older systems, the L2 cache was on a separate set of chips on the motherboard. You can compare one CPU to another according to the size of its L1 and L2 caches.

On some CPUs, the L2 cache operates at the same speed as the CPU itself; on others, the cache speed is only half the CPU speed. Chips with full-speed L2 caches have better performance.

Some newer systems also have an *L3 cache*, which is external to the CPU. It sits between the CPU and RAM to optimize data transfer between them.

CPU Voltage

A CPU's voltage is the amount of electricity provided to it by the motherboard. Older CPUs have higher voltages (around +5V); newer ones have lower voltages (less than +2V in some cases).

One reason a given motherboard cannot support many different CPUs is that it must provide the correct voltage. To get around this issue, some motherboards have *voltage regulator modules (VRMs)* that are able to change the voltage based on the CPU.

CPU Manufacturers

The market leader in the manufacture of chips is Intel Corporation, with Advanced Micro Devices (AMD) gaining market share in the home PC market. Other competitors include Cyrix, Motorola, and IBM.

Intel Processors

The first commercially successful Intel CPU was the 8086, developed in the late 1970s. It was used in the IBM XT, one of the early home and business personal computers. Other early Intel CPUs included the 80286, 80386, and 80486. You might find it useful to learn about the specifications of these CPUs for your own knowledge, but they are not covered on the current A+ exam.

PENTIUM

Intel introduced the Pentium processor in 1993. This processor has 3.1 million transistors using a 64-bit data path, a 32-bit address bus, and a 16KB on-chip cache, and it comes in speeds from 60MHz to 200MHz. With the release of the Pentium chips, *dual pipelining* was introduced (also called *superscalar architecture*), allowing the chip to process two operations at once.

The term *Pentium* refers to three separate CPUs: first-generation, second-generation, and MMX. First-generation Pentiums were 273-pin PGA CPUs (Socket 4) drawing +5V. They ran at 60MHz or 66MHz. The second-generation Pentiums were 296-pin models (Socket 5 or Socket 7) drawing +3.3V. They ran at between 75Mhz and 200MHz.

Third-generation (MMX) Pentiums, released in 1997, added multimedia extensions (MMX) to help the CPU work with graphic-intensive games. They used Socket 7 sockets, drew +2.8V, and ran at 166MHz to 233MHz. Due to the voltage difference between the Pentium MMX CPU and other Socket 7 CPUs, the MMX CPU required a motherboard that either was specifically for that CPU or had a VRM that could take the voltage down to that level.

PENTIUM PRO

The Pentium Pro, released in 1995, came between the second- and third-generation Pentiums. Physically, the Pentium Pro was a PGA-style, rectangular chip with 387 pins, using a Socket 8 socket drawing +3V. It was designed primarily for server usage and was optimized for 32-bit operating systems. On a 16-bit OS like Windows 3.1, the Pentium Pro ran more slowly than a Pentium, so it failed to gain widespread consumer support.

The Pentium Pro included *quad pipelining*, which processed four operations at once. It was also the first CPU to include an on-chip L2 cache. Another advantage of the Pentium Pro was *dynamic processing*, which allowed it to run instructions out of order whenever it was waiting for something else to happen.

PENTIUM II

Intel next released the Pentium II: This chip's speeds ranged from 233MHz to over 400MHz. It was introduced in 1997 and was designed to be a multimedia chip with special on-chip multimedia instructions and high-speed cache memory. It has 32KB of L1 cache, dynamic execution, and MMX technology. The Pentium II uses a Single Edge Connector Cartridge (SECC) to attach to the motherboard instead of the standard PGA package used with the earlier processor types.

When released, the Pentium II was designed for single-processor-only applications. Intel also released a separate processor, known as the Pentium II Xeon, to fill the need for multiprocessor applications such as servers. The Xeon's primary advantage is a huge L2 cache (up to 2MB) that runs at the same speed as the CPU. The Xeon uses a special size of SECC-style slot called Slot 2.

Different voltages have been used for the Pentium II over its lifespan, ranging from +2.8V to +2.0V. When you're using a Pentium II, it is important that the motherboard provide the correct voltage to it. This can be achieved with a VRM on the motherboard that detects the CPU's needs and adjusts the voltage provided.

CELERON

To offer a less-costly alternative and to keep its large market share, Intel released the Celeron. In some cases, the Celeron was priced as low as half the retail price of the Pentium II. Because it was developed after the Pentium II, it benefited from some advancements and in certain aspects outperformed its more expensive counterpart. Intel has also named its low-budget Pentium III CPUs Celeron.

The Celeron CPU has come in several package types, including a 370-pin PGA socket (Socket 370) and a SECC variant called Single Edge Processor (SEP) that is similar to the circuit board inside an SECC cartridge but without the plastic outer shell.

PENTIUM III

The Pentium III was released in 1999 and uses the same SEC connector as its predecessor, the Pentium II. It included 70 new instructions and a processor serial number (PSN), a unique number electronically encoded into the processor. This number can be used to uniquely identify a system during Internet transactions.

The Pentium III has two styles: an SECC-style cartridge called SECC2, and a PGA-style chip with 370 pins. The Pentium III PGA chip has the CPU chip mounted on the top rather than the bottom of the ceramic square; it's called a flip chip (FC), or FC-PGA.

 Like the Pentium II, the Pentium III has a multiprocessor Xeon version as well.

PENTIUM 4

The Pentium 4 was released in 2002. It runs on a motherboard with a fast system bus (between 400MHz and 800MHz) and provides some incremental improvements over the Pentium III. It is a PGA-style CPU.

One of the improvements the Pentium 4 offers is *hyperthreading* technology. This feature that enables the computer to multitask more efficiently between CPU-demanding applications.

SUMMARY OF INTEL PROCESSORS

Table 4.1 provides a summary of the history of the Intel processors. Table 4.2 shows the physical characteristics of Pentium (and higher) class processors.

TABLE 4.1   The Intel Family of Processors

Chip	Year Added	Data Bus Width (in Bits)	Address Bus Width (in Bits)	Speed (in MHz)
8080	1974	8	8	2
8086	1978	16	20	5–10
8088	1979	8	20	4.77
80286	1982	16	24	8–12
386DX	1985	32	32	16–33
386SX	1988	32	24	16–20
486DX	1989	32	32	25–50
486SX	1991	32	32	16–33
487SX	1991	32	32	16–33
486DX2	1991	32	32	33–66
486DX4	1992	32	32	75–100
Pentium	1993	64	32	60–166
Pentium Pro	1995	64	32	150–200
Pentium II	1997	64	64	233–300
Pentium II Xeon	1998	64	64	400–600

TABLE 4.1   The Intel Family of Processors *(continued)*

Chip	Year Added	Data Bus Width (in Bits)	Address Bus Width (in Bits)	Speed (in MHz)
Celeron	1999	64	64	400–600
Pentium III	1999	64	64	350–1000
Pentium III Xeon	1999	64	64	350–1000
Pentium 4	2002	64	64	1000–3000

TABLE 4.2   Physical Characteristics of Pentium-Class Processors

Processor	Speeds (MHz)	Socket	Pins	Voltage
Pentium-P5 (first generation)	60–66	4	273	+5V
Pentium-P54C (second generation)	75–200	5 or 7	296	+3.3V
Pentium-P55C (third generation)	166–233	7	321	+2.8V
Pentium Pro	150–200	8	387	+3V
Pentium II	233–450	SECC	N/A	+2.0V–+2.8V
Pentium III	450–1130	SECC2 or Socket 370	370	+2.0V
Pentium 4	1300–3000 (at this writing)	Socket 423 or Socket 478	423 or 478	+1.53V–+1.75V

Intel Clones and Others

Intel *clones* are processors that are based on the *x*86 architecture and are produced by other vendors; the most notable is AMD. AMD's competitor to the Pentium II is the K6. The original K6 ran at between 166MHz and 300MHz. The K6-2, at 266MHz to 475MHz, added 3DNow! Technology, for improved multimedia. The K6-3, at 400MHz to 450MHz, adds a full-speed L2 cache. Because all the K6 chips are PGA, whereas Pentiums are SECC, you need a special motherboard for the K6 chips designed specifically for them.

AMD's competitor to the Pentium III is the Athlon. It uses an SECC-style slot called Slot A that is physically the same but not pin-compatible with Intel-style Slot 1 SECC. AMD also has a low-budget version called the Duron that has less L2 cache.

The surest way to determine which CPU your computer is using is to open the case and view the numbers stamped on the CPU. Another way to determine a computer's CPU is to save your work, exit any open programs, and restart the computer. Watch closely as the computer returns to its normal state. You should see a notation that tells you which chip you are using. If you are using MS-DOS, you can also run Microsoft Diagnostics to view the processor type (that is, unless your computer has a Pentium processor, in which case it will report a very fast 486).

Exam Essentials

Understand the processor's job.   The processor is the brain of the PC. Most actions performed by the PC require use of the processor to accomplish their task.

Understand the differences between the different classes of Pentium chips.   The Intel Pentium has gone through several changes since its release. You will need to understand the differences between the various classes in terms of their physical packaging, speeds, voltages, and caches.

Know what a VRM is.   A voltage regulator module (VRM) on a motherboard allows it to change the voltage that it provides to the CPU to accommodate a wider range of CPUs.

4.2 Identifying the Types of RAM

To pass the A+ exam and be a productive computer technician, you must be familiar with memory. Not only will you be tested on this subject, but one of the most common upgrades performed on a PC is adding memory. Adding memory is a simple task, but before you can add memory you must have the correct type.

Critical Information

When we say *memory*, we are most often referring to Random Access Memory (RAM). However, there are other types of memory. We will discuss them all in this section. Be familiar with the various types and their usage.

Physical Memory

Physically, memory is a collection of integrated circuits that store data and program information as patterns of 1s and 0s (on and off states) in the chip. Most memory chips require constant power (also called a constant *refresh*) to maintain those patterns of 1s and 0s. If power is lost, all those tiny switches revert back to the off position, effectively erasing the data from memory. Some memory types, however, do not require a refresh.

There are many types of Random Access Memory (RAM). In this section, we examine each type in detail.

SRAM

Static RAM (SRAM) stores whatever is placed in it until it is changed. Unlike Dynamic RAM, it does not require constant electrical refreshing. Another name for it is Non-Volatile RAM (NVRAM). It is expensive, so it is not typically used for the main memory in a system.

DRAM

Dynamic RAM (DRAM) is an improvement over SRAM. DRAM uses a different approach to storing the 1s and 0s. Instead of using transistors, DRAM stores information as charges in very small capacitors. If a charge exists in a capacitor, it's interpreted as a 1. The absence of a charge is interpreted as a 0.

Because DRAM uses capacitors instead of switches, it needs to use a constant refresh signal to keep the information in memory. DRAM requires more power than SRAM for refresh signals and, therefore, is mostly found in desktop computers.

DRAM technology allows several memory units, called *cells*, to be packed to a high density. Therefore, these chips can hold very large amounts of information. Most PCs today use DRAM of one type or another.

Let's take a brief look at some of the different types of DRAM:

Fast Page Mode (FPM)   An older type of RAM (almost always 72-pin SIMM packaging) that is not synchronized in speed with the motherboard. It is rated in nanoseconds of delay, with lower numbers being better (for example, 60ns). FPM is now obsolete.

Extended Data Out (EDO)   Like FPM, an older type of RAM, usually in 72-pin SIMM form. It performs a bit better than normal FPM RAM because it needs to be refreshed less frequently. Like FPM, it is now obsolete.

Synchronous DRAM (SDRAM)   Synchronized to the speed of the motherboard's system bus. Synchronizing the speed of the systems prevents the address bus from having to wait for the memory because of different clock speeds. SDRAM typically comes in the form of 168-pin DIMMs or 184-pin RIMMs.

Double Data Rate (DDR) SDRAM   Essentially, clock-doubled SDRAM. The memory chip can perform reads and writes on both sides of any clock cycle (the up, or start, and the down, or ending), thus doubling the effective memory executions per second. So, if you are using DDR SDRAM with a 100MHz memory bus, the memory will execute reads and writes at 200MHz and transfer the data to the processor at 100MHz. The advantage of DDR over regular SDRAM is increased throughput, and thus increased overall system speed.

Direct Rambus   A relatively new and extremely fast (up to 800MHz) technology that uses, for the most part, a new methodology in memory system design. Direct Rambus is a memory bus that transfers data at 800MHz. Direct Rambus memory models (often called Rambus Inline

Memory Modules [RIMMs]), like DDR SDRAM, can transfer data on both the rising and fall-ing edges of a clock cycle. That feature, combined with the 16-bit bus for efficient transfer of data, results in the ultra-high memory transfer rate (800MHz) and the high bandwidth of up to 1.6GBps.

Memory Chip Package Types

The memory chips themselves come in many different types of packages. The ones most frequently encountered are discussed in the following sections.

Dual Inline Package (DIP)

Dual Inline Package (DIP) memory is so named because the individual RAM chips use the DIP-style package for the memory module. Older computers, such as the IBM AT, arranged these small chips like rows of caskets in a small memory "graveyard." This type of memory has long been obsolete.

SIMMs

Single Inline Memory Modules (SIMMs) were developed because DIPs took up too much real estate on the logic board. Someone got the idea to put several DIP chips on a small circuit board and then make that board easily removable.

Each of these RAM circuit boards is a *stick* of RAM. There are two sizes of SIMMs: 30-pin and 72-pin. The 30-pin are older, 8-bit sticks. The 72-pin are 32-bit sticks. Figure 4.1 shows one of each. SIMMs are called *single* because they are single sided. When you count the number of pins (the metal tabs) along the bottom, there are 30 or 72 of them. In contrast, DIMMs (Dual Inline Memory Modules) are double-sided; for example, a 168-pin DIMM has 84 pins on each side.

FIGURE 4.1   Single Inline Memory Modules (SIMMs)

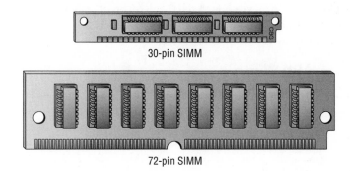

30-pin SIMM

72-pin SIMM

DIMMs and RIMMs

Dual Inline Memory Modules (DIMMs) are double-sided memory chips used in modern sys-tems (Pentium and higher). They typically have 168 pins and are 64 bits in width. Figure 4.2 shows a DIMM.

FIGURE 4.2   Dual Inline Memory Module (DIMM)

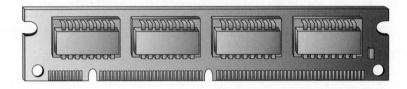

A RIMM is just like a DIMM, except it's a Rambus DRAM stick, has 184 pins, and is slightly longer in size.

SoDIMMs and MicroDIMMs

Portable computers (notebooks and subnotebooks) require smaller sticks of RAM because of their smaller size. Two types are Small Outline DIMM (SoDIMM) and MicroDIMM.

Parity and Non-Parity RAM

Some sticks of RAM have a parity bit on them for error correction. It works by adding up the number of 1s in a particular row of data in RAM (for example, 32-bit RAM has 32 individual binary digits). It then adds either 1 or 0 to that total to make it come out even. When retrieving the data from RAM, it re-adds the 1s again, and if the parity bit doesn't come out the same, it knows an error has occurred.

You can identify a parity SIMM by counting the number of chips on the stick. If there are nine, it's parity RAM. If there are eight, it's non-parity.

When do you choose parity RAM? Usually the motherboard requires either parity or non-parity; a few motherboards will accept either. Nowadays parity RAM is rarely needed because advances in RAM technology have created reliable RAM that seldom makes errors.

One type of parity RAM is ECC (Error Correction Code). This is a now-obsolete type of parity RAM. Most RAM today is non-ECC.

RAM Banks and Bit Width

As explained earlier, 30-pin SIMMs are 8-bit, 72-pin SIMMs are 32-bit, and DIMMs are 64-bit. The motherboard has an address bus that carries data from the RAM to the CPU and chipset. It has a certain width. On Pentium and higher systems, it's 64-bit; on earlier systems it's 32-bit (386 and 486) or less (286 and below). A bank of RAM is a single stick or a group of sticks where the collective bit width adds up to the width of the address bus.

For example, on a Pentium motherboard, a single bank consists of a single 64-bit DIMM or a pair of two 32-bit SIMMs. For a 486 motherboard, a single bank is a single 32-bit SIMM or four 8-bit SIMMs.

Video RAM

Video memory (also called Video RAM [VRAM]) is used to store image data for processing by the video adapter. The more video memory an adapter has, the better the quality of image that it can display. Also, more VRAM allows the adapter to display a higher resolution of image.

Exam Essentials

Know the differences among RAM types.   Make sure you can differentiate among all the acronyms, such as SRAM, DRAM, SDRAM, DDR SDRAM, EDO DRAM, and so on.

Understand the different RAM packaging.   Be able to differentiate between SIMMs and DIMMs, including the number of pins each has and their bit widths.

Know the purpose of parity in RAM.   Understand how a parity bit is used for error correction.

4.3 Identifying Types of Motherboards

The motherboards is the backbone of a computer. The components of the motherboard provide basic services needed for the machine to operate and provide a platform for devices such as the processor, memory, disk drives, and expansion devices.

Critical Information

For this objective, you should study the types of motherboards, their ports and memory, the types of CPU sockets, and the types of expansion slots.

System Board Form Factors

Form factor refers to the size and shape of a component. There are three popular motherboard form factors for desktop PCs: AT, ATX, and NLX.

AT

AT is an older style of motherboard. A slightly more modern variant of it is the baby AT, which is similar but smaller. Its key features are a two-piece power supply connector, ribbon cables that connect the I/O ports to the board, and an AT-style keyboard connector. The expansion slots are parallel to the wide edge of the board. See Figure 4.3.

FIGURE 4.3 An AT-style motherboard

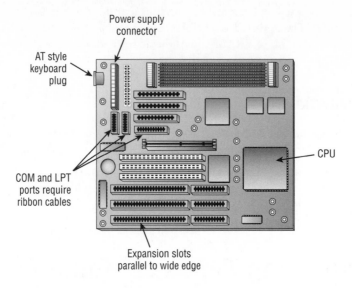

ATX

Most system boards today use the ATX form factor. It contains many design improvements over the AT, including I/O ports built directly into the side of the motherboard, the CPU positioned such that the power supply fan helps cool it, and allowing the PC to be turned on and off via software. It uses a PS/2 style connector for the keyboard. The expansion slots are parallel to the narrow edge of the board. See Figure 4.4.

FIGURE 4.4 An ATX-style motherboard

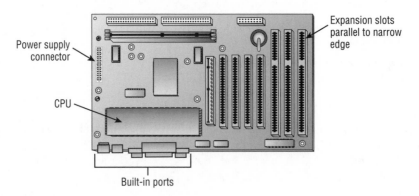

NLX

This form factor is used in low-profile case types. This design incorporates expansion slots that are placed on a *riser board* to accommodate the reduction in case size. However, this design adds another component to troubleshoot.

Buses

A *bus* is a set of signal pathways that allows information and signals to travel between components inside or outside a computer. A motherboard has several buses, each with its own speed and width.

The *external data bus*, also called the *system bus*, connects the CPU to the chipset. On modern systems it is 64-bit. The *address bus* connects the RAM to the CPU. On modern systems it is 64-bit.

The *expansion bus* connects the I/O ports and expansion slots to the chipset. There are usually several different expansion buses on a motherboard. Expansion buses can be broken into two broad categories: internal and external. Internal expansion buses include ISA, PCI, and AGP; they are for circuit boards. External expansion buses include serial, parallel, USB, FireWire, and infrared. The following sections explain some of the most common buses.

 There are many obsolete bus types, including VESA Local Bus (VLB), Microchannel Architecture (MCA), and Enhanced ISA (EISA). These are not on the A+ test.

Industry Standard Architecture (ISA) Bus

This is a 16-bit bus (originally 8-bit on the oldest computers) that operates at 8MHz. Its slots are usually black. New motherboards might not have this type of slot, because the ISA bus is old technology and is being phased out.

Besides the slow speed and narrow width, another drawback of the ISA bus is that each ISA device requires separate system resources, including separate IRQs. In a heavily loaded system, this can cause an IRQ shortage. (PCI slots, in contrast, can share some resources.)

Peripheral Component Interconnect (PCI)

The PCI bus is a fast (33MHz), wide (32-bit or 64-bit) expansion bus that is the modern standard in motherboards today for general-purpose expansion devices. Its slots are typically white. PCI devices can share IRQs and other system resources with one another in some cases. All modern motherboards have at least three PCI slots. Figure 4.5 shows some PCI slots.

FIGURE 4.5   PCI bus connectors

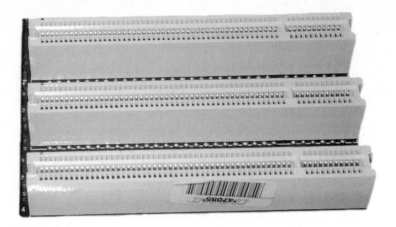

Accelerated Graphics Port (AGP)

As systems got faster, PC game players wanted games that had better graphics, more realism, and more speed. However, as the computers got faster, the video technology couldn't seem to keep up, even with the PCI bus. The Accelerated Graphics Port (AGP) bus was developed to meet this need.

The AGP slot is usually brown, and there is only one of them. It is a 32-bit or 64-bit bus, and it runs very fast (66MHz or faster). It is used exclusively for the video card. If you use a PCI video card, the AGP slot remains empty. See Figure 4.6.

FIGURE 4.6   An AGP slot on a motherboard

AGP slot

Legacy Parallel and Serial

These buses are called *legacy* because they are old technology and are being phased out. The legacy serial port, also called an RS-232 port, is a 9-pin or 25-pin male connector. It sends data one bit at a time and is usually limited to about 115Kbps in speed.

The legacy parallel port transfers data 8 bits at a time. It is a 25-pin female connector. A system typically has only one parallel port, but because many printers are now coming with USB interfaces, this is no longer the inconvenience that it used to be.

Universal Serial Bus (USB)

Universal Serial Bus (USB) is a newer expansion bus type that is used almost exclusively for external devices. All motherboards today have at least two USB ports. Some of the advantages of USB include hot-plugging and the capability for up to 127 USB devices to share a single set of system resources. USB 1.1 runs at 12Mbps, and USB 2.0 runs at 480Mbps. Because USB is a serial interface, its width is 1 bit.

IEEE 1394/FireWire

Some newer motherboards have a built-in IEEE 1394/FireWire port, although this port is more typically found on a PCI expansion board. It transfers data at 400Mbps and supports up to 63 chained devices on a single set of resources. It is hot-pluggable, like USB.

Motherboard RAM Slots

RAM was discussed extensively under Objective 4.2; review that information to study the RAM portion of Objective 4.3. The RAM and the RAM slots on the motherboard must match.

Processor Sockets

Objective 4.1 covered CPUs; review that information here. In addition, review Table 4.3, which lists the various CPU slots and sockets you may find in a motherboard and explains which CPUs will fit into them.

TABLE 4.3 Processor Sockets and Slots

Slot/Socket	CPU Used
Slot 1	Pentium II
Slot 2	Pentium III
Slot A	AMD Athlon
Socket A	AMD Athlon
Socket 7	Pentium (second and third generation), AMD K6

TABLE 4.3   Processor Sockets and Slots *(continued)*

Slot/Socket	CPU Used
Socket 8	Pentium Pro
Socket 423	Pentium 4
Socket 478	Pentium 4
Socket 370	Pentium III

On-Motherboard Cache

On older motherboards, the L2 cache is on its own RAM-like stick made of very fast SRAM. It is known as *cache on a stick (COAST)*. On newer systems, the L2 cache is built into the CPU packaging.

Some newer systems also have an L3 cache, which is an external cache on the motherboard that sits between the CPU and RAM.

IDE and SCSI On-Motherboard Interfaces

You studied IDE and SCSI interfaces in detail in Objectives 1.6 and 1.7; review that technical data about those buses with motherboards in mind. Most motherboards include two IDE channels but do not include built-in SCSI.

A consideration when choosing a motherboard for IDE is that it needs to support the desired level of UltraDMA to match the capabilities of the hard drive you want to use. Refer to Objective 1.6.

Chipsets

The *chipset* is the set of controller chips that monitors and directs the traffic on the motherboard between the buses. It usually consists of two or more chips. There are two basic chipset designs in motherboards: the *north/south bridge chipset* and the *hub chipset*.

North/south bridge is the older of the two. The north bridge c connects the system bus to the other relatively fast buses (AGP and PCI). The south bridge connects ISA, IDE, and USB. A third chip, SuperIO, connects the legacy parallel and serial ports.

The hub chipset includes a memory controller hub (equivalent to the north bridge), an I/O controller hub (equivalent to the south bridge), and a SuperIO chip.

Exam Essentials

Know the motherboard form factors.   Understand the differences between AT, ATX, and NLX.

Distinguish among ISA, PCI, and AGP.   Know their bus widths and maximum speeds, and that they're all used for expansion boards inside the PC.

Distinguish among I/O ports on a motherboard.   Know the different types of ports, such as USB, IEEE 1394, legacy parallel, and legacy serial.

Know the sizes and shapes of CPU slots/sockets.   Be able to specify what type of socket or slot various CPUs require.

4.4 Understanding CMOS Memory

You can adjust a computer's base-level settings through a BIOS Setup program, which you access by pressing a certain key at startup such as F1 or Delete (depending on the system). Another name for this setup program is CMOS Setup, which is what the A+ exam objectives call it. Objective 4.4 tests your familiarity with the settings in this utility and your ability to adjust them to solve certain problems.

Critical Information

The most common settings to adjust in CMOS include port settings (parallel, serial, USB), drive types, boot sequence, date and time, and virus/security protections.

Accessing CMOS Setup

Your PC keeps these settings in a special memory chip called the Complementary Metal Oxide Semiconductor (CMOS) chip. The CMOS chip must have a constant source of power to keep its settings. To prevent the loss of data, motherboard manufacturers include a small battery to power the CMOS memory. On modern systems this is a coin-style battery, about the same diameter of a dime and about ¼-inch thick.

You can press a certain key or group of keys to access the setup program during the power on self-test (POST). This utility allows you to change the configuration through a group of menus. There are many different CMOS Setup programs, depending on the BIOS make and manufacturer, so it is impossible to provide specifics here; instead we will look at capabilities.

Load Setup Defaults

The purpose of this setting is to configure the PC back to the default settings set by the factory. If you make changes to your settings and the machine becomes disabled, in most cases selecting this menu item will return the machine to a usable state. You may then try different settings until you achieve your desired configuration. This is an important setting to know about before making any other changes.

Date and Time

One of the most basic things you can change in CMOS Setup is the system date and time. You can also change this from within the operating system.

CPU Settings

In most modern systems the BIOS detects the CPU's type and speed automatically, so any CPU setting in CMOS Setup is likely to be read-only.

Memory Speed/Parity

Most systems today detect the RAM amount and speed automatically. Some motherboards can use different types of RAM, such as parity and non-parity, or different speeds, and the CMOS Setup program may provide the opportunity to change those settings. Increasingly, however, RAM is becoming a read-only part of CMOS Setup programs.

Power Management

The Power Management settings determine the way the PC will act after it has been idle for certain time periods. For example, you may have choices like Minimum, Maximum, and User Defined. The Minimum and Maximum settings control the HDD Off After, Doze Mode, Standby Mode, and Suspend Mode settings with predefined parameters. If you select User Defined, you must manually configure these settings to your personal preferences.

Ports and Peripherals

In CMOS Setup, you can enable or disable integrated components, such as built-in video cards, sound cards, or network cards. You might disable them in order to replace them with different models on expansion boards, for example.

You can also disable the on-board I/O ports for the motherboard, including parallel, serial, and USB. Depending on the utility, there may also be settings that enable or disable USB keyboard usage, Wake on LAN, or other special features.

In addition to enabling or disabling legacy parallel ports, you can also assign an operational mode to the port. Table 4.4 lists the common modes for a parallel port. When you're troubleshooting parallel port problems, sometimes trying a different mode will help.

TABLE 4.4 Printer or Parallel Port Settings

Setting	Description	Use
EPP (Enhanced Parallel Port)	Supports bidirectional communication and high transfer rates	Newer inkjet and laser printers that can utilize bidirectional communication, and scanners
ECP (Enhanced Communications Port)	Supports bidirectional communication and high transfer rates	Newer inkjet and laser printers that can utilize bidirectional communication, connectivity devices, and scanners
SPP (Standard Printer Port)	Supports bidirectional communication	Older inkjet and laser printers and slower scanners

Passwords

In most CMOS Setup programs, you can set a supervisor password. Doing so requires a password to be entered in order to use the CMOS Setup program, effectively locking out users from making changes to it. You may also be able to set a user password, which restricts the PC from booting unless the password is entered.

To reset a forgotten password, you can remove the CMOS battery to reset everything. There also may be a Reset jumper on the motherboard.

Virus Protection

Some CMOS Setup programs have a rudimentary virus-protection mechanism that prevents applications from writing to the boot sector of a disk without your permission. If this setting is turned on, and you install a new operating system, a confirmation box may appear at some point warning you that the operating system's Setup program is trying to write to the boot sector. Let it.

HDD Auto Detection

Some CMOS Setup programs have a feature that polls the IDE channels and provides information about the IDE devices attached to them. You can use this feature to gather the settings for a hard disk. However, most hard disks these days are fully Plug and Play, so they automatically report themselves to the CMOS Setup.

Drive Configuration

You can specify how many floppy drives are installed and what types they are. Floppy drives are not automatically detected. The settings needed for a floppy drive are size (3½-inch or 5¼-inch) and density (double-density or high-density). You can also set each floppy drive to be enabled or disabled from being bootable. Almost all floppy drives today are high-density 3½-inch.

Hard drives, on the other hand, can be auto-detected by most systems if the IDE setting is set to Auto. The settings detected may include the drive's capacity; its geometry (cylinders, heads, and sectors); and its preferred PIO, DMA, or UltraDMA operating mode. You can also configure a hard drive by entering its CHS values manually, but doing so is almost never necessary anymore.

 CHS stands for Cylinders, Heads, and Sectors. This is also called the drive geometry, as together these three numbers determine how much data the disk can hold. Most CMOS setup programs are able to automatically detect the CHS values.

Boot Sequence

Each system has a default boot order, which is the order in which it checks the drives for a valid operating system to boot. Usually this order is set for floppy first, then hard disk, and finally CD-ROM, but these components can be placed in any boot order. For example, you might set CD-ROM first to boot from a Windows XP Setup disk on a system that already contained an operating system.

Exiting the CMOS Setup

The CMOS Setup program will include an Exit command, with options including Save Changes and Discard Changes. In most programs, Esc is a shortcut for exiting and discarding changes, and F10 is a common shortcut for exiting and saving changes.

Exam Essentials

Know what the CMOS Setup utility does.   The CMOS Setup utility allows you to configure the characteristics of certain portions of the PC.

Be familiar with the common menu items listed.   Knowing these common menu items and their function can greatly aid troubleshooting.

Understand the different printer port settings.   Although there is no good rule of thumb on which of these settings will fix a communication error, in most cases you can resolve the issue by systematically trying the different settings.

Review Questions

1.   On modern systems, what is the relationship between a CPU's internal and external speeds?

2.   Which cache is also known as the back-side cache?

3.   What is the purpose of a VRM on a motherboard?

4.   What is the purpose of a parity bit on a SIMM?

5.   In a system with a 64-bit address bus, how many SDRAM DIMMs form a single bank of memory?

6.   What two essential system components are connected to one another via the address bus?

7.   Which type of expansion slot uses a 33MHz, 32-bit expansion bus and is the most common choice for general-purpose expansion in a modern system?

8.   What is the difference between USB 1.1 and USB 2.0?

9.   Besides Standard and Bidirectional, what are two parallel printer port modes you can choose in BIOS Setup?

10.   What chip holds the changes you make in BIOS Setup?

Answers to Review Questions

1. The internal speed is a multiple of the external speed.

2. The L2 cache

3. To provide different voltages for different CPUs

4. Error correction

5. One

6. The CPU and the RAM

7. PCI

8. Speed. USB 1.1 runs at 12Mbps, and USB 2.0 runs at 400 Mbps.

9. EPP (Enhanced Parallel Port) and ECP (Enhanced Communications Port)

10. CMOS

Chapter

5

Domain 5 Printers

COMPTIA A+ EXAM OBJECTIVES COVERED IN THIS CHAPTER:

- ✓ 5.1 Identify printer technologies, interfaces, and options/upgrades.
- ✓ 5.2 Recognize common printer problems and techniques used to resolve them.

You will likely encounter many printer-related questions when you take the A+ exam, especially regarding laser printing. Objective 5 tests your knowledge of the printing process, your ability to identify printer interfaces, and your troubleshooting and preventive maintenance skills for printers.

5.1 Identifying Printer Technologies, Interfaces, and Options/Upgrades

Objective 5.1 tests your knowledge of how printers work and how they connect to computers. Although the A+ exam has traditionally focused on laser printers most heavily, you may also see questions about other printer types.

Critical Information

The two major areas of study for this objective are printer technologies and printer interfaces. The technologies include laser, ink-jet (sometimes called ink dispersion), dot matrix, solid ink, thermal, and dye sublimation. The interfaces include parallel, network, and USB, among others.

The following sections provide details about various technologies of printers. These printers may be differentiated from one another in several ways, including the following:

Impact vs. Non-Impact   Impact printers physically strike an inked ribbon, and therefore can print multipart forms; non-impact printers deliver ink onto the page without striking it. Dot matrix is impact; everything else is non-impact.

Continuous Feed vs. Sheet Fed   Continuous-feed paper feeds through the printer using a system of sprockets and tractors. Sheet-fed printers accept plain paper in a paper tray. Dot matrix is continuous feed; everything else is sheet fed.

Line vs. Page   Line printers print one line at a time; page printers compose the entire page in memory and then place it all on the paper at once. Dot matrix and ink-jet are line printers; laser is a page printer.

Dot-Matrix Printers

A dot-matrix printer is an impact printer; it prints by physically striking an inked ribbon, much like a typewriter. It is an impact, continuous-feed line printer.

The print head on a dot-matrix printer consists of a block of metal pins that extend and retract. These pins are triggered to extend in patterns that form letters and numbers as the print head moves across the paper. Early models, known as NLQ (near letter quality), printed using only nine pins. Later models used 21 pins and produced much better LQ (letter quality) output.

The main advantage of dot matrix is its impact. Because it strikes the paper, you can use it to print on multipart forms. Non-impact printers can't do that. Dot-matrix printers are not commonly found in most offices these days because of their disadvantages, including noise, slow speed, and poor print quality.

Ink-Jet Printers

Ink-jet printers are one of the most popular types in use today. This type of printer sprays ink on the page to print text or graphics. It is a non-impact, sheet-fed line printer.

Figure 5.1 shows an ink cartridge. Some cartridges, like this one, contain the print head for that color of ink; you get a new print head each time you replace the cartridge. On other printer models, the ink cartridge is just an ink reservoir, and the heads do not need replacing.

FIGURE 5.1   A typical ink cartridge (size: approximately 3 inches by 1½ inches)

There are two kinds of ink-jet printers: *thermal* and *piezoelectric.* These terms refer to the way the ink is sprayed onto the paper. A thermal ink-jet printer heats the ink to about 400° F, creating vapor bubbles that force the ink out of the cartridge. Thermal ink-jets are also sometimes called *bubble-jets.* A piezoelectric printer does the same thing but with electricity instead of heat.

Ink-jet printers are popular because they can print in color and are inexpensive. However, their print quality is not quite as good as that of a laser printer, and the per-page cost of ink is much higher than for a laser printer. Therefore most businesses prefer laser printers for their main printing needs, perhaps keeping one or two ink-jet printers around for situations requiring color printing.

Laser Printers

Laser printers are referred to as *page printers* because they receive their print job instructions one page at a time. They are sheet-fed, non-impact printers. Another name for a laser printer is an *electrophotographic (EP)* printer.

LED printers are much like laser printers except they use light-emitting diodes (LEDs) instead of lasers. Their process is similar to that of laser printers. They are covered in more detail later in this chapter.

Parts of a Laser Printer

An electrophotographic laser printer consists of the following major components:

Printer Controller   A large circuit board that acts as the motherboard for the printer. It contains the processor and RAM to convert data coming in from the computer into a picture of a page to be printed.

Toner Cartridge and Drum   A powdery mixture of plastic resin and iron oxide. The plastic allows it to be melted and fused to the paper, and the iron oxide allows it to be moved around via positive or negative charge. Toner comes in a cartridge, like the one shown in Figure 5.2.

The drum is light sensitive; it can be written to with the laser scanning assembly. The toner cartridge in Figure 5.2 contains the print drum, so every time you change the toner cartridge, you get a new drum. In some laser printers, the drum is a separate part that lasts longer, so you don't have to change it every time you change the toner.

FIGURE 5.2   An EP toner cartridge

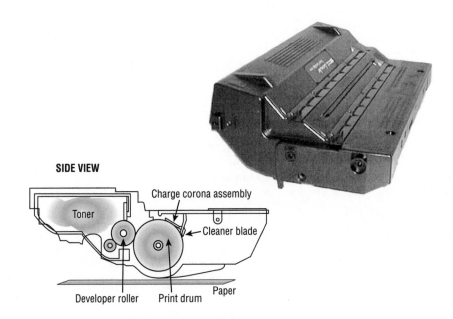

Primary Corona (Charging Corona)   Applies a uniform negative charge (around –600V) to the drum at the beginning of the printing cycle.

Laser Scanning Assembly   Uses a laser beam to neutralize the strong negative charge on the drum in certain areas, so toner will stick to the drum in those areas. The laser scanning assembly uses a set of rotating and fixed mirrors to direct the beam, as shown in Figure 5.3.

FIGURE 5.3   The EP laser scanning assembly (side view and simplified top view)

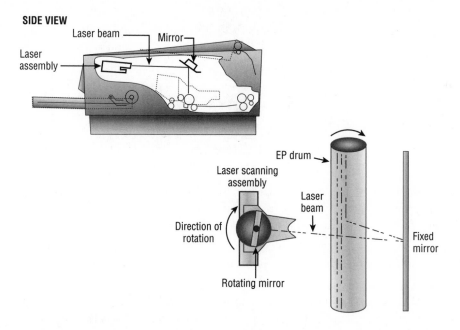

Paper Transport Assembly   Moves the paper through the printer. The paper transport assembly consists of a motor and several rubberized rollers. These rollers are operated by an electronic stepper motor. See Figure 5.4 for an example.

FIGURE 5.4   Paper transport rollers

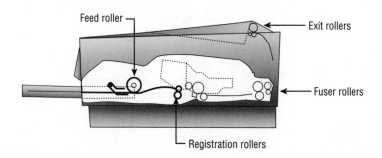

Transfer Corona   Applies a uniform positive charge (about +600V) to the paper. When the paper rotates past the drum, the toner jumps off the drum and onto the paper. Then the paper passes through a static eliminator that removes the positive charge from it. (See Figure 5.5.) Some printers use a transfer corona wire; others use a transfer corona roller.

FIGURE 5.5   The transfer corona assembly

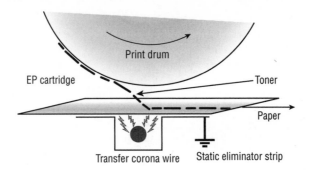

High-Voltage Power Supply (HVPS)   Delivers the high voltages needed to make the printing process happen. It converts ordinary 120V household AC current into high DC voltages used to energize the primary and transfer corona wires (discussed later).

DC Power Supply   Delivers lower voltages to components in the printer that need much lower voltages than the corona wires do (such as circuit boards, memory, and motors).

Fusing Assembly   Melts the plastic resin in the toner so that it adheres to the paper. The fusing assembly contains a halogen heating lamp, a fusing roller made of Teflon-coated aluminum, and a rubberized pressure roller. The lamp heats the fusing roller, and as the paper passes between the two rollers, the pressure roller pushes the paper against the hot fusing roller, melting the toner into the paper. (See Figure 5.6.)

FIGURE 5.6   The fusing assembly

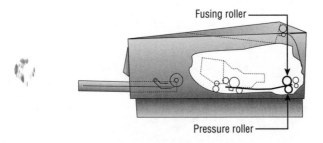

The Laser Printing Process

The laser (EP) print process consists of six steps. Here are the steps in the order you will see them on the exam:

1. Cleaning
2. Conditioning (or charging)
3. Writing
4. Developing
5. Transferring
6. Fusing

STEP 1: CLEANING

In the first part of the laser print process, a rubber blade inside the EP cartridge scrapes any toner left on the drum into a used-toner receptacle inside the EP cartridge, and a fluorescent lamp discharges any remaining charge on the photosensitive drum (remember that the drum, being photosensitive, loses its charge when exposed to light). This step is called the *cleaning step* (Figure 5.7).

FIGURE 5.7 The cleaning step of the EP process

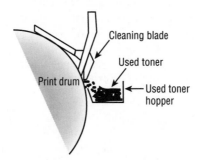

The EP cartridge is constantly cleaning the drum. It may take more than one rotation of the photosensitive drum to make an image on the paper. The cleaning step keeps the drum fresh for each use. If you didn't clean the drum, you would see ghosts of previous pages printed along with your image.

 The actual amount of toner removed in the cleaning process is quite small. The cartridge will run out of toner before the used toner receptacle fills up.

STEP 2: CONDITIONING

In the *conditioning step* (Figure 5.8), a special wire (called a *primary corona* or *charging corona*) within the EP toner cartridge (above the photosensitive drum) gets a high voltage from the

HVPS. It uses this high voltage to apply a strong, uniform negative charge (around –600VDC) to the surface of the photosensitive drum.

FIGURE 5.8   The conditioning step of the EP process

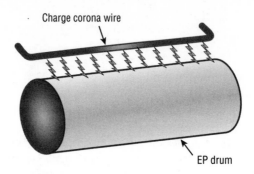

Charge corona wire

EP drum

STEP 3: WRITING

In the *writing step* of the EP process, the laser is turned on and scans the drum from side to side, flashing on and off according to the bits of information the printer controller sends it as it communicates the individual bits of the image. In each area where the laser touches the photosensitive drum, the drum's charge is severely reduced from –600VDC to a slight negative charge (around –100VDC). As the drum rotates, a pattern of exposed areas is formed, representing the images to be printed. Figure 5.9 shows this process.

FIGURE 5.9   The writing step of the EP process

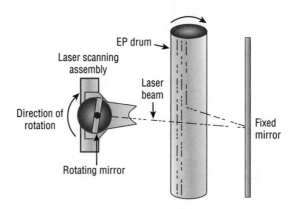

EP drum

Laser scanning
assembly

Laser
beam

Direction of
rotation

Fixed
mirror

Rotating mirror

At this point, the controller sends a signal to the pickup roller to feed a piece of paper into the printer, where it stops at the registration rollers.

STEP 4: DEVELOPING

Now that the surface of the drum holds an electrical representation of the image being printed, its discrete electrical charges need to be converted into something that can be transferred to a piece of paper. The EP process *developing step* accomplishes this (Figure 5.10). In this step, toner is transferred to the areas that were exposed in the writing step.

FIGURE 5.10   The developing step of the EP process

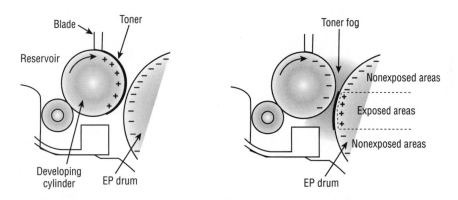

A metallic *developing roller* inside an EP cartridge acquires a –600VDC charge (called a *bias voltage*) from the HVPS. The toner sticks to this roller because there is a magnet located inside the roller and because of the electrostatic charges between the toner and the developing roller. While the developing roller rotates toward the photosensitive drum, the toner acquires the charge of the roller (–600VDC). When the toner comes between the developing roller and the photosensitive drum, the toner is attracted to the areas that have been exposed by the laser (because these areas have a lesser charge, of –100VDC). The toner also is repelled from the unexposed areas (because they are at the same –600VDC charge, and like charges repel). This toner transfer creates a fog of toner between the EP drum and the developing roller.

The photosensitive drum now has toner stuck to it where the laser has written. The photosensitive drum continues to rotate until the developed image is ready to be transferred to paper in the next step.

STEP 5: TRANSFERRING

At this point in the EP process, the developed image is rotating into position. The controller notifies the registration rollers that the paper should be fed through. The registration rollers move the paper underneath the photosensitive drum, and the process of transferring the image can begin, with the *transferring step*.

The controller sends a signal to the corona wire or corona roller (depending on which one the printer has) and tells it to turn on. The corona wire/roller then acquires a strong *positive* charge (+600VDC) and applies that charge to the paper. The paper, thus charged, pulls the toner from the photosensitive drum at the line of contact between the roller and the paper, because the paper and toner have opposite charges. Once the registration rollers move the paper past the corona wire, the static-eliminator strip removes all charge from that line of the paper. Figure 5.11 details this step. If the strip didn't bleed this charge away, the paper would attract itself to the toner cartridge and cause a paper jam.

FIGURE 5.11   The transferring step of the EP process

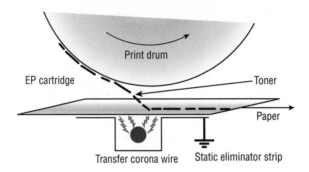

The toner is now held in place by weak electrostatic charges and gravity. It will not stay there, however, unless it is made permanent, which is the reason for the fusing step.

STEP 6: FUSING

In the final step, the *fusing step*, the toner image is made permanent. The registration rollers push the paper toward the fuser rollers. Once the fuser grabs the paper, the registration rollers push for only a short time more. The fuser is now in control of moving the paper.

As the paper passes through the fuser, the fuser roller melts the polyester resin of the toner, and the rubberized pressure roller presses it permanently into the paper (Figure 5.12). The paper continues on through the fuser and eventually exits the printer.

FIGURE 5.12   The fusing step of the EP process

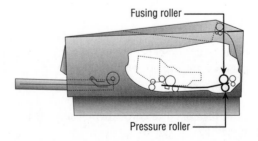

Once the paper completely exits the fuser, it trips a sensor that tells the printer to finish the EP process with the cleaning step. At this point, the printer can print another page and the EP process can begin again.

SUMMARY OF THE EP PRINT PROCESS

Figure 5.13 summarizes all the EP process printing steps. First, the printer uses a rubber scraper to clean the photosensitive drum. Then the printer places a uniform, negative, –600VDC charge on the photosensitive drum by means of a charging corona. The laser paints an image onto the photosensitive drum, discharging the image areas to a much lower voltage (–100VDC). The developing roller in the toner cartridge has charged (–600VDC) toner stuck to it. As it rolls the toner toward the photosensitive drum, the toner is attracted to (and sticks to) the areas of the photosensitive drum that the laser has discharged. The image is then transferred from the drum to the paper at its line of contact by means of the corona wire (or corona roller) with a +600VDC charge. The static-eliminator strip removes the high, positive charge from the paper, and the paper, now holding the image, moves on. The paper then enters the fuser, where the fuser roller and the pressure roller make the image permanent. The paper exits the printer, and the printer starts printing the next page or returns to its ready state.

FIGURE 5.13   The EP print process

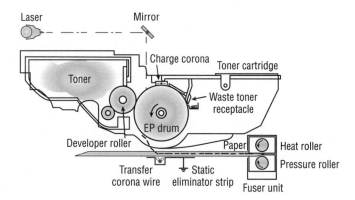

LED Printers

An LED printer uses a light-emitting diode instead of a laser. The LED is not built into the toner cartridge; it is separate, so that when you replace the toner cartridge, all you get is new toner.

The LED printing process uses a row of small LEDs very close to the drum to expose it. Each LED is about the same size as the diameter of the laser beam used in a laser printer. Except for the writing stage, the operation is the same as the laser printing process.

LED printers are cheaper and smaller than lasers. However, they are considered lower-end printers, and they have a lower maximum dots per inch (dpi)—under 800dpi versus 1,200 or more for a laser printer.

Other Printer Technologies

Besides the aforementioned technologies, you might see a question or two about several less popular ones on the A+ exam. They are all high-end color graphics printers designed for specialty professional usage:

Color Laser   Works much like a regular laser printer except that it makes multiple passes over the page, one for each ink color. Consequently, the printing speed is rather low.

Thermal Wax Transfer   A color non-impact line printer that uses a solid, wax-like ink. A heater melts the wax and then sprays it onto the page, somewhat like an ink-jet. The quality is very high, but so is the price ($2,500 or so). However, the wax is cheaper per page than ink-jet ink. The quality is as good as a color laser, but the speed is much faster because it needs only one pass.

Dye Sublimation   Another color non-impact line printer. This one converts a solid ink into a gas that is then applied to the paper. Color is applied in a continuous tone, rather than individual dots, and the colors are applied one at a time. The ink comes on film rolls. The paper is very expensive, as is the ink. Print speeds are very low. The quality is extremely high.

Printer Interfaces

Besides understanding the printer's operation, for the exam you need to understand how the printer talks to a computer. A printer's *interface* is the collection of hardware and software that allows the printer to communicate with a computer. Each printer has at least one interface, but some printers have several, in order to make them more flexible in a multiplatform environment. If a printer has several interfaces, it can usually switch between them on the fly so that several computers can print at the same time.

Communication Types

When we say *communication types*, we're talking about the hardware technologies involved in getting the printed information from the computer to the printer. There are eight major types:

Legacy Serial   This is the traditional RS-232 serial port found on most PCs. The original printer interface on the earliest computers, it has fallen out of favor and is seldom used anymore for printing because it is so slow.

Legacy Parallel   Until recently, the parallel port on a PC was the overwhelming favorite interface for connecting printers, to the point where the parallel port has become synonymous with *printer port*. It sends data 8 bits at a time (in parallel), and uses a cable with a male DB-25 connector at the computer and a 36-bin Centronics male connector at the printer. Its main drawback is its cable length, which must be less than 10 feet.

Universal Serial Bus (USB)   The most popular type of printer interface as this book is being written is the Universal Serial Bus (USB). It is actually the most popular interface for just about every peripheral. The benefit for printers is that it has a higher transfer rate than either serial or parallel and it automatically recognizes new devices. USB is also fully Plug-and-Play, and it allows several printers to be connected at once without adding additional ports or using up additional system resources.

Network   Most large environment printers (primarily laser and LED printers) have a special interface that allows them to be hooked directly to a network. These printers have a network interface card (NIC) and ROM-based software that let them communicate with networks, servers, and workstations.

The type of network interface used on the printer depends on the type of network the printer is being attached to. For example, if you're using a Token Ring network, the printer should have a Token Ring interface.

SCSI   Although it is not a common interface for printers, external SCSI can be used for a printer. See Objective 1.7 for more information about SCSI.

IEEE 1394/FireWire   This is a high-speed serial alternative to USB. It is less commonly used for printers than USB is, but FireWire printer interfaces do exist.

Infrared   BlueTooth is an infrared technology that can connect a printer to a computer at a range of about 35 feet, provided there is an unblocked line of sight.

Wireless   A network-enabled printer that has a wireless adapter can participate in a wireless Ethernet (IEEE 802.11b, a, or g) network, just as it would as a wired network client.

Exam Essentials

Know the common types of printers.   Know and understand the types of printers such as impact printers, ink-jet printers, and laser printers (page printers), as well as their interfaces and print media.

Understand the process of printing for each type of printer.   Each type of printer puts images or text on paper. Understand the process that each type of printer uses to accomplish this task.

Know the specific components of each type of printer.   Each type of printer uses similar components to print. Know the different components that make up each type of printer and their job.

Know and understand the print process of a laser printer.   You will almost certainly be asked questions about certain processes of a laser printer. Know and understand the different steps that make up the print process of a laser printer.

Know the possible interfaces that can be used for printing.   The eight types are legacy parallel, legacy serial, USB, FireWire, network, wireless, infrared, and SCSI.

5.2 Recognizing and Resolving Common Printer Problems

Not only is printer troubleshooting on the test, but you may have to accomplish these tasks on a daily basis. Your ability to get a down printer working will make you more valuable to your employer.

Critical Information

In the real world, you will find that large portion of all service calls relate to printing problems. This section will give you some general guidelines and common printing solutions to resolve printing problems.

Printer Driver Issues

Many problems with a printer that won't work with the operating system or that prints the wrong characters can be traced to problems with its software. Computers and printers can't talk to each other by themselves. They need interface software to translate software commands into commands the printer can understand.

For a printer to work with a particular operating system, a driver must be installed for it. This driver specifies the *page description language (PDL)* that the printer understands, as well as information about the printer's characteristics (paper trays, maximum resolution, and so on). For laser printers, there are two popular PDLs: Adobe PostScript and Hewlett Packard Printer Control Language (PCL). Almost all laser printers use one or both of these.

If the wrong printer driver is selected, the computer will send commands in the wrong language. If that occurs, the printer will print several pages of garbage (even if only one page of information was sent). This "garbage" isn't garbage at all, but in fact the printer PDL commands printed literally as text instead of being interpreted as control commands.

Although HP does not recommend using any printer driver other than the one designed for the specific printer, in some cases, you can increase the printing performance (speed) of HP LaserJet and DeskJet printers by using older drivers that do not support the newer high-definition printing. I have also had cases where software packages would not function with newer HP drivers. To increase speed or correct printing problems with HP LaserJet printers, try this rule of thumb: If you are using a 5 series printer (5Si), try a 4 series driver; if that does not work, reduce the driver by one series. If a LaserJet III does not work, try the LaserJet driver, which should be last on your list of the default drivers built into Windows. In 90 percent of cases, this driver will fix printing problems with some applications.

Firmware Updates

A printer resembles a computer in many ways. Like a computer, it has its own motherboard, its own memory, and its own CPU. It also has firmware—that is, software permanently stored on a chip. If you are using an old computer with a new operating system, an update may be available for the printer's firmware. You can find out that information at the printer manufacturer's website, and download the update from there along with a utility program for performing the update.

Memory Errors

A printer can have several types of memory errors. The most common is insufficient memory to print the page. Sometimes this problem can be circumvented by doing any of the following:

- Turn off the printer to flush out its RAM, and then turn it back on and try again.
- Print at a lower resolution. (Adjust this setting in the printer's properties in Windows.)
- Change the page being printed so it is less complex.
- Try a different printer driver if your printer supports more than one PDL. (For example, try switching from PostScript to PCL or vice versa.) Doing so involves installing another printer driver.

Printer Hardware Troubleshooting

This section covers the most common types of hardware printer problems you will run into. We'll break the information into three areas, for the three main types of printers in use today.

Dot-Matrix Printer Problems

Dot-matrix printers are relatively simple devices. Therefore, only a few problems usually arise. We'll cover the most common problems and their solutions here.

LOW PRINT QUALITY

Problems with print quality are easy to identify. When the printed page comes out of the printer, the characters may be too light or have dots missing from them. Table 5.1 details some of the most common print-quality problems, their causes, and their solutions.

TABLE 5.1 Common Dot-Matrix Print-Quality Problems

Characteristics	Cause	Solution
Consistently faded or light characters	Worn-out print ribbon	Replace ribbon with a new, vendor-recommended ribbon.
Print lines that go from dark to light as the print head moves across the page	Print ribbon advance gear slipping	Replace ribbon advance gear or mechanism.
A small, blank line running through a line of print (consistently)	Print head pin stuck inside the print head	Replace the print head.
A small, blank line running through a line of print (intermittently)	A broken, loose, or shorting print-head cable or a sticking print head	Secure or replace the print-head cable. Replace the print head or clean it.

TABLE 5.1   Common Dot-Matrix Print-Quality Problems *(continued)*

Characteristics	Cause	Solution
A small, dark line running through a line of print	Print-head pin stuck in the out position	Replace the print head. (Pushing the pin in may damage the print head.)
Printer makes a printing noise, but no print appears on the page	Worn, missing, or improperly installed ribbon cartridge, or the print head gap set too large	Replace the ribbon cartridge correctly or adjust the print-head gap.
Printer prints garbage	Cable partially unhooked, wrong driver selected, or a bad printer control board (PCB)	Hook up cable correctly, select the correct driver, or replace the PCB (respectively).

PRINTOUT JAMS INSIDE THE PRINTER

A paper jam happens when something prevents the paper from advancing through the printer evenly. Print jobs jam for two major reasons: an obstructed paper path or stripped drive gears.

An obstructed paper path is often difficult to find. Usually it means disassembling the printer to find the bit of paper or other foreign substance that's blocking the paper path. A very common obstruction is a piece of the *perf*—the perforated sides of tractor-feed paper—that has torn off and gotten crumpled up and then lodged into the paper path. It may be necessary to remove the platen roller and feed mechanism to get at the obstruction.

STEPPER MOTOR PROBLEMS

A *stepper motor* is a motor that can move in very small increments. Printers use stepper motors to move the print head back and forth as well as to advance the paper (these are called the *carriage motor* and *main motor*, respectively). These motors get damaged when they are forced in any direction while the power is on. This includes moving the print head over to install a printer ribbon as well as moving the paper feed roller to align paper. These motors are very sensitive to stray voltages. And, if you are rotating one of these motors by hand, you are essentially turning it into a small generator, thereby damaging it!

A damaged stepper motor is easy to detect. Damage to the stepper motor will cause it to lose precision and move farther with each step. Lines of print will be unevenly spaced if the main motor is damaged (which is more likely). Characters will be scrunched together if the print head motor goes bad. In fact, if the motor is bad enough, it won't move at all in any direction. It may even make high-pitched squealing noises. If any of these symptoms show themselves, it's time to replace one of these motors. Stepper motors are usually expensive to replace—about half the cost of a new printer. However, because dot-matrix printers are old technology and difficult to find, you may have no choice but to replace the motor if the printer is essential and is no longer available new.

Ink-jet Printers

Ink-jet printers are the most commonly sold printers for home use. For this reason, you need to understand the most common problems with ink-jet printers so your company can service them effectively.

PRINT QUALITY

The majority of ink-jet printer problems are quality problems. Ninety-nine percent of these can be traced to a faulty ink cartridge. With most ink-jet printers, the ink cartridge contains the print head and the ink. The major problem with this assembly can be described by "If you don't use it, you lose it." The ink will dry out in the small nozzles and block them if they are not used at least once a week.

An example of a quality problem is when thin blank lines or colored stripes appear on the page. This is caused by a plugged hole in at least one of the small, pinhole ink nozzles in the print cartridge. Replacing the ink cartridge solves this problem easily. You may also be able to clear the clogged ink jet by running the printer's cleaning routine, either by pressing buttons on the printer or by issuing a command through the printer's driver in Windows.

If an ink cartridge becomes damaged or develops a hole, it can put too much ink on the page, and the letters will smear. Again, the solution is to replace the ink cartridge. (However, a very small amount of smearing is normal if the pages are laid on top of each other immediately after printing.)

One final print quality problem that does not directly involve the ink cartridge is characterized by the print quickly going from dark to light, and then to nothing. As we already mentioned, ink cartridges dry out if not used. That's why the manufacturers included a small suction pump inside the printer that primes the ink cartridge before each print cycle. If this priming pump is broken or malfunctioning, this problem will manifest itself and the pump will need to be replaced.

If the problem of the ink quickly going from dark to light and then disappearing ever happens to you, and you really need to print a couple of pages, try this trick I learned from a fellow technician: Take the ink cartridge out of the printer. Squirt some window cleaner on a paper towel and gently tap the print head against the wet paper towel. The force of the tap plus the solvents in the window cleaner should dislodge any dried ink, and the ink will flow freely again.

PAPER JAMS

Ink-jet printers usually have very simple paper paths. Therefore, paper jams due to obstructions are less likely. They are still possible, however, so an obstruction shouldn't be overlooked as a possible cause of jamming.

Paper jams in ink-jet printers are usually due to one of two things:

- A worn pickup roller
- The wrong type of paper

The pickup roller usually has one or two D-shaped rollers mounted on a rotating shaft. When the shaft rotates, one edge of the D rubs against the paper, pushing it into the printer. When the roller gets worn, it becomes smooth and doesn't exert enough friction against the paper to push it into the printer.

If the paper used in the printer is too smooth, it causes the same problem. Pickup rollers use friction, and smooth paper doesn't offer much friction. If the paper is too rough, on the other hand, it acts like sandpaper on the rollers, wearing them smooth. Here's a rule of thumb for paper smoothness: Paper slightly smoother than a new dollar bill will work fine.

Laser and Page Printers

Most of the problems with laser printers can be diagnosed with knowledge of the inner workings of the printer and a little common sense.

PAPER JAMS

Laser printers today run at copier speeds. As a result, their most common problem is paper jams. Paper can get jammed in a printer for several reasons. First, feed jams happen when the paper feed rollers get worn (similar to feed jams in ink-jet printers). The solution to this problem is easy: Replace the worn rollers.

> If your paper-feed jams are caused by worn pickup rollers, there is something you can do to get your printer working while you're waiting for the replacement pickup rollers. Scuff the feed roller(s) with a Scotch-Brite pot-scrubber pad (or something similar) to roughen up the feed rollers. This trick works only once. After that, the rollers aren't thick enough to touch the paper.

Another cause of feed jams is related to the drive of the pickup roller. The drive gear (or clutch) may be broken or have teeth missing. Again, the solution is to replace it. To determine if the problem is a broken gear or worn rollers, print a test page, but leave the paper tray out. Look into the paper feed opening with a flashlight and see if the paper pickup roller(s) are turning evenly and don't skip. If they turn evenly, the problem is more than likely worn rollers.

Worn exit rollers can also cause paper jams. These rollers guide the paper out of the printer into the paper-receiving tray. If they are worn or damaged, the paper may catch on its way out of the printer. These types of jams are characterized by a paper jam that occurs just as the paper is getting to the exit rollers. If the paper jams, open the rear door and see where the paper is. If the paper is very close to the exit roller, the exit rollers are probably the problem.

The solution is to replace all the exit rollers. You must replace all of them at the same time, because even one worn exit roller can cause the paper to jam. Besides, they're inexpensive. Don't be cheap and skimp on these parts if you need to have them replaced.

Paper jams can be the fault of the paper. If your printer consistently tries to feed multiple pages into the printer, the paper isn't dry enough. If you live in an area with high humidity, this could be a problem. I've heard some solutions that are pretty far out but that work (like keeping the paper in a Tupperware-type of airtight container or microwaving it to remove moisture). The best all-around solution, however, is humidity control and to keep the paper wrapped until it's needed. Keep the humidity around 50 percent or lower (but above 25 percent if you can, in order to avoid problems with electrostatic discharge).

Finally, a metal, grounded strip called the *static eliminator strip* inside the printer drains the corona charge away from the paper after it has been used to transfer toner from the EP cartridge. If that strip is missing, broken, or damaged, the charge will remain on the paper and may cause it to stick to the EP cartridge, causing a jam. If the paper jams after reaching the corona assembly, this may be the cause.

BLANK PAGES

Blank pages are a somewhat common occurrence in laser and page printers. Somehow, the toner isn't being put on the paper. The toner cartridge is the source for most quality problems, because it contains most of the image-formation pieces for laser and page printers. Let's start with the obvious. A blank page will come out of the printer if there is no toner in the toner cartridge. It's very easy to check: Just open the printer, remove the toner cartridge, and shake it. You will be able to hear if there's toner inside the cartridge. If it's empty, replace it with a known, good, manufacturer-recommended toner cartridge.

Another issue that crops up rather often is the problem of using refilled or reconditioned toner cartridges. During their recycling process, these cartridges may be filled with the wrong kind of toner (for example, one with an incorrect charge). This may cause toner to be repelled from the EP drum instead of attracted to it. Thus, there's no toner on the page because there was no toner on the EP drum to begin with. The solution is to replace the toner cartridge with the type recommended by the manufacturer.

A third problem related to toner cartridges happens when someone installs a new toner cartridge and forgets to remove the sealing tape that is present to keep the toner in the cartridge during shipping. The solution to this problem is as easy as it is obvious: Remove the toner cartridge from the printer, remove the sealing tape, and reinstall the cartridge.

Another cause of blank pages is a damaged or missing corona wire. If a wire is lost or damaged, the developed image won't transfer from the EP drum to the paper. Thus, no image appears on the printout. To determine if this is causing your problem, do the first half of the self-test (described later in this section). If there is an image on the drum but not on the paper, you will know that the corona assembly isn't doing its job.

To check if the corona assembly is causing the problem, open the cover and examine the wire (or roller, if your printer uses one). The corona wire is hard to see, so you may need a flashlight. You will know if it's broken or missing just by looking (it will either be in pieces or just not there). If it's not broken or missing, the problem may be related to the HVPS. The corona wire (or roller) is a relatively inexpensive part and can be easily replaced with the removal of two screws and some patience.

The HVPS supplies high-voltage, low-current power to both the charging and transfer corona assemblies in laser and page printers. If it's broken, neither will work properly. If the self-test shows an image on the drum but none on the paper, and the corona assembly is present and not damaged, then the HVPS is at fault.

ALL-BLACK PAGES

This happens when the charging unit (the charging corona wire or charging corona roller) in the toner cartridge malfunctions and fails to place a charge on the EP drum. Because the drum is grounded, it has no charge. Anything with a charge (like toner) will stick to it. As the drum rotates, all the toner will be transferred to the page, and a black page will form.

This problem wastes quite a bit of toner, but it can be fixed easily. The solution (again) is to replace the toner cartridge with a known, good, manufacturer-recommended one. If that doesn't solve the problem, then the HVPS is at fault (it's not providing the high voltage the charging corona needs to function).

REPETITIVE SMALL MARKS OR DEFECTS

Repetitive marks occur frequently in heavily used (as well as older) laser printers. The problem may be caused by toner spilled inside the printer. It can also be caused by a crack or chip in the EP drum (this mainly happens with recycled cartridges). These cracks can accumulate toner. In both cases, some of the toner will get stuck onto one of the rollers. Once this happens, every time the roller rotates and touches a piece of paper, it will leave toner smudges spaced a roller circumference apart.

The solution is simple: Clean or replace the offending roller. To help you figure out which roller is causing the problem, the service manuals contain a chart like the one in Figure 5.14. To use the chart, place the printed page next to the chart. Align the first occurrence of the smudge with the top arrow. The next smudge will line up with one of the other arrows. The arrow it lines up with tells you which roller is causing the problem. (This chart in Figure 5.14 is only an example; your printer will have different-size rollers and will need a different chart. Also, this chart is not to scale.)

FIGURE 5.14   Laser printer roller circumference chart

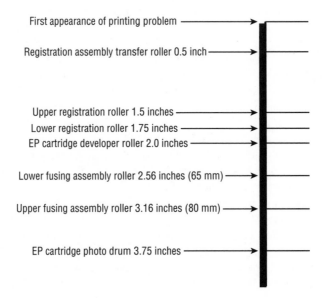

VERTICAL BLACK LINES ON THE PAGE

A groove or scratch in the EP drum can cause the problem of vertical black lines running down all or part of the page. Because a scratch is lower than the surface, it doesn't receive as much (if any) of a charge as the other areas. The result is that toner sticks to it as though it were discharged.

Because the groove may go around the circumference of the drum, the line may go all the way down the page.

Another possible cause of vertical black lines is a dirty charging corona wire. A dirty charging corona wire will prevent a sufficient charge from being placed on the EP drum. Because the EP drum will have almost zero charge, toner will stick to the areas that correspond to the dirty areas on the charge corona wire.

The solution to the first problem is, as always, to replace the toner cartridge (or EP drum if your printer uses a separate EP drum and toner). You can also solve the second problem with a new toner cartridge, but in this case that would be an extreme solution. It's easier to clean the charge corona with the brush supplied with the cartridge.

VERTICAL WHITE LINES ON THE PAGE

Vertical white lines running down all or part of the page are relatively common problems on older printers, especially ones that see little maintenance. They are caused by foreign matter (more than likely toner) caught on the transfer corona wire. The dirty spots keep the toner from being transmitted to the paper (at those locations, that is), with the result that streaks form as the paper progresses past the transfer corona wire.

The solution is to clean the corona wires. Some printers come with a small corona-wire brush to help in this procedure. To use it, remove the toner cartridge and run the brush in the charge corona groove on top of the toner cartridge. Replace the cartridge and use the brush to brush away any foreign deposits on the transfer corona. Be sure to put it back in its holder when you're finished.

IMAGE SMUDGING

If you can pick up a sheet from a laser printer, run your thumb across it, and have the image come off on your thumb, then you have a fuser problem. The fuser isn't heating the toner and fusing it into the paper. This could be caused by a number of things—but all of them can be taken care of with a fuser replacement. For example, if the halogen light inside the heating roller has burned out, that will cause the problem. The solution is to replace the fuser. The fuser can be replaced with a rebuilt unit, if you prefer. Rebuilt fusers are almost as good as new fusers, and some even come with guarantees. Plus, they cost less.

The whole fuser may not need to be replaced. You can order fuser components from parts suppliers and then rebuild them. For example, if the fuser has a bad lamp, you can order a lamp and replace it in the fuser.

Another, similar problem happens when small areas of smudging repeat themselves down the page. Dents or cold spots in the fuser heat roller cause this problem. The only solution is to replace either the fuser assembly or the heat roller.

GHOSTING

Ghosting means you can see light images of previously printed pages on the current page. This is caused by one of two things: bad erasure lamps or a broken cleaning blade. If the erasure lamps are bad, the previous electrostatic discharges aren't completely wiped away. When the EP drum rotates toward the developing roller, some toner sticks to the slightly discharged areas. A broken cleaning blade, on the other hand, causes old toner to build up on the EP drum and consequently present itself in the next printed image.

Replacing the toner cartridge solves the second problem. Solving the first problem involves replacing the erasure lamps in the printer. Because the toner cartridge is the least expensive cure, you should try that first. Usually, replacing the toner cartridge will solve the problem. If it doesn't, you will then have to replace the erasure lamps.

PRINTER PRINTS PAGES OF GARBAGE

This has happened to everyone at least once. You print a one-page letter and 10 pages of what looks like garbage come out of the printer. This problem comes from either the print driver software or the formatter board:

Printer Driver   The correct printer driver needs to be installed for the printer you have. For example, if you have an HP LaserJet III, then that is the driver you need to install. Once the driver has been installed, it must be configured for the correct page description language: PCL or PostScript. Most HP LaserJet printers use PCL (but can be configured for PostScript). Determine what page description your printer has been configured for and set the print driver to the same setting. If this is not done, you will get garbage out of the printer.

 Most printers with LCD displays indicate that they are in PostScript mode with a *PS* or *PostScript* somewhere in the display.

If the problem is the wrong driver setting, the garbage the printer prints looks like English. That is, the words are readable, but they don't make any sense.

Formatter Board   The other cause of several pages of garbage being printed is a bad formatter board. This circuit board takes the information the printer receives from the computer and turns it into commands for the various components in the printer. Problems with the formatter board generally produce wavy lines of print or random patterns of dots on the page.

It's relatively easy to replace the formatter board in a laser printer. Usually this board is installed underneath the printer and can be removed by loosening two screws and pulling the board out. Typically, replacing the formatter board also replaces the printer interface; another possible source of garbage printouts.

Problems with Consumables

Just as it is important to use the correct printer interface and printer software, you must use the correct printer supplies. These supplies include the print media (what you print on) and the consumables (what you print with). The quality of the final print job has a great deal to do with the print supplies.

Paper

Most people don't give much thought to the kind of paper they use in their printers. It's a factor that can have a tremendous effect on the quality of the hard-copy printout, however, and the topic is more complex than people think. For example, if the wrong paper is used, it can cause the paper to jam frequently and possibly even damage components.

Transparencies

Transparencies are still used for presentations made with overhead projectors, even with the explosion of programs like Microsoft PowerPoint and peripherals like LCD computer displays, both of which let you show a whole roomful of people exactly what's on your computer screen. PowerPoint has an option to print slides, and you can use any program to print anything you want on a transparent sheet of plastic or vinyl for use with an overhead projector. The problem is, these "papers" are *exceedingly* difficult for printers to work with. That's why special transparencies were developed for use with laser and ink-jet printers.

Each type of transparency was designed for a particular brand and model of printer. Again, check the printer's documentation to find out which type of transparency works in that printer. Don't use any other type of transparency.

WARNING   *Never* run transparencies through a laser printer without first checking to see if it's the type recommended by the printer manufacturer. The heat from the fuser will melt most other transparencies, and they will wrap themselves around it. It is impossible to clean a fuser after this has happened. The fuser will have to be replaced. *Use only the transparencies that are recommended by the printer manufacturer.*

Ink, Toner, or Ribbon

Besides print media, other things in the printer run out and need to be replenished. These items are the print consumables. Most consumables are used to form the images on the print media. Printers today use two main types of consumables: ink and toner.

To avoid problems relating to the ink, toner, or ribbon, use only brand-new supplies from reputable manufacturers. Do not use remanufactured or refilled cartridges.

Cleaning Pads

Some toner cartridges come with a cleaning pad. It's a long, thin strip of felt mounted on a piece of plastic. If a toner cartridge includes one, that means that somewhere inside the printer is a dirty felt pad that needs to be swapped out with the new one. Failing to do this when you change toner cartridges can cause problems.

Environmental Issues for Printers

Just like computers, printers can suffer from operating in an inhospitable environment such as one that is extreme in temperature or very dusty or smoky. Printers work best in a cool, clean environment where the humidity is between 50 and 80 percent.

Exam Essentials

Know the common printing problems listed.   Understand the most common problems that occur in an environment.

Know the possible fixes for the common problem types.   Each type of printer has its own common issues. Be familiar with the most likely repair options for each common problem.

Know how to select good-quality, appropriate consumables.   Using appropriate paper and new (not remanufactured) toner, ink, or ribbon can prevent many problems.

Review Questions

1. Give two examples of line printers.
2. What advantage does dot matrix have over other printer technologies?
3. What is the purpose of the primary corona in the laser printing process?
4. List the six steps in the laser printing process in the correct order.
5. If there is loose toner on the paper after a laser print, which part is defective?
6. What are some advantages of USB as a printer interface, as opposed to legacy parallel?
7. What do you need to do if there are stripes on an ink-jet printout?
8. True or false: A laser printer that prints a completely black page may be suffering from a nonfunctioning fuser.
9. Why should you not use transparency film designed for an ink-jet printer in a laser printer?
10. What is the most common cause of small marks or defects in the same spot on every page of a laser printer's printout?

Answers to Review Questions

1. Answer: Ink-jet, dot matrix
2. Answer: The ability to print on multipart forms
3. Answer: It applies a uniform negative charge to the drum.
4. Answer: Cleaning, conditioning, writing, developing, transferring, fusing
5. Answer: Fuser
6. Answer: USB is fully Plug-and-Play, it allows several printers to be connected at once without adding additional ports or using up additional system resources, and it is faster.
7. Answer: Clean the ink jets; one or more is clogged.
8. Answer: False. A completely black page results from the primary (charging) corona malfunctioning.
9. Answer: Because the laser printer's fuser will melt it
10. Answer: A scratch on the drum

Chapter

6

Domain 6 Basic Networking

COMPTIA A+ EXAM OBJECTIVES COVERED IN THIS CHAPTER:

- ✓ 6.1 Identify the common types of network cables, their characteristics and connectors.
- ✓ 6.2 Identify basic network concepts including how a network works.
- ✓ 6.3 Identify common technologies available for establishing Internet connectivity and their characteristics.

The A+ exam will test your basic networking skills—those skills needed to effectively troubleshoot and repair desktop PCs in a corporate environment. To pass the test and be effective in your troubleshooting, you need to understand the basic concepts and terminology in this chapter. This objective has been greatly expanded in the latest exam revision and has been split into three subobjectives, whereas it had previously been a single one.

6.1 Identifying Network Cables

The latest revision of the A+ exam increases the number of cable and connector types that it specifically lists in the objective. You should be able to identify various connector types by sight and specify which cable should be used with which network systems.

Critical Information

When data travels between network nodes, it uses cable (or wireless infrared or radio frequency [RF] signal). The cabling you choose must support both the network architecture and topology. There are three main types of cabling methods: twisted-pair cable, coaxial cable, and fiber optic cable.

Twisted-Pair

Twisted-pair is one of the most popular methods of cabling because of its flexibility and low costs. It consists of several pairs of wire twisted around each other within an insulated jacket, as shown in Figure 6.1. Twisted-pair is most often found in 10/100BaseT Ethernet networks, although other systems can use it.

FIGURE 6.1   Twisted-pair cable

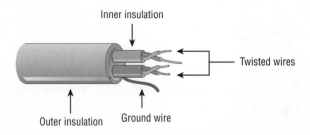

Twisted-pair cable can be unshielded (UTP) or shielded (STP). This refers to its level of protection against electromagnetic interference (EMI). STP has a braided foil shield around the twisted wires, whereas UTP does not.

Unshielded Twisted-Pair (UTP)

UTP comes in several grades to offer different levels of protection against electrical interference:

- *Category 1*—For voice-only transmissions. Used in most phone systems today. It contains two twisted pairs.
- *Category 2*—Transmits data at speeds up to 4Mbps. It contains four twisted pairs of wires.
- *Category 3*—Transmits data at speeds up to 10Mbps. It contains four twisted pairs of wires with three twists per foot.
- *Category 4*—Transmits data at speeds up to 16Mbps. It contains four twisted pairs of wires.
- *Category 5*—Transmits data at speeds up to 100Mbps. It contains four twisted pairs of copper wire to give the most protection.
- *Category 5e*—Transmits data at speeds up to 1Gbps. It also contains four twisted pairs of copper wire, but they are physically separated and contain more twists per foot than Category 5 to provide maximum interference protection.
- *Category 6*—Transmits data at speed up to 2Gbps. It contains four twisted pairs of copper wire.

Most network UTP cable uses RJ-45 connectors, which are like fat versions of telephone connectors. Instead of two or four metal tabs on the connector like a phone cable has, the RJ-45 connector has eight.

Shielded Twisted Pair (STP)

STP cable is differentiated by type, rather than category, and uses an IBM Data Connector (IDC) or Universal Data Connector (UDC) connector on one end for connecting to the Token Ring network. The types for STP cable are:

- *Type 1*—The most common STP cable type. Contains two pairs.
- *Type 2*—Like Type 1 but adds two pairs of voice wires.
- *Type 3*—Contains four pairs.
- *Type 6*—Patch cable, used for connecting token ring hubs.
- *Type 8*—A flat type of STP cable used for running under carpets.
- *Type 9*—A two-pair, high-grade type of STP.

Coaxial

The next choice of cable for most LANs is coaxial cable. The cable consists of a copper wire surrounded by insulation and a metal foil shield, as shown in Figure 6.2. It is very similar to the cable used to connect cable television.

FIGURE 6.2   Coaxial cable

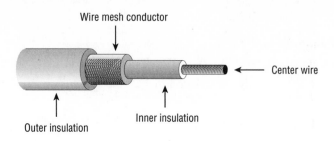

Another name for coaxial cable is RG. Coaxial cable comes in many thicknesses and types, including these:

- *RG-58*—50-ohm cable. Used for 10Base2 (Thinnet) Ethernet.
- *RG-59*—75-ohm cable. Used for broadband transmission such as cable TV.
- *RG-6*—Used for satellites. A double- or quad-shielded cable that offers superior performance and minimal signal leakage.
- *RG-8*—50-ohm cable. Used for 10Base5 (Thicknet) Ethernet.

The connectors on coaxial cable are usually BNC (Bayonet Neil Connector or British Naval Connector), a connector that may be familiar to cable television users. It consists of a metal wire core in the center with a threaded metal ring around it. An exception: 10Base5 (Thicknet) coaxial cable uses an AUI (Attachment Unit Interface) connector to connect to the PC network card.

Fiber Optic

Fiber optic cabling consists of a thin, flexible glass fiber surrounded by a rubberized outer coating (see Figure 6.3). It provides transmission speeds from 100Mbps up to 1Gbps and a maximum distance of several miles. Because it uses pulses of light instead of electric voltages to transmit data, it is completely immune from electric interference and from wiretapping.

FIGURE 6.3   Fiber optic cable

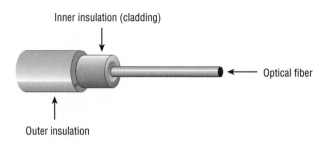

Fiber optic cable has not become a standard in networks, however, because of its high cost of installation. Networks that need extremely fast transmission rates, transmissions over long distances, or have had problems with electrical interference in the past often use fiber optic cabling.

There are several types of fiber optic cable, differentiated by their fiber thickness, coating thickness, and mode (single or multi). A single-mode cable uses injection laser diodes (ILDs) to send data. It is a high-bandwidth, expensive cable. Multimode cable uses light-emitting diodes (LEDs).

Fiber optic cable can use either ST or SC connectors. ST is a barrel-shaped connector; SC is a newer, squared type that is easier to connect in a cramped space.

Summary of Cabling Types

Each type of cabling has its own benefits and drawbacks. Table 6.1 details the most common types of cabling in use today. As you look at this table, pay particular attention to the cost, length, and maximum transmission rates of each cabling type.

TABLE 6.1   Cable Types

Characteristics	Unshielded Twisted-Pair	Shielded Twisted-Pair	Coaxial	Fiber Optic
Cost	Least expensive	Moderate	Moderate	Expensive
Maximum Length	100m (328ft)	100m (328ft)	185m (607ft) to 500m (1640ft)	>10 miles
Transmission Rates	10Mbps to 2Gbps	10Mbps to 2Gbps for Ethernet, Fast Ethernet and Gigabit Ethernet. 16Mbps for Token Ring	10Mbps	100Mbps or more
Flexibility	Most flexible	Fair	Fair	Fair
Ease of Installation	Very easy	Very easy	Easy	Difficult
Interference	Susceptible	Not susceptible	Moderate	Not susceptible
Special Features	Various categories; must choose the right kind for the job	Various types; must choose the right kind for the job		Supports voice, data, and video at highest transmission speeds
Preferred Uses	10/100/1000BaseT	10/100/1000BaseT or Token Ring	10Base2, 10Base5	Network segments requiring high-speed transmission

TABLE 6.1   Cable Types *(continued)*

Characteristics	Unshielded Twisted-Pair	Shielded Twisted-Pair	Coaxial	Fiber Optic
Connector	RJ-45	RJ-45 for Ethernet; IDC/UDC for Token Ring	BNC or AUI	ST/SC
Physical Topology	Star	Star or ring	Bus	Star (typically)

Exam Essentials

Know the cable types for Ethernet networks.   Given the task of cabling a 100BaseT, 10Base5, or 10Base2 network, you should be able to specify the types of cable you would need and their connectors.

Know the UTP categories.   Understand the situations for which Cat3, Cat5, Cat5e, and Cat6 cable would be required.

6.2 Understanding Basic Network Concepts

This objective tests your knowledge of basic networking terms and concepts such as networking models and protocols, as well as practical skills like installing a NIC and physically connecting a network.

Critical Information

A *network* links two or more computers together to communicate and share resources. A computer network allows computers to link to each other's resources. For example, in a network every computer does not need a printer connected locally to print. Instead, one computer can have a printer connected to it and allow the other computers to access this resource. Because they allow users to share resources, networks offer an increase in performance as well as a decrease in the outlay for new hardware and software.

LANs vs. WANs

A local area network (LAN) is a network within a limited area, such as a single office. Wide area networks (WANs) expand the LANs to include networks outside of the local environment and also to distribute resources across distances.

Network Types

There are two basic network types: client/server and peer-to-peer:

Client/Server   A network that has one or more computers dedicated for use as a server, with a special server operating system and responsibilities. Can be any size, but typically has 10 or more client computers. See Figure 6.4.

FIGURE 6.4   The server-based model

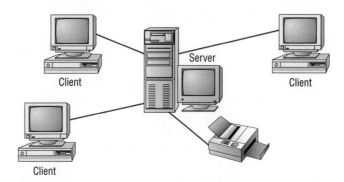

Peer-to-Peer   A network in which all computers are clients, or equal participants, with no server. Usually limited to 10 or fewer computers. See Figure 6.5.

FIGURE 6.5   The peer-to-peer model

Servers

The server is a core component of a client/server network, providing a link to the resources necessary to perform a task. For example, a server might route requests between clients, deliver centrally stored files, provide Internet access, or deliver a print job to a printer.

Servers offer networks the capability of centralizing the control of resources and can thus reduce administrative difficulties. They can be used to distribute processes for balancing the load on the computers, thereby increasing speed and performance. They can also departmentalize files for improved reliability. That way, if one server goes down, not all of the files are lost.

Servers perform several tasks. For example, servers that provide files to the users on the network are called *file servers*. Likewise, servers that host printing services for users are called *print servers*. (There are other tasks as well, such as remote access services, administration, mail, and so on.) Servers can be multipurpose or single-purpose. If they are multipurpose, they can be, for example, both a file server and a print server at the same time. If the server is a single-purpose server, it is a file server only or a print server only.

Clients

Clients are the computers on which the users on a network do their work, such as word processing, database design, graphic design, e-mail, and other office or personal tasks. Clients are regular computers, except for the fact that they are connected to a network that offers additional resources. As clients, they are allowed to communicate with the servers in the network in order to use the network's resources.

In some companies, *thin clients* are used to save expenses. A thin client is a computer that lacks some component, such as disk storage, such that it can't function very well as a stand-alone model. It relies on the network server to make up for its deficiency.

A network client must have a network interface card (NIC), a special expansion card that allows the PC to talk on a network. The NIC is then connected to the network via cable (see Objective 6.1). And you must install some special software, called *client software*, which allows the computer to talk to the network. Once you've accomplished all this, the computer will be on the network.

The purpose of a client being connected to the network is to participate in the pool of shared resources available there. A *resource* (as far as the network is concerned) is any item that can be used on a network. Resources can include a broad range of items, including printers, files, applications, and disk storage space.

Network Topologies

A *topology* is a way of laying out the network. Topologies can be either physical or logical. *Physical topologies* describe how the cables are run. *Logical topologies* describe how the network messages travel. Deciding which type of topology to use is the next step when designing your network.

You must choose the appropriate topology in which to arrange your network. Each type differs by its cost, ease of installation, fault tolerance (how the topology handles problems like cable breaks), and ease of reconfiguration (like adding a new workstation to the existing network).

There are five primary topologies (some of which can be both logical and physical):

- Bus (can be both logical and physical)
- Star (physical only)
- Ring (can be both logical and physical)
- Mesh (can be both logical and physical)
- Hybrid (usually physical)

Each topology has advantages and disadvantages. At the end of this section, check out the table that summarizes the advantages and disadvantages of each topology.

Bus

A *bus* is the simplest physical topology. It consists of a single cable that runs to every workstation, as shown in Figure 6.6. This topology uses the least amount of cabling but also covers the shortest distance. Each computer shares the same data and address path. With a logical bus topology, messages pass through the trunk, and each workstation checks to see if the message is addressed to itself. If the address of the message matches the workstation's address, the network adapter copies the message to the card's on-board memory.

FIGURE 6.6   The bus topology

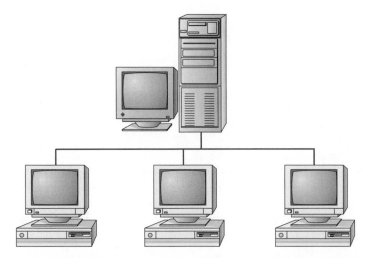

Cable systems that use the bus topology are easy to install. You run a cable from the first computer to the last computer. All the remaining computers attach to the cable somewhere in between. Because of the simplicity of installation, and because of the low cost of the cable, bus topology cabling systems (such as 10Base2 and 10Base5 Ethernet) are the cheapest to install.

Although the bus topology uses the least amount of cabling, it is difficult to add a workstation to this configuration. If you want to add another workstation, you have to completely reroute the cable and possibly run two additional lengths of it. Also, if any one of the cables breaks, the entire network is disrupted. Therefore, it is very expensive to maintain.

Star

A *physical star topology* branches each network device off a central device called a *hub*, making it very easy to add a new workstation. Also, if any workstation goes down, it does not affect the entire network. (But, as you might expect, if the central device goes down, the entire network goes down.) Modern Ethernet (10BaseT, 100BaseT, and Gigabit Ethernet) uses a physical star topology, as does Token Ring. Figure 6.7 gives an example of the organization of the star network.

FIGURE 6.7   The star topology

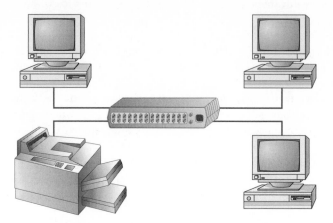

Star topologies are easy to install. A cable is run from each workstation to the hub. The hub is placed in a central location in the office (for example, a utility closet). Star topologies are more expensive to install than bus networks because several more cables need to be installed, in addition to the cost of the hubs that are required.

Ring

A *physical ring topology* is a unique topology. Each computer connects to two other computers, joining them in a circle, creating a unidirectional path where messages move from workstation to workstation. Each entity participating in the ring reads a message, then regenerates it and hands it to its neighbor on a different network cable. See Figure 6.8 for an example of a ring topology.

FIGURE 6.8   The ring topology

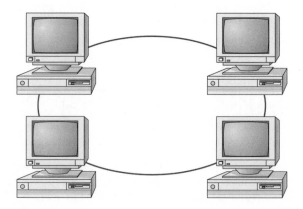

The ring makes it difficult to add new computers. Unlike a star topology network, the ring topology network will go down if one entity is removed from the ring. Few physical ring topology systems still exist, mainly because the hardware involved was fairly expensive and the fault tolerance was very low. However, one type of logical ring still exists: IBM's Token Ring technology. We'll discuss this technology later in the "Network Architectures" section.

Mesh

The *mesh topology* is the simplest logical topology, in terms of data flow, but it is the most complex in terms of physical design. In this physical topology, each device is connected to every other device, as shown in Figure 6.9. This topology is rarely found in LANs, mainly because of the complexity of the cabling. If there are x computers, there will be $(x \times (x-1)) \div 2$ cables in the network. For example, if you have five computers in a mesh network, it will use $5 \times (5-1) \div 2$, which equals 10 cables. This complexity is compounded when you add another workstation. For example, your 5-computer, 10-cable network will jump to 15 cables just by adding one more computer. Imagine how the person doing the cabling would feel if you told them you had to cable 50 computers in a mesh network—they'd have to come up with $50 \times (50-1) \div 2 = 1,225$ cables!

FIGURE 6.9   The mesh topology

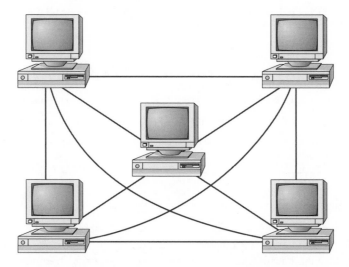

Because of its design, the physical mesh topology is very expensive to install and maintain. Cables must be run from each device to every other device. The advantage you gain from it is high fault tolerance. With a logical mesh topology, there will always be a way of getting the data from source to destination. It may not be able to take the direct route, but it can take an alternate, indirect route. For this reason, the mesh topology is still found in WANs to connect multiple sites across WAN links. It uses devices called *routers* to search multiple routes through the mesh and determine the best path. However, the mesh topology does become inefficient with five or more entities.

Hybrid

The *hybrid topology* is simply a mix of the other topologies. It would be impossible to illustrate it, because there are many combinations. Most networks today are not only hybrid, but heterogeneous (by *heterogeneous* I mean they include a mix of components of different types and brands). The hybrid network may be more expensive than some types of network topologies, but, on the other hand, it takes the best features of all the other topologies and exploits them.

Summary of Topologies

Table 6.2 summarizes the advantages and disadvantages of each type of network topology. This table is a good study aid for the A+ exam. (In other words, memorize it!)

TABLE 6.2   Topologies—Advantages and Disadvantages

Topology	Advantages	Disadvantages
Bus	Cheap. Easy to install.	Difficult to reconfigure. A break in the bus disables the entire network.
Star	Cheap. Easy to install. Easy to reconfigure. Fault tolerant.	More expensive than bus.
Ring	Efficient. Easy to install.	Reconfiguration is difficult. Very expensive.
Mesh	Simplest. Most fault tolerant.	Reconfiguration is extremely difficult. Extremely expensive. Very complex.
Hybrid	Combines the best features of each topology used.	Complex (less so than mesh, however).

Network Protocols

You have chosen the type of network and arrangement (topology). Now the computers need to understand how to communicate. Network communications use protocols. A *protocol* is a set of rules that govern communications. Protocols detail which language the computers are speaking when they talk over a network. If two computers are going to communicate, they both must be using the same protocol.

TCP/IP

The most common protocol used today is *Transmission Control Protocol/Internet Protocol (TCP/IP)*. It is used for Microsoft networking and also for the Internet. This is actually not one single protocol, but rather a suite of interrelated protocols and standards.

TCP/IP uses IP addresses to uniquely identify each computer on the network. An IP address is a string of four numbers (between 1 and 255) separated by periods, like this: 192.168.2.200.

It is a single 64-bit binary string of digits, but is broken up and converted to decimal for ease of use.

A portion of the IP address represents the domain (group) that the resource belongs to, much like an area code in a phone number; this is called its *network address*. Another portion represents its unique address within that group; this is called its *host address*.

Unlike in a phone number, however, the dividing point between the network address and the host address is not a fixed point. It varies depending on the *subnet mask* that is used. The subnet mask specifies where the dividing line is between the network and host portions of the IP address. For example, in the IP address 192.168.2.200, if the subnet mask was 255.255.0.0, then 192.168 would be the network portion of the IP address and 2.200 would be the host address.

IP addresses may be assigned to a PC statically (that is, manually entered at each PC), or dynamically through a *Dynamic Host Configuration Protocol (DHCP) server*. This is a server utility that assigns IP addresses to each client as it logs on to the network according to assignment rules that the network administrator configures.

IPX/SPX

Stands for Internet Packet eXchange/Sequenced (or Sequential) Packet eXchange. This protocol is for Netware networks, and is seldom used anymore because most networking is Microsoft-based. Windows provides an IPX/SPX-compatible protocol that enables a PC to connect to a Novell Netware network, but it does not install it by default in the newer Windows versions.

AppleTalk

This protocol enables a computer to connect to a Macintosh-based network. It is not installed by default, and the necessary software does not come with Windows, so it must be obtained from Apple. We'll discuss AppleTalk more in the "Network Architectures" section later in this chapter.

NetBEUI/NetBIOS

NetBIOS Extended User Interface (NetBEUI) is an older protocol for Windows networking. It has some limitations, such as being unable to work with routers, that make it unsuitable for large-scale networking, but it is a very fast and efficient protocol.

With NetBEUI, each computer is known by a NetBIOS name rather than an IP address. This is a plain-text name. When you enter a computer name in the networking properties in Windows, it will use that name as a NetBIOS name when communicating through a NetBEUI-enabled network.

Network Architectures

Network architectures define the structure of the network, including hardware, software, and layout. We differentiate each architecture by the hardware and software required to maintain optimum performance levels. The major architectures in use today are Ethernet, Token Ring, and AppleTalk.

Ethernet

Ethernet has several specifications, each one specifying the speed, communication method, and cable. The original Ethernet was given a designation of 10Base5. The *10* in Ethernet 10Base5 stands for the 10Mbps transmission rate, *Base* stands for the baseband communications used, and *5* stands for the maximum distance of 500 meters. This method of identification soon caught on, and as vendors changed the specifications of the Ethernet architecture, they followed the same pattern in the way they identified them.

After the 10Base5 came 10Base2 and 10BaseT. These quickly became standards in Ethernet technology. Many other standards (including 100BaseF, 10BaseF, and 100BaseT) have developed since then, but those three are the most popular.

Ethernet 10Base2 uses thin coaxial cables ($\frac{1}{4}$-inch) and bus topology and transmits at 10Mbps, with a maximum distance of 185 meters. Ethernet 10BaseT uses twisted-pair cabling (*T* stands for twisted), transmitting at 10Mbps, with a maximum distance of 100 meters, and physical star topology with a logical bus topology. 100BaseT Ethernet is the same except that it works at 100Mbps.

Token Ring

Token Ring uses a physical star, logical ring topology. All workstations are cabled to a central device, called a *multistation access unit* (*MAU*). The ring is created within the MAU by connecting every port together with special circuitry. Token Ring can use shielded or unshielded cable and can transmit data at either 4Mbps or 16Mbps.

AppleTalk

AppleTalk is a proprietary network architecture for Macintosh computers. It uses a bus and either shielded or unshielded cable. There are a few things to note about AppleTalk.

AppleTalk uses a Carrier Sense Multiple Access with Collision Avoidance (CSMA/CA) technology to put data on the cable. Unlike Ethernet, which uses a Carrier Sense Multiple Access with Collision Detection (CSMA/CD) method, this technology uses "smart" interface cards to detect traffic *before* it tries to send data. A CSMA/CA card listens to the wire. If there is no traffic, it sends a small amount of data. If no collisions occur, it follows that amount of data with the data it wants to transmit. In either case, if a collision happens, it backs off for a random amount of time and tries to transmit again.

Another interesting point about AppleTalk is that it's fairly simple. Most Macintosh computers already include AppleTalk, so it is relatively inexpensive. It assigns itself an address. In its first revision (Phase I), it allowed a maximum of 32 devices on a network. With its second revision (Phase II), it supports faster speeds and multiple networks with EtherTalk and TokenTalk. EtherTalk allows AppleTalk network protocols to run on Ethernet coaxial cable (used for Mac II and above.) TokenTalk allows the AppleTalk protocol to run on a Token Ring network.

The Network Interface Card

The network interface card (NIC) provides the physical interface between computer and cabling. It prepares data, sends data, and controls the flow of data. It can also receive and translate data into bytes for the CPU to understand. It communicates at the Physical layer of the OSI model and comes in many shapes and sizes.

Installation

The physical installation of a NIC is the same as with any other internal circuit board. It fits into an ISA or PCI expansion slot in the motherboard.

When choosing a NIC, use one that fits the bus type of your PC. If you have more than one type of bus in your PC (for example, a combination ISA/PCI), use a NIC that fits into the fastest type (PCI, in this case). This is especially important in servers, because the NIC can quickly become a bottleneck if this guideline isn't followed.

Configuration

The NIC's configuration includes such things as a manufacturer's hardware address, IRQ address, base I/O port address, and base memory address. Some NICs may also use DMA channels to offer better performance.

Each card has a unique hardware address, called a *media access control (MAC) address,* which is hard-wired into the card during its manufacture. It consists of six two-digit hexadecimal numbers; the first three represent the manufacturer and the second three are the unique serial number of the card. The MAC address is separate from any logical address that might be assigned to the PC by the networking system, such as an IP address.

Configuring a NIC is similar to configuring any other type of expansion card. The NIC usually needs a unique IRQ channel and I/O address, and possibly a DMA channel. Token Ring cards often have two memory addresses that must be allocated in reserved memory for them to work properly.

Drivers

For the computer to use the NIC, it is very important to install the proper device drivers. These drivers communicate directly with the network redirector and adapter. They operate in the Media Access Control sublayer of the Data Link layer of the OSI model.

Media Access Methods

You have put the network together in a topology. You have told the network how to communicate and send the data, and you have told it how to send the data to another computer. You also have the communications medium in place. The next problem you need to solve is how to put the data on the cable. What you need now are the *cable access methods*, which define a set of rules for how computers put data on and retrieve it from a network cable. The four methods of data access are shown here:

- Carrier Sense Multiple Access with Collision Detection (CSMA/CD)
- Carrier Sense Multiple Access with Collision Avoidance (CSMA/CA)
- Token passing
- Polling

Carrier Sense Multiple Access with Collision Detection

As we've already discussed, NICs that use CSMA/CD listen to, or "sense," the cable to check for traffic. They compete for a chance to transmit. Usually, if access to the network is slow, it means that too many computers are trying to transmit, causing traffic jams.

Carrier Sense Multiple Access with Collision Avoidance

Instead of monitoring traffic and moving in when there is a break, CSMA/CA allows the computers to send a signal that they are ready to transmit data. If the ready signal transmits without a problem, the computer then transmits its data. If the ready signal is not transmitted successfully, the computer waits and tries again. This method is slower and less popular than CSMA/CD.

Token Passing

As previously discussed, token passing is a way of giving every NIC equal access to the cable. A special packet of data is passed from computer to computer. Any computer that wants to transmit has to wait until it has the token. It can then transmit its data.

Polling

Polling is an old method of media access that is still in use. Not many topologies support polling anymore, mainly because it has special hardware requirements. This method requires a central, intelligent device (meaning that the device contains either hardware or software intelligence to enable it to make decisions) that asks each workstation in turn if it has any data to transmit. If the workstation answers "yes," the controller allows the workstation to transmit its data.

The polling process doesn't scale very well—that is, you can't take this method and simply apply it to any number of workstations. In addition, the high cost of the intelligent controllers and cards has made the polling method all but obsolete.

Wireless Networks

One of the most fascinating cabling technologies today—actually, it doesn't really *use* cable— is wireless. Wireless networks offer the ability to extend a LAN without the use of traditional cabling methods. Wireless transmissions are made through the air by infrared light, laser light, narrow-band radio, microwave, or spread-spectrum radio.

Wireless LANs are becoming increasingly popular as businesses are becoming more mobile and less centralized. You can see them most often in environments where standard cabling methods are not possible or wanted.

Wireless networking requires much the same type of equipment as traditional networking; the main difference is that the special versions of each item rely on RF signals or infrared instead of cables. So, for example, each node needs a NIC that has a transceiver in it instead of a cable jack; and there needs to be a central wireless access point (WAP), the equivalent of a hub, with which the wireless NICs communicate.

The first wireless networking standard to become commercially popular was *IEEE 802.11b*, which could send and receive at up to 11Mbps. At this writing a newer standard, *IEEE 802.11a*, has extended that to 54Mbps and will reach over 100Mbps in the next two years.

BlueTooth is an infrared wireless standard that uses light rather than radio waves. It is limited to about 35 feet in range and requires a clear line of sight, so it has not become widespread in use except for communications between notebook PCs and PDAs.

Connectivity Devices

In addition to clients, servers, and the cables between them, certain other "boxes" are required to help manage and facilitate connections. The following sections discuss some of them.

Repeaters

Repeaters are simple devices. They allow a cabling system to extend beyond its maximum allowed length by amplifying the network voltages so they travel farther. Repeaters are nothing more than amplifiers and, as such, are very inexpensive.

The main disadvantage of repeaters is that they just amplify signals. These signals include not only the network signals, but any noise on the wire as well. Eventually, if you used enough repeaters, you could possibly drown out the signal with the amplified noise. For this reason, repeaters are used only as a temporary fix.

Hubs

Hubs are devices used to link several computers together. They are most often used in 10/100BaseT Ethernet networks. They are essentially just multiport repeaters. They repeat any signal that comes in on one port and copy it to the other ports (a process that is also called *broadcasting*).

There are two types of hubs: active and passive. *Passive hubs* connect all ports together electrically and are usually not powered. *Active hubs* use electronics to amplify and clean up the signal before it is broadcast to the other ports. The category of active hubs also includes a class called *intelligent hubs*, which are hubs that can be remotely managed on the network.

Bridges

Bridges join similar topologies and are used to divide network segments. Bridges keep traffic on one side from crossing to the other. For this reason, they are often used to increase performance on a high-traffic segment.

For example, with 200 people on one Ethernet segment, performance would be mediocre, because of the design of Ethernet and the number of workstations fighting to transmit. If you divided the segment into two segments of 100 workstations each, the traffic would be much lower on either side and performance would increase.

Bridges cannot distinguish one protocol from another. If a bridge is aware of the destination address, it is able to forward packets; otherwise, a bridge forwards the packets to all segments. Bridges are more intelligent than repeaters but are unable to move data across multiple networks simultaneously. Unlike repeaters, bridges *can* filter out noise.

The main disadvantage of bridges is that they can't connect dissimilar network types or perform intelligent path selection. For that function, you need a router.

Routers

Routers are highly intelligent devices that connect multiple network types and determine the best path for sending data. They can route packets across multiple networks and use routing tables to store network addresses to determine the best destination.

The advantage of using a router over a bridge is that routers can determine the best path data can take to get to its destination. Like bridges, they can segment large networks and filter out noise. However, they are slower than bridges because they are more intelligent devices; as such, they analyze every packet, causing packet-forwarding delays. Because of this intelligence, they are also more expensive.

Routers are normally used to connect one LAN to another. Typically, when a WAN is set up, at least two routers are used.

Switches

Like hubs, *switches* are devices used to link several computers together. They differ from hubs in a few important ways. Switches repeat signals to the ports like hubs do, with one exception: Rather than send network traffic to all ports, switches have enough intelligence to send the traffic directly to the port the packet was intended for. All switches are active, and some are manageable. *Manageable hubs* allow remote management and in higher-end devices can also act similarly to a router. This feature can be used to logically divide the network into segments and reduce network traffic.

Brouters

Brouters are truly an ingenious idea because they combine the best of both worlds—bridges and routers. They are used to connect dissimilar network segments and also to route only one specific protocol. The other protocols are bridged instead of being dropped. Brouters are used when only one protocol needs to be routed or where a router is not cost-effective (as in a branch office).

Gateways

Gateways connect dissimilar network environments and architectures. Some gateways can use all levels of the OSI model, but they are frequently found in the Application layer. It is there that gateways convert data and repackage it to meet the requirements of the destination address. This makes gateways slower and more costly than other connectivity devices. An example of a gateway is the NT Gateway Service for NetWare, which, when running on a Windows NT Server, can connect a Microsoft Windows NT network with a Novell NetWare network.

Exam Essentials

Understand local area networks (LANs) and wide area networks (WANs). LANs are small in area, such as a single office. WANs encompass a large geographic area, possibly even among cities or countries.

Understand peer-to-peer and client/server. In a peer-to-peer network, the computers act as both workstations and servers, and there is no dedicated server with special server software. A client/server network contains at least one server, such as a file server, print server, DHCP server, and so on.

Know the role of TCP/IP in networking.   TCP/IP is the protocol used for the Internet and most Ethernet networks these days. It assigns each PC a unique IP address.

6.3 Establishing Internet Connectivity

This is a brand-new objective on the A+ Core Hardware exam; previously the Internet was covered only on the OS Technologies exam. It is still covered there, but this new objective deals with the hardware side of Internet connectivity. A good PC technician should be able to select appropriate Internet connectivity methods for a given situation and install and configure that technology.

Critical Information

For each of the following technologies, you should be able to provide a definition, identify the speed range, identify advantages and disadvantages, and explain how the connection functions.

Dial-Up

Dial-up Internet uses a modem and dial-up networking (DUN) in Windows to establish a connection between a PC and an Internet Service Provider (ISP). A dial-up connection is not always on; it is established when needed and disconnected when not needed. It uses standard telephone lines and ties up the phone while it is operating.

Dial-up speed is limited to between 52Kbps and 56Kbps. Its primary disadvantages are its low speed and the inconvenience of tying up the phone line. Its advantage is price; it is the cheapest type of Internet connection.

To configure a modem dial-up connection, install the modem in the PC, make sure dial-up networking is installed in Windows, and then create a new DUN connection for the ISP's phone number.

ISDN

Integrated Services Digital Network (ISDN) is a special digital type of phone line that is able to carry data faster than a regular dial-up. An ISDN phone line can carry two channels of data at once, at up to 64Kbps each, for a total of about 128Kbps maximum. It also has a separate voice channel, so you can place voice calls while connected to the Internet. It requires special phone lines from the phone company.

ISDN is a dial-up connection, so it uses dial-up networking. However, it establishes the connection much more quickly than a standard dial-up, usually within 5 seconds.

ISDN's advantage over regular dial-up is its speed and the ability to use the phone for voice calls simultaneously with the Internet. Its disadvantage is that better, faster Internet options currently exist at lower prices than ISDN, such as ADSL and cable. It is not very popular anymore.

To configure ISDN access, install the ISDN terminal adapter in Windows as you would any new piece of hardware. Connect it to the ISDN telephone line, and then create a new DUN connection for the ISP's phone number. Your ISP must specifically support ISDN for this to work, and you may need a special type of ISP account.

DSL

Digital Subscriber Line (DSL) is a technology that uses regular telephone lines to carry high-speed Internet. Like ISDN, it allows voice calls to take place while you're connected to the Internet.

DSL is much faster than ISDN. Its top speed can reach 2Mbps or higher, although there are many different types of DSL and not all of them are that fast.

The two major types of DSL are Asynchronous (*ADSL*) and Synchronous (*SDSL*). ADSL is cheaper and more common. It provides faster download speeds than upload speeds. SDSL has the same speed in both directions.

The advantages of DSL are its convenience, its always-on nature (no dialing up), its ability to use standard telephone lines, and its attractive price in relation to its speed. The disadvantage is that it is not available in all areas, especially rural areas, because of the limitation in distance between the PC and the local telephone switching station.

To configure DSL access, connect the DSL terminal adapter to your phone line and then connect it to the PC. This may be a USB connection, or it may be an Ethernet networking connection. If it's the latter, you need a 10BaseT or 100BaseT Ethernet card in the PC to connect it to. From that point, the PC will see the Internet connect as a LAN connection.

Cable

Cable Internet access is available in most areas that have digital cable TV. It has nothing to do with the phone lines, so it does not require telephone service. Its speed is roughly equivalent to ADSL (1Mbps or more in most cases), and its price is also comparable to ADSL. It is an always-on connection.

The advantages of cable are convenience, always-on access, attractive pricing for the speed provided, and independence from telephone lines. The disadvantage is that it is not available in all areas, and usually is not available to businesses.

Configuring cable is much like configuring DSL. Connect the terminal adapter to your cable TV connection. You may need to install a splitter (see your cable company for details). Then connect the terminal adapter to the PC, either via Ethernet network card or USB connection. The PC will see the Internet connection as a LAN connection.

When you use a broadband Internet connection such as cable or DSL, your computer is participating in a LAN owned by the ISP. In a large company, there may be a full-time broadband connection to the Internet, such as a T1 line, that all the computers in the company share. If that is the case, Internet connectivity is provided through the LAN and no special setup is needed.

Satellite

Satellite Internet service has the advantage of near-global availability, making it a good choice for users in areas not serviced by cable or DSL providers. Its speed ranges from 300Kbps to 1Mbps for downloads and around 128Kbps for uploads, so it is inferior to other broadband choices in speed. It is also more expensive than most cable and DSL plans.

There are two types: one-way and two-way. One-way satellite uses a satellite dish for downloading but a dial-up account with an ISP for uploading. Two-way satellite has no relationship to the telephone; it uses satellite in both directions.

The advantage of satellite is that is can be used virtually anywhere that has a clear view of the southern sky. It is also faster than dial-up. The disadvantage is that it is not as good a value in terms of bandwidth for the money as DSL or cable. The speed is also not as good.

Two-way satellite installation requires a professional installer. Professional installers are also recommended for one-way systems. Installation involves running coaxial cable from the satellite dish to an external terminal adapter, and then connecting the terminal adapter to the PC via USB and running setup software. Two-way satellite requires two separate terminal adapters—one for sending and one for receiving.

Wireless Connectivity

Wireless Internet uses the wireless telephone network to provide service. It is primarily for use with mobile computers and PDAs, but it can also be used for desktop PCs, especially in areas that offer no other broadband options. Its primary advantage is that it can be used anywhere the wireless phone network covers. The disadvantage is the price for the bandwidth you get.

Exam Essentials

Know the broadband options.   Given a scenario, you should be able to make a recommendation as to the best broadband Internet option available in that situation.

Understand how cable, DSL, and satellite operate.   Be familiar with the basics of each technology, including what equipment and connectivity are required, its approximate speed, and its availability issues.

Review Questions

1. What does STP cable have that UTP cable does not?

2. Which category of cable is the minimum required for 100BaseT networking?

3. What common household connector does an RJ-45 connector most resemble?

4. Which type of cable would be used for a 10Base2 (Thinnet) Ethernet network?

5. Which type of cable has either an ST or SC connector?

6. In which type of network are all computers equal participants?

7. Which physical topology connects all nodes to a hub?

8. Which type of server dynamically assigns IP addresses to network nodes?

9. Which type of network uses a multistation access unit (MAU)?

10. Which type of Internet connectivity does not require a telephone?

Answers to Review Questions

1. The *S* in STP stands for *shielded*, referring to shielding from electromagnetic interference (EMI).

2. Cat5 cable can transmit data at up to 100Mbps, which is the maximum speed of 100BaseT.

3. An RJ-45 connector is essentially a wider version of the RJ-11, the common household telephone connector.

4. RG-58 is 50ohm cable designed for use with 10Base2 Ethernet. RG-59 is for television signals, RG-6 is for satellites, and RG-8 is for 10Base5 Ethernet.

5. ST and SC are two types of fiber optic cable connectors.

6. A peer-to-peer network does not have any computers set aside to be servers; all are equal.

7. A star consists of several nodes that all connect to a central hub.

8. A Dynamic Host Configuration Protocol (DHCP) server dynamically assigns IP addresses.

9. Token Ring networks connect all nodes with an MAU in the center. It is a physical star, although it is a logical ring.

10. Cable and two-way satellite do not require a telephone.

A+ Operating System Technologies Exam

Domain 1 Operating System Fundamentals

7

COMPTIA A+ EXAM OBJECTIVES COVERED IN THIS CHAPTER:

- ✓ 1.1 Identify the major desktop components and interfaces, and their functions. Differentiate the characteristics of Windows 9x/Me, Windows NT 4.0 Workstation, Windows 2000 Professional, and Windows XP.

- ✓ 1.2 Identify the names, locations, purposes, and contents of major system files.

- ✓ 1.3 Demonstrate the ability to use command-line functions and utilities to manage the operating system, including the proper syntax and switches.

- ✓ 1.4 Identify basic concepts and procedures for creating, viewing, and managing disks, directories, and files. This includes procedures for changing file attributes and the ramifications of those changes (for example, security issues).

- ✓ 1.5 Identify the major operating system utilities, their purpose, location, and available switches.

A good PC technician must be familiar not only with hardware, but also with a variety of operating systems. Objective 1.0 tests your ability to identify, navigate, and configure Microsoft Windows versions 95, NT 4.0, and higher, all the way up to Windows XP.

1.1 Understanding the Major Desktop Components and Interfaces

This objective deals with two basic questions:

- What desktop components and interfaces form the Windows GUI?
- What are the differences among the various Windows versions?

It's essential to know the answers to both these questions, both for the A+ exam and for real-world work in the PC field. You need to be able to navigate confidently in any OS version and tailor your processes to the specific OS version present.

Critical Information

Some of this information about Windows functionality may be a review for you, but read through it anyway, to make sure nothing slips between the cracks in your education. Pay special attention to the material on differentiating the OS versions from one another, because you are sure to see some test questions on that topic.

Major Operating System Functions

The A+ exam focuses only on Windows-based OSs available from Microsoft, and we will give those systems the most time in this chapter. Although Macintosh has a strong following in certain niche markets, Intel/Windows machines dominate the corporate market almost completely.

The *operating system* provides a consistent environment for other software to execute commands. The OS gives users an interface with the computer so they can send commands to it (input) and receive feedback or results back (output). To do this, the OS must communicate with the computer hardware to perform the following tasks:

- Disk and file management
- Device access
- Memory management
- Input/output

Disk and File Management

The OS must be able to store and retrieve files on disks; this is one of its most primary functions. The system components involved in disk and file management include:

The Filesystem   The organizational scheme that governs how files are stored and retrieved from a disk. There are four major filesystems: the original 16-bit FAT system (a carryover from MS-DOS), the 32-bit version of it called FAT32, the NT File System (NTFS 4.0) supported by Windows NT 4.0, and the improved version of NTFS called NTFS 5.0, supported by Windows 2000/XP. Table 7.1 lists the filesystems and the OSs that support them.

TABLE 7.1   Major Filesystems

OS	FAT16	FAT32	NTFS 4.0	NTFS 5.0
Windows NT 4.0	Yes	No	Yes	No
Windows 95a	Yes	No	No	No
Windows 95b	Yes	Yes	No	No
Windows 98	Yes	Yes	No	No
Windows Me	Yes	Yes	No	No
Windows 2000	Yes	Yes	No (must convert)	Yes
Windows XP	Yes	Yes	No (must convert)	Yes

Windows Explorer   The primary file-management interface in Windows. It displays the list of files in the current location at the right and a folder tree of other locations at the left. (See Figure 7.1.) It starts with the My Documents folder as its default location when opened. Windows Explorer is available in all Windows versions and works approximately the same way in each.

FIGURE 7.1 The Windows Explorer interface

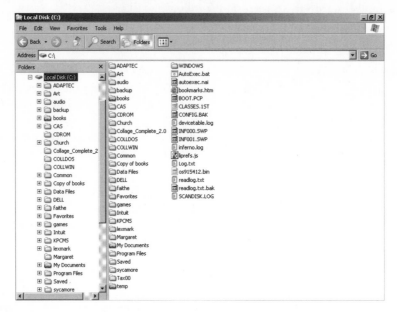

My Computer Basically the same interface as Windows Explorer, except it does not show the folder tree by default and it starts with a list of local drives. Originally the two were separate, but in modern versions of Windows you can click the Folders button on the toolbar to turn that folder tree on/off, making the two interfaces practically identical.

Network Neighborhood/My Network Places Again this is basically the same interface as the others, except it is designed for browsing network computers and drives rather than local ones. In early versions of Windows it was called Network Neighborhood; starting with Windows 2000, the name was changed to My Network Places.

Objective 1.3 discusses the specific user interfaces and procedures involved in using them in more detail.

Device Access

Another responsibility of the OS is to manage the way that software on the system interacts with the computer's hardware. More advanced OSs have the ability to avoid conflicts between devices and to prevent applications from interfering with each other.

Windows handles device management by itself in most cases. In instances where the user needs to get involved, he can use the Device Manager interface. Device Manager is covered in detail under objective 2.4.

One quirk about Device Manager is that the procedure for opening it differs among Windows versions. In Windows 95/98/Me, Device Manager is a tab in the System Properties box. (Right-click My Computer and choose Properties.) In Windows 2000/XP, you must display the System Properties box, click the Hardware tab, and then click Device Manager.

Memory Management

Computers are designed so that in order for information to be used by the processor, it must be in the machine's memory (RAM). How the OS manages the transfer of information from storage on the hard drive to a place in RAM is referred to as *memory management.*

Back in the days of MS-DOS, applications could run only in conventional memory—the first 640KB of RAM in the system. This severely limited the size of the applications that could be written, so various schemes for getting around that limitation were devised. Windows 95 and higher get around it in the following ways:

Extended Memory   PCs today have many megabytes and even gigabytes of RAM, and everything except the first megabyte is considered *extended memory.* Windows can address extended memory and apportion it out to applications as needed.

Virtual Machines   Windows can multitask (that is, run more than one application at the same time) by creating a separate memory space for each application. It's almost like each of the applications is running on a separate PC, with the OS interface tying them all together. The separate space in which an application runs is called a *virtual machine.*

Virtual Memory   Windows is such a large OS and requires so much overhead that sometimes a PC does not have enough RAM to accommodate its needs. Rather than giving an *out of memory* error message to the user, Windows has a workaround technique whereby it uses an unused part of the hard disk to simulate additional RAM, swapping data into and out of it from the real RAM. This is called *virtual memory.* The file on the hard disk used for the simulation is called a *paging file* or *swap file.*

Input/Output

Generally called *I/O,* this is the process by which the machine accepts instructions (from the mouse, keyboard, and so on) and provides output (to a monitor, file, or printer). These operations happen behind the scenes with no user intervention in most cases. The user clicks the mouse or types on the keyboard, and input happens. Keyboard and mouse settings can be fine-tuned through Control Panel.

Major Operating System Components

All Windows versions have a similar look and feel in their user interface. Figure 7.2 shows Windows 2000, for example.

FIGURE 7.2 The Windows 2000 interface

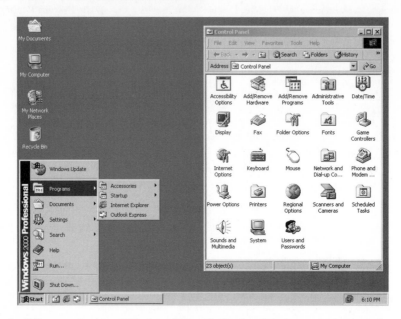

The main differences between Windows XP and all other Windows versions are the redesigned Start menu and the rounded look of the dialog boxes. Figure 7.3 shows a typical Windows XP screen.

FIGURE 7.3 The Windows XP interface

Much of this information will be review for those of you who have experience using Windows OSs, but you may want to refresh your mind as to the specific names and attributes of these components.

The Desktop

The Desktop is the virtual desk upon which all of your other programs and utilities run. By default it contains the Start menu, the Taskbar, and a number of icons. The Desktop can also contain additional elements, such as web page content, through the use of the Active Desktop option. Because it is the base on which everything else sits, how the Desktop is configured can have a major effect on how the GUI looks and how convenient it is for users.

You can change the Desktop's background patterns, screensaver, color scheme, and size by right-clicking any area of the Desktop that doesn't contain an icon. The menu that appears allows you to do several things, such as create new Desktop items, change how your icons are arranged, and select a special command called Properties. Right-click the Desktop and choose Properties to work with display properties.

 Windows is designed to allow each user to access information in the way they are most comfortable with, and as such there are generally at least two ways to do everything. When you're getting ready for the test, try to make sure you know *all* the ways to perform a task, not just the way you are used to.

The Taskbar

The *Taskbar* runs along the bottom of the Windows display. At the left is the Start button, which opens the menu system. At the right is the clock and the *System Tray*. The System Tray holds icons for programs that are running in the background, such as virus checkers, and also sometimes icons for frequently needed controls such as the sound volume.

 Another name for the System Tray is *notification area*. That's the terminology Microsoft appears to be switching to in its documentation.

In its center, the Taskbar displays buttons for each of the open windows To bring a window or program to the front (or to maximize it if it is minimized), click its button on the Taskbar. As the middle area of the Taskbar fills up with buttons, the buttons become smaller so there is room to display them all.

There are different methods of managing situations where you have too many Taskbar buttons. One method is to drag the top border of the Taskbar upward, creating an extra row for the buttons. Another, which works only in later Windows versions like XP, is to allow Taskbar buttons to be grouped. For example, if you have four file-management windows open, they will appear as a single button on the Taskbar. You can click that button to see the windows in menu form and make your selection. To set this up, right-click the Taskbar and choose Properties, and then mark the Group Similar Taskbar Icons check box. If there's no such check box, your version of Windows doesn't support this feature.

You can move the Taskbar to the top or sides of the screen by clicking the Taskbar and dragging it to the new location. This is important to know, because sometimes users accidentally do this and need help dragging the Taskbar back to the bottom.

The Start Menu

The Start button opens the Start menu, an entry point into a well-organized system of shortcuts to various utilities and applications you can run. Its top level has a few shortcut icons for some critical features, but most of the shortcuts are contained in a hierarchical system of submenus. To display a submenu, point at any item that has a right-pointing arrow to its right.

PROGRAMS SUBMENU

The Programs submenu holds the program groups and program icons that you can use. In Windows XP it is called All Programs rather than Programs, but it's basically the same thing.

Shortcuts to programs are placed in the Programs menu when they are installed using a Windows-based setup utility, or when you manually place them there. There are a number of ways to create a new item on the Start menu or reorganize items that are already there:

- Right-click the Taskbar and choose Properties. Depending on the Windows version, different options may be available through this Properties box for customizing the Start menu.

- Right-click the Start button and choose Open. The Start menu's content appears in a file-management window, and you can add and remove shortcuts to it.

- Drag-and-drop a shortcut from the Desktop. This works only in later Windows versions. Drag an icon to the Start menu, but don't release the mouse button. Just pause, and the Start menu will open. Then, pause over the Programs menu, and it will open. Keep going until you find the right spot, and then release the mouse button.

Within the Programs submenu is one especially important submenu that is specifically mentioned in the exam objective: the Accessories/System Tools submenu. This menu is important because it contains shortcuts to some of the utilities needed for troubleshooting and preventive maintenance of a system. See objective 1.5 for more details.

DOCUMENTS SUBMENU

The Documents submenu has only one function: to keep track of the last 15 data files you opened. Whenever you open a file, a shortcut to it is automatically added to this menu. Click the document in the Documents menu to reopen it in its associated application. In Windows XP, this submenu is called My Recent Documents.

SETTINGS SUBMENU

The Settings submenu provides easy access to the Windows configuration. It contains a shortcut to Control Panel, for example, and to the Printers folder. Additional menus are available depending on which version of Windows you are using. Windows XP has no Settings submenu; the shortcuts it would contain appear directly on the top level of the Start menu, instead.

SEARCH (FIND) SUBMENU

The name of this menu changes between Windows 98 and Windows 2000, but its purpose doesn't. The Windows 98 Find submenu is used to locate information on your computer or on a network. The Search submenu of Windows 2000/Me/XP has the same functionality. In Windows XP, Search is a command that opens a Search window, rather than a submenu.

HELP COMMAND

Windows includes a *very* good Help system. Not only is it arranged by topic, but it is also fully indexed and searchable. Because of its usefulness and power, it was placed on the Start menu for easy access. When you select the Help command, it brings up Windows Help. From this screen, you can double-click a manual to show a list of subtopics and then click a subtopic to view the text of that topic. You can also view indexed help files or do a specific search through the help documents' text.

RUN COMMAND

The Run command can be used to start programs if they don't have a shortcut on the Desktop or in the Programs submenu. To execute a particular program, type its name and path in the Open field. If you don't know the exact path, you can browse to find the file by clicking the Browse button. Once you have typed in the executable name and path, click OK to run the program.

SHUT DOWN COMMAND

You probably already know that you should never shut down a Windows-based computer by pressing the power switch, because of the possibility of file corruption. Instead you should shut it down through Windows' Shut Down command.

When you select Shut Down, you are provided a choice of several shutdown methods. They vary depending on the Windows version:

Shut Down   This option writes any unsaved data to disk, closes any open applications, and either gets the computer ready to be powered off (on AT systems) or shuts off the computer's power (on ATX systems).

Restart   This option works the same as the first option, but instead of shutting down completely, it automatically reboots the computer with a warm reboot.

Restart the Computer in MS-DOS Mode (Windows 9x Only)   This option is special. It does the same tasks as the previous options, except upon reboot, Windows 9x executes the command prompt only and does not start the graphical portion of Windows 9x. You can then run DOS programs as though the machine were a DOS machine. When you have finished running these programs, type **exit** to reboot the machine back into the full Windows 9x with the GUI.

Log Off   If you have user profiles enabled, a Log Off option is available either from this menu or as a separate menu command. Profiles are automatic on NT/2000 and optional on 95/98.

Stand By   On laptops or other machines with power-management capability through their BIOS, the Stand By option may be available. It allows the machine to go into a sleep mode where it shuts down most functions to save energy. Utilizing Stand By can significantly extend battery time on laptops.

Hibernate   Hibernate copies the content of RAM to a reserved area on the hard disk and then shuts down the computer completely. When you turn it back on, it copies the data back into RAM, and startup is much faster than normal. This option is available only in later Windows versions, and only on systems that support it through the BIOS.

Using a Command-Line Interface within Windows

Occasionally you may need to run commands from an MS-DOS–style command prompt. To do so, there is a special command: either MS-DOS Prompt or Command Prompt, depending on the OS version. It may be on the first-level Programs menu, or it may be on the Accessories sub-menu, depending on the version.

   This command opens a window containing a command prompt. From there, you can type commands and press Enter to execute them. Objective 1.3 discusses some of these commands in detail.

Contrasts between Windows Versions

There are two main families of Windows versions: Windows 95, 98, and Me (collectively called Windows 9x); and Windows NT 4.0, 2000, and XP. They are all similar in their user interface, but the way they operate behind the scenes is substantially different. Each family has a very different startup process (see objective 2.3 in Chapter 8), and in some cases different troubleshooting utilities (see objective 1.5 later in this chapter and objective 3.2 in Chapter 9).

A Brief Version History

Early Windows versions had completely separate platforms for home and business use. Windows NT 4.0 offered stability and networking for the corporate world but lacked user-friendly features such as Plug and Play (PnP). Windows 95 was easy to install and configure but crashed frequently. Over the years, Windows 98/Me were incremental improvements on Windows 95, and Windows 2000 was an incremental improvement on Windows NT 4.0, adding some user-friendliness but retaining stability.

   Today, Windows XP is the dominant OS; it is based on Windows 2000 (which, in turn, was based on Windows NT 4.0). So, the Windows 9x platform is essentially going away. Although

Windows XP comes in both Professional and Home versions, both are NT-based. The Home version is just the Pro version with some features stripped off.

User Interface Differences

The user interface is virtually identical for Windows NT 4.0, 95, 98, Me, and 2000. Windows XP is the different one, and the main differences are in its Start menu and differently styled windows. However, Windows XP can be set up to look just like Windows 2000. In the Display Properties, choose the Windows Classic appearance theme. Then, in the Taskbar Properties, select the Classic Start menu.

System File Differences

The files required to start up Windows, access Registry settings, and run utilities are different between the 9x versions and the NT versions. These are covered in detail in objective 1.2.

Security and Networking Differences

The 9x versions of Windows have very little local security. A login box can be set up to appear, but users can bypass it by clicking Cancel. These versions also offer no security among multiple users who locally share a PC. For example, there is a single My Documents folder, and everyone has access to it.

The NT-based versions are much more flexible and robust in their security settings. Each user has her own settings and her own My Documents folder, and can hide or restrict files from other local users. The NT-based versions are also stronger in networking features, especially when connecting to a domain-based network.

Differences in Included Utilities

The newer the Windows version, the more and better utilities it has. For example, Windows Me/XP come with a System Restore utility for undoing bad Registry changes. Such utilities are addressed in greater detail in other objectives.

There is also a division of utilities between the 9x and the NT versions. For example, in the 9x versions, ScanDisk is the utility for checking hard disks, whereas in NT versions that utility is called Check Disk. In addition, Windows 2000/XP come with additional management utilities such as Computer Management, Disk Management, and an entire class of Administrative Tools in Control Panel.

Differences in Application Compatibility

Windows 9x is designed for backward compatibility with 16-bit Windows programs (for Windows 3.x) and MS-DOS, so it includes some features that help with that specifically, including MS-DOS Mode in Windows 95/98.

Although Windows 2000/XP make no claims about universal backward compatibility, in reality most MS-DOS and 16-bit Windows programs work fine under them. In addition, Windows XP comes with an Application Compatibility feature that helps the system emulate the earlier versions when needed.

Exam Essentials

Know the major functions of Windows.   You should understand what an OS does, what systems it manages, and how it communicates with the human user.

Know which filesystems work with which Windows versions.   Refer back to Table 7.1 if you need to review this.

Understand virtual memory.   You should know the purpose of virtual memory and how it operates in terms of hard disk and physical RAM.

Be able to identify Windows display components.   Make sure you can point out the Taskbar, Start button, System Tray, Desktop, and other key features of the OS interface.

Understand version differences.   Be able to group the Windows versions according to similarity and explain how one group differs from the other in terms of system files (see objective 1.2) and functionality.

1.2 Understanding Major System Files

This is a new objective, which has been split off from objective 1.1 in the latest revision of the exam. It tests your knowledge of the names of the files that each version of Windows uses to start up and to operate.

Critical Information

By understanding the files used by various Windows versions for behind-the-scenes operations, you will be better able to troubleshoot problems when they occur. That's the real purpose of memorizing all these filenames.

Windows 9x Major System Files

The following are important files for systems with a 9x version of Windows installed:

IO.SYS   A startup file that interacts with the BIOS and the hardware. It is the first file executed at startup after the BIOS runs its POST test. See objective 2.3 (Chapter 8) for more detail about the boot process.

MSDOS.SYS   Under MS-DOS, this file shared startup duties with IO.SYS, but under Windows 9x it is a plain-text configuration file that works as a companion to IO.SYS.

SYSTEM.INI and WIN.INI   Initialization files exist only for backward compatibility with 16-bit (Windows 3.x) applications.

WIN.INI and SYSTEM.INI served the same function under Windows 3.x that the Registry serves in modern Windows versions.

WIN.COM The main executable program for the Windows 9x OS.

COMMAND.COM The command interpreter, required for the user to interact with the OS via a command prompt.

CONFIG.SYS An initialization file that loads real-mode device drivers at startup. This file isn't required in most cases, because Windows handles its own device drivers.

AUTOEXEC.BAT An initialization file that loads Terminate and Stay Resident (TSR) programs at startup. It isn't required anymore in most cases, because Windows loads the programs it needs at startup.

HIMEM.SYS The extended memory-management utility, required for Windows to be able to handle extended memory. It can be loaded through CONFIG.SYS, but if it is not, Windows loads it automatically when it starts up.

EMM386.EXE An expanded memory-management utility. It isn't required for Windows 9x, because Windows handles memory management for itself, but it may still be loaded through CONFIG.SYS on systems that were upgraded from MS-DOS.

 Expanded memory (EMS) was originally a totally different type of extra memory above the 1MB mark, introduced in 80286 computers. It is now obsolete, but some very old programs require it rather than extended memory (XMS). The original purpose of the EMM386.EXE utility was to apportion out memory as needed to programs that required one type or another.

USER.DAT One of the two files that compose the Registry. It contains environmental settings for each user who logs in to Windows 9x. By default, Windows 9x uses a single profile for all users, and in that case only a single USER.DAT is maintained in the Windows directory. If users each have their own profile, though, a separate USER.DAT file is created and maintained for each user. This file is stored in the user's profile directory.

SYSTEM.DAT The other file that makes up the Registry. It contains information about the hardware configuration of the computer on which Windows is running. The SYSTEM.DAT file is stored in the Windows directory and is shared by all users of the computer.

USER.DAT and SYSTEM.DAT cannot be edited with a text editor because they aren't text files (like AUTOEXEC.BAT, CONFIG.SYS, or the .ini files). To edit the Windows 9x Registry, you need to use a tool specifically designed for that purpose: the aptly named Registry Editor (REGEDIT.EXE). See objective 1.5 for more information about it.

Windows 2000 Major System Files

Almost all of the files needed to boot Windows 9x are unnecessary for Windows NT 4.0, 2000, and XP. Here are the files for those OSs:

NTLDR   *Bootstraps* the system. In other words, starts the loading of an OS on the computer.

BOOT.INI   Holds information about which OSs are installed on the computer. Used when dual-booting, to display the boot menu.

NTDETECT.COM   Parses the system for hardware information each time Windows is loaded. This information is then used to create dynamic hardware information in the Windows Registry.

NTBOOTDD.SYS   Used to recognize and load the SCSI interface on a system with a SCSI boot device with the SCSI BIOS disabled. On EIDE systems or SCSI systems with the BIOS enabled, this file is not needed and is not even installed.

System Files   Besides the previously listed files, all of which are located in the root of the C: partition on the computer, Windows 2000 also needs a number of files from its system directories, including the hardware abstraction layer (HAL.DLL) and the Windows 2000 command file (WIN.COM).

Numerous other DLL (dynamic link library) files are also required, but usually the lack or corruption of one of them produces a noncritical error, whereas the absence of WIN.COM or HAL.DLL causes the system to be nonfunctional.

The Windows NT/2000/XP Registry

The Registry in Windows NT/2000/XP has the same purpose as the Windows 9x Registry. Unlike Windows 9x, though, NT/2000 and XP require that each user have their own profile and maintains that profile automatically for them. The current user's settings are stored in the NTUSER.DAT file.

Instead of USER.DAT and SYSTEM.DAT, these Windows versions use the following files to store the Registry settings:

SAM   Stores the machine's Security Accounts Management database, which is where the Registry stores information about user accounts and passwords.

SECURITY   Stores information about file and folder security on the machine.

SOFTWARE   Holds configuration data for programs and utilities installed on the machine. Also has numerous areas corresponding to the OS itself.

SYSTEM   Holds information that affects the OS's operation, especially during startup.

Exam Essentials

Know the names of the system files for each Windows version.   You should be able to list the files for a particular OS; or, given a filename, you should be able to say which OS it goes with.

Know the files that make up the Registry.   They're different for 9x versions versus NT versions; make sure you can differentiate between them.

1.3 Using Command-Line Functions and Utilities

This is yet another objective that has been split off from objective 1.1 in the latest revision of the exam guidelines. It tests your ability to display a command prompt and enter common commands using the correct syntax.

Critical Information

Both for the test and for real life, you should know the various ways of displaying command prompts and the way that command syntax is constructed. For the exact syntax of individual commands, you can always get help by typing the command followed by /?.

Displaying a Command Prompt

Because 9x versions of Windows are much closer to MS-DOS (a command-prompt OS) than NT versions are, there are more ways of displaying a command prompt under Windows 9x. To display a command prompt from Windows 9x, you can:

- Boot from a startup floppy that you create with the Add/Remove Programs applet in Control Panel.
- Restart the PC in MS-DOS mode (Windows 95 and 98 only).
- Choose Start ➤ Run, type **COMMAND**, and click OK.
- Choose Start ➤ Programs ➤ MS-DOS Prompt, or Start ➤ Programs ➤ Accessories ➤ MS-DOS Prompt, depending on the Windows version.

   To display a command prompt from Windows NT/2000/XP, you can:

- Choose Start ➤ Run, type **CMD**, and click OK.
- Choose Start ➤ Programs ➤ Accessories ➤ Command Prompt.

Most commands can be executed through the command prompt that appears with any of these methods. To return to Windows, type **EXIT** and press Enter. If that doesn't work, restart the computer.

> When you start a command prompt from within Windows, it is sometimes called *shelling out to DOS*, which means you are creating a *shell*, or user environment, that resembles MS-DOS from within Windows. EXIT returns you to Windows from a shell in most cases.

Using Wildcards at a Command Prompt

Many of the commands covered later in this section involve entering file specifications. This can be the name of an individual file or a combination of text and wildcard characters that have the effect of selecting multiple files.

The most common wildcard is the asterisk (*). It stands for any number of characters. So, for example, a file specification of *.TXT would include all files with a .TXT extension, whereas DOCUMENT.* would include all files named DOCUMENT regardless of their extension. One more example: D*.* would include all files that began with the letter *D*, regardless of extension.

The other wildcard is the question mark (?). It stands for any single character. So, for example, D????.* would find all files that begin with *D* and are exactly five characters in name length, with any extension.

Internal vs. External Commands

Internal commands are built into the command interpreter (COMMAND.COM), so they do not need any external files in order to work. DIR, DEL, and COPY are examples.

External commands are mini-programs that exist either in the current folder or somewhere within the search path. For example, FORMAT and FDISK don't work unless FORMAT.COM and FDISK.EXE are available.

Under MS-DOS, all the external commands needed for the OS were stored in the C:\MSDOS folder. Under Windows, the location of the external command-prompt commands depends on the OS version, but they are usually found in C:\Windows\Command.

> The *search path* is a list of locations where the OS looks for a command's needed file when you try to execute it. You can set a path statement in AUTOEXEC.BAT with the PATH= command, with the names of the folders separated by semicolons. When you run a command prompt from within Windows, the folder containing the external OS commands is automatically included in the path for that prompt; so, you should not have any problem with errors due to the path statement. When you're working at a command prompt from a startup floppy, however, you may need to remember to change to the folder containing the external command you want to run.

Understanding Command Syntax

To issue a command from the command prompt, you need to know the structure that the command uses, generally referred to as its *syntax*. Over time, you will memorize the command syntax for the commands you use most often, but until that happens, you can rely on the Help system.

Type the command followed by a forward slash (/) and a question mark (?). Doing so displays all the options for that command and how to use them properly, as shown in Figure 7.4.

FIGURE 7.4   Options available for ATTRIB.EXE

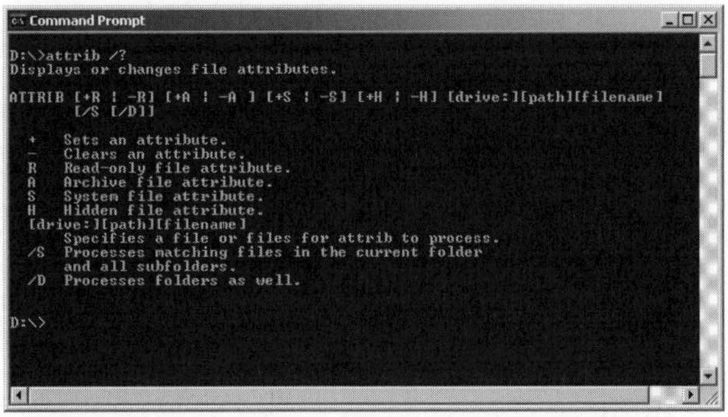

Common Commands

The A+ objective's topic list expects you to know how to use certain specific commands at a prompt. The following list summarizes them:

DIR   Displays the contents of the current folder. Can be used by itself or with a file specification to narrow down the listing. Here are some examples:

> **DIR**   Displays all files in the current folder.

> **DIR ????.***   Displays all files that are exactly four letters in name length, with any extension.

> **DIR /w**   Displays the listing in wide (multicolumn) format, with names only (fewer details).

> **DIR /p**   Displays the listing one screenful at a time. Press Enter to see the next screenful.

ATTRIB   Displays or changes the attributes for one or more files. Used by itself, it displays a list of all files in the current location with attributes set. The attributes are Read Only (R), Hidden (H), System (S), and Archive (A). They can be turned off with a minus sign or turned on with a plus sign. Here are some examples:

> **ATTRIB -R TEE.DOC**   Removes the read-only attribute from TEE.DOC.

> **ATTRIB +H *.***   Adds the Hidden attribute to all files in the current location.

VER   Displays the current OS name and version.

MEM   Displays memory usage data. If more than one screenful of data scrolls by quickly, try adding the /p switch for one screenful at a time. For example:

> *MEM*   Provides standard memory information.

> *MEM /C*   Provides more detailed memory information.

SCANDISK   Runs the ScanDisk utility. Works only under MS-DOS or Windows 9x startup disks.

DEFRAG   Runs the Disk Defragmenter utility. Works only under MS-DOS or Windows 9x startup disks.

EDIT   Opens the MS-DOS Editor utility, a text editor similar to Notepad. A filename can be added to open that file (if it exists) or create a new file (if it doesn't exist). For example:

> *EDIT CONFIG.SYS*   Opens CONFIG.SYS if it's present in the current folder; otherwise creates it and opens it.

COPY   Copies files from one location to another. If the location for either the source or the destination is not included in the command, it is assumed to be the current folder. Here are some examples:

> *COPY *.* A:*   Copies all files from the current folder to the A: drive.

> *COPY C:\Windows\Myfile.txt*   Copies Myfile.txt from C:\Windows to the current folder.

XCOPY   Like COPY but also duplicates any subfolders. For example:

> *XCOPY C:\BOOKS A:*   Copies everything from C:\BOOKS to the A: drive and also copies any subfolders and their contents.

FDISK   Under MS-DOS and Windows 9x, prepares a hard disk for formatting by creating one or more formattable partitions. Not for use with floppy disks, and not for use under Windows NT/2000/XP.

FORMAT   Prepares a floppy or hard disk for use by applying a certain filesystem to it.

SETVER   An older command that provided a way of tricking applications into running under versions of MS-DOS that they were not designed for. This command isn't used much anymore. You can use it by itself to see a list of currently version-set commands. Use it with a command name and version number to add one to the list. For example:

> *SETVER RAIDER.EXE 5.0*   When the file RAIDER.EXE is run, the OS will report to the program that it is MS-DOS version 5.0.

SCANREG   Checks the Registry for errors. Not usually necessary, because the Registry scans itself automatically at startup.

MD/CD/RD   Directory (folder) management commands. MD is Make Directory, CD is Change Directory, and RD is Remove Directory. When they're used without specifying a location, the current location is assumed. Some examples include:

> *MD BACKUP*   Makes a new directory called Backup in the current directory.

CD C:\SYSTEM   Changes to the System directory.

RD C:\SYSTEM   Deletes the System directory (assuming it is empty).

DELTREE   Removes non-empty directories and everything in them, including subdirectories. Not supported in the latest versions of Windows.

DEL   Deletes specified files. Doesn't work on folders (directories). Examples:

DEL C:\SYSTEM\BACKUP.DOC   Deletes the specified file in the specified location.

DEL *.*   Deletes all files in the current location.

DEL does not act on hidden or read-only files. They will be ignored.

REN   Renames the specified file(s). You must specify both the old and new names. For example:

REN MYFILE.DOC YOURFILE.DOC   Renames MYFILE.DOC to YOURFILE.DOC.

REN S*.PCX T*.PCX   Renames all files that start with *S* and have a PCX extension so that their first letters are now *T*, but otherwise their names remain the same.

Windows does not let you rename a group of files in a single operation, as in the second example. This is one case where it is very helpful to use a command prompt instead of Windows.

TYPE   Shows the text contained in the specified file on-screen. Useful for browsing through a group of text files without having to open them in an editing program. For example:

TYPE CONFIG.SYS   Displays the complete contents of the file CONFIG.SYS on-screen.

ECHO   Used in batch files (such as AUTOEXEC.BAT) to display certain text on-screen. For example:

ECHO Good Morning Friend!   During startup, if you want the message *Good Morning Friend!* to appear on the screen, you can add this line to AUTOEXEC.BAT.

SET   A command used mostly in AUTOEXEC.BAT to set a variable. Seldom used anymore except on older systems.

PING   Allows you to check a particular IP address or domain name on a network for reachability. For example:

PING Microsoft.com   Tells you whether Microsoft's website is up. (It probably is.)

PING 127.0.0.1   To check your own computer, ping the loopback address.

Exam Essentials

Know how to open a command prompt and enter text commands.   Go through each of the commands listed in the objectives and read through their help screens. Find out which switches are available for each command, and what they do.

1.4 Creating, Viewing, and Managing Disks, Directories, and Files

The wording of this objective makes it sound like it'll be testing end-user skills like moving, copying, and renaming files, but there's much more to it than that. This objective addresses topics like disk partitioning and formatting, filesystems, directory structures, and file compression, encryption, and permissions.

Critical Information

This objective tests your ability to build up a filesystem from scratch, starting with a totally blank hard disk. You must be able to partition it, format it, create the directory structures, and apply attributes, compression, encryption, and permission settings to those structures.

Creating and Managing Partitions

Once the drives are in the machine and the controller is set up, you need to prepare the hard drives for use before an OS can be installed on the machine. This generally consists of two steps: partitioning and formatting.

Partitioning

Partitioning refers to establishing large allocations of hard-drive space. A *partition* is a continuous section of sectors that are next to each other. In DOS and Windows, a partition is referred to by a drive letter, such as C: or D:. Partitioning a drive into two or more parts gives it the appearance of being two or more physical hard drives.

When a drive is partitioned in DOS, the first partition you create is a *primary partition*. A primary partition is a bootable one. A disk can have more than one primary partition, but it is not customary.

Only one primary partition can be active. The *active partition* is the one that the system attempts to boot from. It is possible for no partitions to be marked active on a particular drive. In this case, the machine cannot boot to the drive, and you must use FDISK to set an active partition before you will be able to properly install Windows 9x.

If there is additional space, a second partition called an *extended partition* can be created. One or more *logical partitions* must be defined within the extended partition, and they can then have drive letters attached to them so users can access them. Due to limitations with the way that DOS and Windows 9x access partition structures, only one primary and one extended partition can be created per disk using the Windows 9x disk utility, FDISK.

Windows NT/2000/XP all have a partitioning utility built into their Setup programs. You can partition and format the drive as you install the OS. With Windows 9x, however, you must partition using the FDISK utility, and then format using the FORMAT utility, before you start Windows Setup. You run these from a startup floppy disk, which you can create on an existing Windows installation using Add/Remove Programs.

You cannot alter the partition that contains the OS after setup (except with third-party utilities), but you can create and manage other partitions on the system later. To do this from Windows 9x, you can go to a command prompt and rerun FDISK; to do it in Windows NT, use Disk Administrator; and in 2000/XP, use Disk Management.

Using *FDISK*

With FDISK, you can create partitions, delete partitions, mark a partition as active, or display available partitioning information. FDISK can be run off the Windows 9x startup disk, as discussed earlier, or from a command prompt within Windows 9x. Figure 7.5 shows an example of the FDISK interface.

FIGURE 7.5 The FDISK utility (Windows Me version)

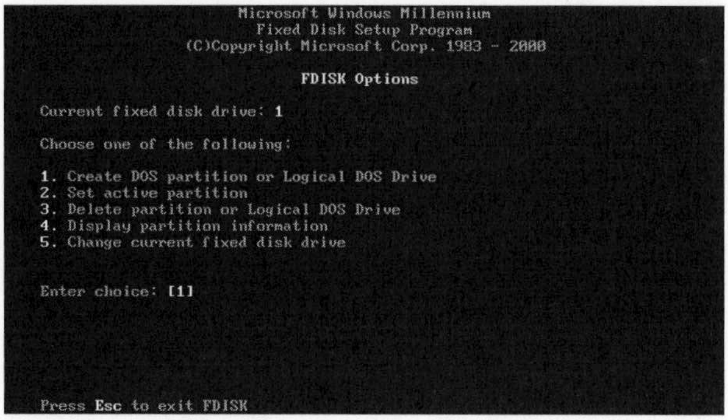

```
                    Microsoft Windows Millennium
                      Fixed Disk Setup Program
            (C)Copyright Microsoft Corp. 1983 - 2000

                           FDISK Options

  Current fixed disk drive: 1

  Choose one of the following:

  1. Create DOS partition or Logical DOS Drive
  2. Set active partition
  3. Delete partition or Logical DOS Drive
  4. Display partition information
  5. Change current fixed disk drive

  Enter choice: [1]



  Press Esc to exit FDISK
```

FDISK has a number of major functions:

Creating Partitions and Logical Drives   Partitions are created from unused space on the drive. Until the space has been partitioned, it is unusable by most systems.

Deleting Partitions and Logical Drives   If a partition is no longer needed, and you need to make space on the drive for the creation of other partitions, deleting a partition removes all information about the partition and also deletes any information that had been stored on the partition. Think before you do this!

Setting a Partition as Active   In order to boot the system, the computer must know where to look for the bootstrap files that start the system load phase. Setting a partition as active identifies it as the place to look for these files.

Viewing the Partitions on a Disk   FDISK also allows you to browse through the partition information on a disk. If the machine has more than one disk, you can choose which one to look at.

Disk Administrator/Disk Management

Windows NT and 2000/XP use different tools to manage partitions. Windows NT has an icon for Disk Administrator in its Administrative Tools folder, whereas Windows 2000 has a Disk Management tool within its Computer Management utility.

> Where's Disk Management? In Windows 2000/XP, go to Control Panel, choose Administrative Tools, and choose Computer Management. One of the items on the folder tree in the window that appears is Disk Management.

The two utilities are very similar; both allow you to modify partition information in a graphical manner. Figure 7.6 shows the Windows XP version of Disk Management.

FIGURE 7.6   The Disk Management utility (Windows XP version)

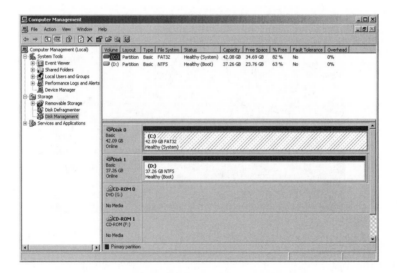

Among the important differences between FDISK and these advanced disk tools is the ability of Disk Administrator and Computer Management to do the following:

- Format partitions
- Change drive letters
- Check other drive properties
- Create more than one primary partition per physical drive

Disk Formatting

The next step in the management of a hard drive is formatting, initiated by the FORMAT command or through the Windows interface. During a format, the surface of the hard-drive platter is briefly scanned to find any possible bad spots, and the areas surrounding a bad spot are marked as bad sectors. After this, magnetic tracks are laid down in concentric circles. These tracks are where information is eventually encoded.

Beyond this, there are a number of options regarding how the system will store information. Each of these methods of storing information is known as a *filesystem*, and you need to know about several of these for the test:

FAT   Short for File Allocation Table. The FAT keeps track of where information is stored and how to retrieve it.

FAT16   Used with DOS and Windows 3.x, as well as early versions of Windows 95. FAT16 (generally just called FAT) has a number of advantages. First, it is extremely fast on small (under 500MB) drives. Second, it is a filesystem that nearly all OSs can agree on, making it excellent for dual-boot system. However, FAT also has limitations that began causing problems as Windows got bigger and faster. First, FAT has a limit of 4GB per partition. When you have hard drives that are 10GB to 30GB, this becomes a serious issue. Also, sectors on hard drives are arranged in what is called a *cluster* or *allocation unit*. In general, as a FAT16-formatted drive or drive partition increases in size, the number of sectors per cluster increases. A drive between 16MB and 128MB has four sectors per cluster, whereas a drive of up to 256MB has eight sectors per cluster, and drives of up to 512MB have 16 sectors per cluster.

Another aspect of FAT is so wonderfully obscure that test preparers rarely can resist it. The root of any FAT drive (C:\, D:\) has a hard-coded limit of 512 entries. This includes directories, files, and so on. Also, long filenames may take up more than one entry. If users reach this limit, they will be unable to save any other files in the root. This limit does not apply to subdirectories or to FAT32 or NTFS drives.

FAT32   Introduced with Windows 95 OSR2. FAT32 is similar to FAT but has a number of advantages. It supports larger drives and smaller allocation units. As a comparison of how the new system saves you space, a 2GB drive with FAT16 has clusters of 32KB; with FAT32, the clusters sizes are 4KB. If you save a 15KB file, FAT needs to allocate an entire 32KB cluster; FAT32 uses four 4KB clusters, for a total of 16KB. FAT32 wastes an unused 1KB, but FAT wastes 15 times as much!

The disadvantage of FAT32 is that it is not compatible with older DOS, Windows 3.x, and Windows 95 OSs. This means that when you boot a Windows 95 Rev B. or Windows 98 FAT32-formatted partition with a DOS boot floppy, you can't read the partition.

Windows 98 includes the FAT32 Drive Converter tool (CVT1.EXE), which allows you to upgrade FAT disks to FAT32 without having to reformat them. This preserves all the information on the drive but allows you to take advantage of FAT32's enhancements.

NTFS4   Windows NT's filesystem. NTFS4 includes enhanced attributes for compressing files or for setting file security. Updating a FAT drive to NTFS is relatively easy and can be done through a command called CONVERT. This conversion does not destroy any information but updates the filesystem. NTFS4 is used only with Windows NT 4.0.

NTFS5   The NTFS system updated with Windows 2000. It includes enhancements such as file encryption. NTFS5 also includes support for larger drive sizes and a new feature called Dynamic Disks that does away with the whole concept of partitioning to improve drive performance. NTFS5 is used only with Windows 2000/XP.

Formatting a Drive

If you are installing Windows 9x, you need to use a boot disk to first partition and then format the drive. The FORMAT command is located on the boot disk and is simple to use. If you want to format the first partition on the system, type **FORMAT C:** to start the process. You will be reminded that this procedure destroys any information currently on the drive and will be asked to verify your decision to format. After the format is complete, you can start the install process.

Windows NT/2000/XP allow you to format as part of the install, so no advance preparation with FDISK or FORMAT is necessary when installing those OSs.

Once Windows is up and running, you can format or reformat drives by using FORMAT from a command prompt or graphically through the Windows interface, which also allows formatting through the Explorer or the My Computer icon. Just right-click on a drive icon in My Computer and choose Format. If the drive icon does not appear in My Computer, it may need to be partitioned; only partitioned drives show up as icons there.

Working with the Filesystem

After you have created and formatted your partitions, you can put information onto them. Generally, the first information to be put onto the drive is placed there by the OS installation program. Once this is done and the system is up and running, you can perform additional modifications as needed. This section of the chapter deals with how users can access and work with the Windows filesystem-management tools.

The Windows filesystem is arranged like a filing cabinet. In a filing cabinet, paper is placed in folders, which are inside dividers, which are in a drawer. In the filesystem, individual files are placed in subdirectories, which are inside directories, which are stored on different disks. Windows also protects against duplicate filenames, because no two files on the system can have exactly the same name and path. A *path* indicates the location of the file on the disk; it is composed of the logical drive letter the file is on and, if the file is located in a directory or subdirectory, the names of those directories. For instance, a file named AUTOEXEC.BAT is located in the root of the C: drive—meaning it is not within a directory—so the path to the file is C:\AUTOEXEC.BAT. Another important file, FDISK.EXE, is located in the COMMAND directory under Windows under the root of C:, so the path to FDISK is C:\WINDOWS\COMMAND\FDISK.EXE (Windows 9x only). The *root* of any drive is the place where the hierarchy of that drive begins. On a C: drive, for instance, C:\ is the root directory of the drive.

File Naming Conventions (Most Common Extensions)

First, let's look at some of the basics. Windows filenames are used to identify particular application, configuration, or data files. Each file must have a unique name within the directory it is created in and must obey certain rules. The following characters are not allowed in filenames in Windows: \ / : * ? " | < >.

Besides the filename itself, each file can also have an optional filename extension, which is one or more characters long and allows Windows to identify the file as being of a certain type. Text files are given a `.txt` extension, batch files are given a `.bat` extension, and executable files are given an `.exe` extension. Each type of file is then handled differently when it is accessed. The behavior of a file with a particular extension is determined by a process called *association*.

When a file extension is associated with a particular filename, the association defines what application will open the file and what the file's default actions are. To check on a file association, use Windows Explorer. Click Tools ➤ Folder Options and go to the File Types tab. From there you can view and modify the extensions for that computer. Table 7.2 shows some of the most common filename extensions.

TABLE 7.2   Filename Extensions

Extension	File Type
`.bat`	Batch files
`.bmp`	Bitmap graphic files
`.dll`	Dynamic Link Library code files
`.doc`	MS Word document files
`.exe`	Executable files
`.inf`	Setup information files
`.ini`	DOS/Windows 3.x application initialization files
`.sys`	System files
`.txt`	Text files
`.xls`	MS Excel spreadsheet files

Although there are many different file types, each with its own extension, the OS breaks them into two essential categories: text and binary. A *text file* contains only ASCII text characters (letters, numbers, symbols); a *binary file* contains program instructions or a mixture of programming and text.

All Windows filenames share the elements we have looked at so far. There are, however, two very different naming schemes in Windows:

Short Filenames   These filenames come out of the DOS legacy. Files that are created using the short *8.3* naming convention are allowed a name of only one to eight characters, with an optional extension of one to three characters. Although this system works fine, it does not allow for names that make a great deal of sense. These names are seldom used anymore; however, both DOS and Windows 3.1 used this naming convention, so the DOS prompt and any Windows 16-bit applications still are likely to use 8.3 naming. Short names do not allow blank spaces.

Long Filenames   Beginning with Windows 95, Microsoft expanded the namespace by allowing names of up to 256 characters (215 in Windows 2000). All newer MS OSs support long filenames, which do allow blank spaces in the name.

File Attributes

In addition to their names, files also have a series of attributes that you can attach to them to further identify or categorize them. In DOS, Windows 3.x, and Windows 9x, there are four such attributes; Windows NT/2000/XP add additional attributes through NTFS (on NTFS-formatted disks only). These attributes are listed here, along with their functions:

Read Only   Prevents the file from being modified or deleted.

Archive   Tells the system whether the file has been modified since it was last backed up and allows the backup program to know which files to process in an incremental or differential backup.

System   Identifies the file as one needed by the system. You will be warned if you attempt to delete a file labeled as System.

Hidden   Indicates system files that are hidden to prevent them from showing up in normal searches of the hard drive. To see a list of hidden files in a directory, type **DIR /ah** at the command prompt.

Compress   Specifies that the file is to be compressed when not in use. This saves space on the drive but slows access to the file (NTFS disks only).

Index   Allows the Index Service to add the file to its indexes. This increases the speed of any searches you do on the system (NTFS5 disks only).

Encrypt   Secures a file through an encryption algorithm. This makes it extremely difficult for anyone other than the user to access the file by encoding it using a public/private key technology (NTFS5 disks only).

The ATTRIB command can be used to set and remove the four base RASH attributes (Read Only, Archive, System, Hidden). Windows Explorer can be used to set any of the attributes that are available by viewing a file's properties.

File Permissions

You can assign two kinds of permissions: sharing permissions and NTFS permissions.

Sharing permissions are in effect when someone accesses your computer from the network. They determine which drives and folders outsiders have access to, and whether they can make changes to those folders. You set up such permissions from the Sharing tab of the Properties box for a folder or drive. You cannot set sharing permissions for an individual file.

NTFS permissions are in effect at the local level, and are based on the user who is logged in. They are set on the Security tab of the Properties box for a folder, drive, or file. NTFS permissions can be set for individual files, although doing so is not recommended because of the potential administrative headaches.

Folders and Files

Now that you understand the basics of file naming and attributes, you also need to know how to view, create, and manage files and folders for the test. *File management* is the process by which a computer stores data and retrieves it from storage. The process of managing files is similar across all current Windows platforms. Most folder and file management is done through a tool called Windows Explorer.

WARNING   Watch out for all the "Explorers" when you're reading test questions. There are three different Explorers in Windows: Internet Explorer, Windows Explorer, and EXPLORER.EXE (the Windows shell program). Make sure you know which one the question is asking you about.

Although it is technically possible to use the command-line utilities provided within the command prompt to manage your files, this is not the most efficient way to accomplish most tasks. The ability to use drag-and-drop techniques and other graphical tools to manage the filesystem makes the process far simpler. Windows Explorer is a utility that allows you to accomplish a number of important file-related tasks from a single graphical interface. Figure 7.7 shows the Windows Explorer interface for Windows XP; other versions are similar.

FIGURE 7.7   Windows Explorer (Windows XP version)

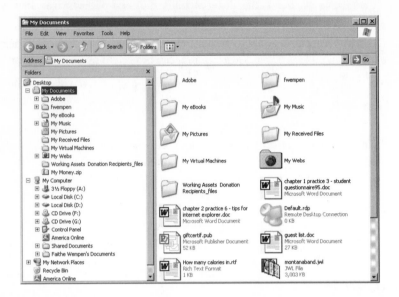

Using Windows Explorer is pretty simple. You need only a few basic instructions to start working with it. The Explorer interface has a number of parts, each of which serves a specific purpose. The top area of Explorer is dominated by a set of menus and toolbars that allow easy access to common commands. The main section of the window is divided into two panes: The left pane displays the drives and folders available to the user, and the right pane displays the contents of the currently selected folder. Along the bottom of the window, the status bar displays information about the used and free space on the current directory.

Some common actions in Explorer include the following:

Expanding a Folder   You can double-click a folder to expand it (show its subfolders in the left panel) and display its contents in the right pane. Clicking the plus sign (+) to the left of a folder expands the folder without changing it.

Collapsing a Folder   Clicking the minus sign (−) next to a folder collapses it.

Selecting a File   If you click a file in the right pane, Windows highlights the file by marking it with a darker color.

Selecting Multiple Files   The Ctrl and Shift keys allow you to select multiple files at once. Holding down Ctrl while clicking individual files selects each new file while leaving the currently selected file or files selected as well. Holding down Shift while selecting two files selects both of them and all files in between.

Opening a File   Double-clicking a file in the right pane opens the program if it is an application; if it is a file, Explorer opens it using the file extension that is configured for it.

Changing the View Type   There are four primary view types: Large Icons, Small Icons, List, and Details. You can move between these views by clicking the View menu and selecting the view you prefer.

Creating New Objects   To create a new file, folder, or other object, navigate to the location where you want to create the object, and then right-click in the right pane. In the menu that appears, select New and then choose the object you want to create.

Deleting Objects   To delete an object, select it and press the Delete key on the keyboard, or right-click the object and select Delete from the menu that appears. Doing so sends the file or folder to the Recycle Bin. To permanently delete the object, you must then empty the Recycle Bin. Alternatively, you can hold down Shift while deleting an object, and it will be permanently deleted immediately.

In addition to simplifying most file-management commands as shown here, Explorer also allows you to easily complete a number of disk-management tasks. You can format and label floppy disks, and copy the Windows system files to a floppy so that a disk may be used to boot a machine. Before you take the test, you should be extremely familiar with the Windows filesystem and how these tasks are accomplished.

Labeling is an optional process of giving a name to a disk. You can label both hard drives and floppies.

Exam Essentials

Be able to partition and format drives.   You should be able to use both `FDISK`/`FORMAT` and Disk Management, as well as various versions of Windows Setup, to perform these tasks.

Know the filesystems.   Make sure you can explain the differences between FAT16, FAT32, NTFS4, and NTFS5 and tell which OSs they are compatible with.

Know the file-naming conventions.   Be able to explain the filename limitations for various OS versions.

Understand file attributes.   You should be able to explain the major file attributes and how to set them.

Use Windows Explorer.   This is somewhat of a no-brainer because it's a basic end-user skill, but you should be thoroughly familiar with using Windows Explorer to manage files and folders.

1.5 Employing Major Operating System Utilities

This is a new objective, but its content is not new; it has been moved from other objectives. This objective covers a host of utility programs included in Windows that help technicians and experienced end-users manage their file storage.

Critical Information

The utilities covered under this objective can be organized into three categories: disk management, system management, and file management.

Disk Management Utilities

These utilities help you work with entire disks as a whole, or help you perform operations that can potentially affect an entire disk, such as backups and disk cleanup.

Disk Defragmenter (*DEFRAG*)

Disk Defragmenter reorganizes the file storage on a disk to reduce the number of files that are stored noncontiguously. This makes file retrieval faster, because the read/write heads on the disk have to move less.

There are two versions of Disk Defragmenter: a DOS version that comes on the startup floppy for Windows 9x and comes with MS-DOS, and a Windows version that runs from within Windows. The Windows version is located on the System Tools submenu on the Start menu.

The available switches for the DOS version (`defrag.exe`) include:

`-a`	Analyze only
`-f`	Force defragmentation even if disk space is low
`-v`	Verbose output

Fixed Disk Utility (*FDISK*)

This utility is only for MS-DOS and Windows 9x versions. It manages disk partitions (FAT and FAT32). It is located in the `MSDOS` folder under DOS, and on the startup floppy and in `C:\Windows\Command` for Windows 9x.

The switches are as follows:

`/STATUS`	Displays partition information
`/S`	Ignores extended partition information

Backup and Restore

Most versions of Windows come with a Backup program (Microsoft Backup). However, the Windows 95/98 utility was pretty rough, and bears little resemblance to the more robust backup utility in Windows 2000/XP.

You can access this utility from the System Tools menu, or from the Tools tab in a hard disk's Properties box. Its purpose is to back up files in a compressed format, so the backups take up less space than the original files would if they were copied. To restore the backup, you must use the same utility again, but in Restore mode.

CHKDSK

CHKDSK is an old MS-DOS utility that predates ScanDisk. It's used to correct logical errors in the FAT. The most common switch for CHKDSK is /F, which fixes the errors that it finds. Without /F, CHKDSK is an "information only" utility.

ScanDisk

ScanDisk is a graphical utility that does the same thing as CHKDSK, except that it also can check for physical errors in the storage media and relocate any readable data away from bad spots. There are two versions: a DOS version, which comes with MS-DOS 5.0 and higher and Windows 9x (used only at startup or from a startup floppy); and a 32-bit Windows version, found in Windows 9x (on the System Tools submenu).

The switches for the DOS version of ScanDisk include:

/ALL	Checks and repairs all local drives
/AUTOFIX	Fixes damage without prompting
/CHECKONLY	Checks but does not repair
/CUSTOM	Configures and runs according to SCANDISK.INI settings
/NOSAVE	With /AUTOFIX, deletes lost clusters rather than saving them as files
/NOSUMMARY	With /CHECKONLY or /AUTOFIX, prevents Scandisk from stopping at summary screens
/SURFACE	Performs a surface scan after other checks
/MONO	Configures ScanDisk for use with a monochrome display

Check Disk

Check Disk (not to be confused with CHKDSK) is a Windows NT/2000/XP graphical utility for doing basically the same thing as ScanDisk—finding and fixing logical errors in the FAT, and optionally also checking each sector of the disk physically and relocating any readable data from damaged spots.

Unlike ScanDisk, Check Disk is not a menu command on the Start menu. To run it, display the Properties box for a hard disk and then select Check Disk for Errors from the Tools tab.

Disk Cleanup

Disk Cleanup is a Windows-based utility found in versions 98 and higher; it helps the user recover disk space by offering to delete unneeded files. It can be run from the System Tools submenu. In some versions of Windows, it automatically runs (or offers to run) when free disk space gets low.

FORMAT

The FORMAT command can be used at a command prompt to format a disk. It is located in the C:\Windows\Command folder, but can be accessed from any prompt.

Its switches are as follows:

/V[:*label*]	Specifies a volume label
/Q	Performs a quick format
/F:*size*	Specifies the formatted size; omit for default
/B	Allocates space on the formatted disk for system files to be added later
/S	Copies system files to the formatted disk
/T:*tracks*	Specifies the number of tracks per disk side
/N:*sectors*	Specifies the number of sectors per track
/1	Formats a single side of a floppy disk
/4	Formats a 5~QF~IN 360KB floppy disk
/8	Formats eight sectors per track
/C	Tests clusters that are currently marked as bad

You can also access a Windows-based Format utility by right-clicking a drive icon in Windows and selecting Format.

System Utilities

These utilities act upon the system in more ways than just disk storage. They affect the way Windows starts up, the way it runs, the way tasks are managed, the way events are logged, and so on.

Device Manager

Device Manager, which you will learn more about in objective 2.4 (Chapter 8), shows a list of all installed hardware and lets you add items, remove items, update drivers, and more. This is a Windows-only utility. In Windows 9x, it is a tab in the System Properties box. In Windows NT/2000/XP, you display the System Properties, click the Hardware tab, and then click the Device Manager button to display it.

Computer Management

The A+ objective lists this as Computer Manager, but the proper name for the utility is Computer Management. This utility, present in Windows NT/2000/XP, provides easy access to a variety of computer-management tools, including Disk Management (the tool for partitioning and formatting drives). Computer manager was not present in NT 4.0. To run Computer Management, go through Control Panel (Administrative Tools ➤ Computer Management).

System Configuration Editor (*MSCONFIG*)

This utility helps troubleshoot startup problems by allowing you to selectively disable individual items that normally are executed at startup. There is no menu command for this utility; you must run it with the Run command (on the Start menu). Choose Start ➤ Run and type **MSCONFIG**. It works in most versions of Windows, although the interface window is slightly different among versions.

Registry Editor (*REGEDIT* and *REGEDT32*)

Configuration information for Windows is stored in a special configuration database known as the Registry. This centralized database contains environmental settings for various Windows programs. It also contains what is known as *registration* information, which details the types of file extensions associated with applications. So, when you double-click a file in Windows Explorer, the associated application runs and opens the file you double-clicked.

The Registry Editor enables you to make changes to the large hierarchical database that contains all of Windows' settings. These changes can potentially disable the entire system, so they should not be made lightly.

Changes made in the Registry Editor are implemented immediately; you do not have the opportunity to save or reject your changes.

As with MSCONFIG, there is no menu command for the Registry Editor. You must run it with the Run command. REGEDIT is the name of the program.

In Windows NT 4.0 and 2000, there is a second Registry Editor program, called REGEDT32. This alternative program accesses the same Registry, but does it in a slightly different way; it shows each of the major key areas in a separate window.

In Windows XP, the command REGEDT32 is still present, but running it launches REGEDIT; they have been rolled into a single utility. Windows 9x does not have a REGEDT32 command at all.

System Editor (*SYSEDIT*)

System Editor is like Notepad except it automatically opens a separate pane for each of several important startup text files, such as AUTOEXEC.BAT, CONFIG.SYS, WIN.INI, and SYSTEM.INI. (Actually these are no longer important files, because they exist only for backward compatibility with MS-DOS and Windows 3.1, but they do still exist.) To run SYSEDIT, use the Run command on the Start menu. Depending on the Windows version, the files that it automatically opens may be slightly different.

Registry Scanner (*SCANREG*)

Windows 9x automatically makes backup copies of the two Registry files USER.DAT and SYSTEM.DAT. Each time Windows 9x restarts, your Registry is examined, and if problems are found, the backup copy of the Registry is located and is used to start Windows. The application used to do this is SCANREG.EXE. You can run this application separately from Windows if you want to verify the Registry at any time. SCANREG is great, as long as the automatic Registry backup is good. Just in case, though, it is always a good idea to back up the Registry files regularly. If both the current and backup copies of the Registry are corrupt, you can save a backup copy of the Registry files over the corrupt files and restart the system.

In Windows NT/2000, the situation is more complex. More files make up the Registry, and they are not backed up automatically. You can back up the Registry in NT/2000 using the Backup program or by creating an emergency repair disk (ERD). Note that when creating an ERD, you have to add the /s switch to back up the security information from the Registry. When the ERD is updated, the /REPAIR directory on the hard drive can also be updated with the same current configuration information that is written to the floppy disk.

Another option in all versions of Windows is to use REGEDIT or REGEDT32 to save the Registry out to a file, which can then be re-added later. This file can include all Registry information or only particular parts of the Registry's hierarchy.

Command Prompt

To open a command prompt from within Windows 9x, use COMMAND. (Run it with the Run command.) To open a command prompt from within an NT-based Windows version (NT/2000/XP), use CMD instead.

Event Viewer

This utility provides information about what's been going on system-wise, to help you troubleshoot problems. Event Viewer shows warnings, error messages, and records of things happening successfully. It's found in NT versions of Windows only. You can access it through Computer Management, or you can access it directly from the Administrative Tools in Control Panel.

Task Manager

Task Manager shows running programs and the system resources they are consuming. It can be used for informational purposes, but it is most often used to shut down a nonresponsive application.

To display the Task Manager, press Ctrl+Alt+Delete. In Windows 9x, it appears immediately, under the guise of the Close Program box. In Windows NT/2000/XP, you must take one more step—click the Task Manager button.

A list of running tasks appears; you can click on one of them and then click End Task to shut it down. Because this shutdown method fails to close files gracefully, you should use it only as a last resort, not as a normal method of shutting down an application.

File Management Utilities

The utilities in this category are designed to help you work with individual files and folders.

EDIT

EDIT is the MS-DOS equivalent to Notepad in Windows. It is a plain text editor program that you might use when working at a command prompt. To run it, type **EDIT** at the command prompt.

TABLE 7.3   The switches for EDIT are as follows:

/B	Forces monochrome mode
/H	Displays the maximum number of lines possible for your hardware
/R	Loads the file(s) in read-only mode
/S	Forces the use of short filenames
/<nnn>	Loads binary file(s), wrapping lines to <nnn> characters wide
[file]	Specifies an initial file to load

ATTRIB

This is the command-line utility for viewing, setting, and removing file attributes. You specify the attribute to remove or add, followed by the filename or wildcard specification. For example, ATTRIB +H Myfile.doc would apply the Hidden attribute to the Myfile.doc file.

The switches are as follows:

/S	Processes all files in all the directories in the specified path
+	Sets an attribute. Followed by R, A, S, or H
–	Removes an attribute. Followed by R, A, S, or H
R	Read-only
A	Archive
S	System
H	Hidden

EXTRACT

This is a cabinet extraction tool. Its purpose is to extract one or more files from the compressed cabinet (CAB) archive files that Microsoft uses to ship the Windows software on the Setup CD.

You can use this utility to replace a missing file in a Windows installation without having to completely reinstall Windows.

The syntax for the command is

EXTRACT x:\path\cabinetfile x:\path\filename

Its switches are as follows:

/Y   Does not prompt before overwriting an existing copy.

/A   Searches all CAB files in the specified location, starting with the one specified by the cabinetfile variable.

/D   Displays the cabinet directory. If you use this switch along with a filename, it displays the list only, and does not extract anything.

/E   Extract all. Can be used instead of *.* for the filename.

/L *dir*   Location to place the extracted files. The default is the current folder.

You can also use EXTRACT to decompress a single compressed file on the Windows Setup CD. These are not CABs; they are just compressed files. They can be identified by the underscore character as the first letter in their file extension. The syntax is

EXTRACT /Y *source* [*newname*]

Windows Explorer

We discussed Windows Explorer earlier in this chapter; you should be familiar with its operation from your everyday usage of Windows.

Exam Essentials

Select the right utility for a scenario.   The test is likely to provide you with a troubleshooting or management scenario and ask you to identify which utility you would use. Familiarize yourself with all the utilities presented in the objective list.

Know the tools available for maintaining the health of a filesystem.   You need to know how and why you would use tools such as DEFRAG and SCANDISK.

Understand how the Registry works and how it is maintained.   Know how REGEDIT and REGEDT32 work, and how the Registry is structured.

Review Questions

1. Which Windows versions do not support FAT32?

2. With what Windows feature is a paging file associated?

3. What is another name for the System Tray?

4. To display a command-line interface in Windows XP, what would you execute from the Run command?

5. Which Windows version uses USER.DAT and SYSTEM.DAT to hold the Registry settings?

6. To select all files that have exactly four letters in their name and an extension that begins with *D*, what file specification would you use?

7. Which type of disk must be partitioned prior to formatting?

8. Which version of Windows supports NTFS encryption on NTFS5 drives?

9. What utility in Windows 2000/XP takes the place of ScanDisk?

10. Which Windows application most resembles the MS-DOS application EDIT?

Answers to Review Questions

1. Windows 95a and Windows NT 4.0 do not support FAT32.

2. Virtual memory creates a paging file, or swap file, and then moves data into and out of RAM to it.

3. Microsoft uses the terms *System Tray* and *notification area* roughly synonymously to refer to the area where the clock and the icons for running background programs appear.

4. In Windows NT/2000/XP you use CMD. COMMAND is used in 9x versions.

5. Windows 95/98/Me use USER.DAT and SYSTEM.DAT. NT-based versions of Windows use SAM, SECURITY, SOFTWARE, SYSTEM, and DEFAULT.

6. You would use ????.D*. The four letters in the name are represented by ????. The extension D* refers to any extension as long as it begins with *D*.

7. Hard disks must be partitioned; removable disks such as CDs and floppy do not need this step.

8. NTFS5 is used only with Windows 2000/XP.

9. Check Disk is the equivalent of ScanDisk in NT-based versions of Windows.

10. EDIT is a plain-text editor, so is the answer is Notepad.

Chapter

8

Domain 2 Installation, Configuration, and Upgrading

COMPTIA A+ EXAM OBJECTIVES COVERED IN THIS CHAPTER:

✓ **2.1 Identify the procedures for installing Windows 9x/Me, Windows NT 4.0 Workstation, Windows 2000 Professional, and Windows XP, and bringing the operating system to a basic operational level.**

✓ **2.2 Identify steps to perform an operating system upgrade from Windows 9x/Me, Windows NT 4.0 Workstation, Windows 2000 Professional, and Windows XP. Given an upgrade scenario, choose the appropriate next steps.**

✓ **2.3 Identify the basic system boot sequences and boot methods, including the steps to create an emergency boot disk with utilities installed for Windows 9x/Me, Windows NT 4.0 Workstation, Windows 2000 Professional, and Windows XP.**

✓ **2.4 Identify procedures for installing/adding a device, including loading, adding, and configuring device drivers and required software.**

✓ **2.5 Identify procedures necessary to optimize the operating system and major operating system subsystems.**

Domain 2 gets into the heart of operating system usage. It covers skills related to selecting, installing, and booting various versions of Windows, as well as configuring hardware devices to run and making system changes to optimize performance. The one topic that is conspicuously absent from domain 2 is troubleshooting; that will be the subject of domain 3.

2.1 Installing Windows

The topics covered in this objective include all the skills required to take a system from empty (that is, a blank hard disk) to having a fully functional copy of an operating system installed. The study challenge here is that so many different OSs are covered, and each one works a little differently. One way to study is to focus on the differences between the two classes of Windows OSs—9x and NT/2000/XP—and not worry too much about the minor differences within a class.

Critical Information

The topic list for this objective is broken down into several conceptual areas, in roughly the order that you would tackle them in real life.

Verifying Compatibility and Requirements

Before installing an OS, you must make sure that the computer on which you will be installing meets the minimum system requirements. Table 8.1 lists the minimum requirements for the OS versions covered on the A+ exam.

TABLE 8.1   Windows System Requirements

Version	CPU	RAM	Hard Disk	Other
NT Workstation 4.0	Pentium	16MB (32MB recommended)	110MB	
95	386DX (486 recommended)	4MB (8MB recommended)	50–55MB	
98	486DX 66 (Pentium recommended)	16MB (24MB recommended)	165–355MB	

TABLE 8.1   Windows System Requirements *(continued)*

Version	CPU	RAM	Hard Disk	Other
Me	150MHz Pentium	32MB	480–645MB	
2000 Professional	133MHz Pentium	64MB	2GB with at least 650MB free	
XP	233 MHz Pentium (300MHz recommended)	64MB (128MB recommended)	1.5GB	Super VGA (800x600)

In addition to basic system compatibility, you must also consider the compatibility of individual devices, such as printers, scanners, and so on. To check on the compatibility for a piece of hardware, consult the Microsoft Hardware Compatibility List (HCL) at www.microsoft.com/hcl.

Installation Options

Before beginning the installation process, you must make several key decisions:

Installation Type   The types vary depending on the OS version, but there is usually a Typical option that installs the most common components and a Custom option that enables you to specify precisely which of the optional components you want. These optional components may include accessory programs, drivers, and so on.

Network Configuration   You must decide how this computer will interact with other computers via network. Will it be part of a peer-to-peer workgroup or a domain? Will it connect directly to the Internet? Will it share its Internet connection with other computers?

Filesystem Type   Recall from earlier chapters that valid filesystems include FAT, FAT32, NTFS 4.0, and NTFS 5.0. Not all OS versions support all types, as you saw in Table 7.1 (Chapter 7). NTFS is usually the best choice for Windows NT 4, 2000, and XP, unless you plan to dual-boot and need that drive to also be accessible from Windows 9x.

Dual-Boot Support   Provided you put them on separate partitions, multiple OS versions can peacefully coexist on a system. NT-based versions of Windows can support dual-booting and can provide a boot menu at startup to allow you to choose each time, but you must install the non-dual-boot-aware OS first (Windows 95, 98, or Me).

Disk Preparation Order

The published guidelines for this objective specifically mark this topic as "conceptual," meaning that for this objective, you only need an overview of the topic. These skills are covered in greater detail under other objectives.

The required order for disk preparation for Windows 9x is as follows:

1. Boot from a bootable floppy
2. Partition using FDISK
3. Reboot
4. Format using FORMAT
5. Start the Setup utility

Disk preparation prior to installing is necessary only with 9x versions of Windows; the Windows NT/2000/XP Setup programs can all partition and format drives automatically.

Selecting an Installation Method

There are several possible ways for Windows Setup to start.

Booting from CD

The Windows NT/2000/XP CDs are bootable, so installing them is pretty simple. Put the disk in, turn on the machine, and wait for Setup to start. The only catch is that if you have an older machine, its BIOS may not allow it to boot from a CD. In that case, you need to resort to another method for the install. Windows 95/98 CDs are not bootable.

 If you have a newer system but it won't boot from a CD, check the CMOS Setup settings to make sure the CD drive is enabled as a boot device.

Booting from Disk to Access a Local CD

With Windows 9x, you cannot boot from the CD; you must boot from a startup floppy and then access the CD from a command prompt.

In Windows 98, the startup disk automatically presents you with an option to load CD-ROM support on startup. Some Windows 95 startup disks also have this option, but if not, you can modify the AUTOEXEC.BAT and CONFIG.SYS files to load a CD-ROM driver. The exact modifications you need to make depend on the type and manufacturer of your CD-ROM drive, but a sample of some lines you may need to add to CONFIG.SYS and AUTOEXEC.BAT follow. In this case, the drivers are for a Panasonic CD-ROM. The drivers you need to load in the DEVICE and MSCDEX.EXE options depend on the drive you are using:

```
CONFIG.SYS:
        Files=25
        Buffers=9,256
        DEVICE=C:\PANCD.SYS /D:PANCD001

AUTOEXEC.BAT
        PATH=C:\;C:\DOS
        MSCDEX.EXE /D:PANCD001
```

Notice that these aren't big changes, but they are crucial to make the CD-ROM functional under DOS; once Windows 95 or 98 is loaded, these files won't be needed because Windows has its own drivers for accessing the CD drive, and they will be loaded during the install. These lines can be added to and later removed from AUTOEXEC.BAT and CONFIG.SYS using any text editor.

Once you have gained access to the CD, you start the setup process by changing to the CD drive (type its letter and a colon and press Enter) and typing **SETUP**.

If you can't boot from CD to install Windows NT/2000/XP, you can use a utility on the Setup CD to make a set of boot disks that will allow you to start up the PC, load the CD drivers, and start the Setup utility. Run the file MAKEBOOT.EXE in the BOOTDISK folder on the Setup CD.

Booting from Disk to Access a Network Install Share

If you are installing a number of machines with any OS, you may find it best to place the installation files on a network file server and then install the workstations over the network. To do this, you need a DOS or Windows 9x boot disk with the proper network interface card (NIC) and client software. This often means that you need to have a different boot disk for every type of network card on your network. Knowing how to access network resources by setting up client software is an important skill and will be covered in domain 4.

When you're doing an install from the network, it is a good idea to copy the install files to the local hard drive and then start the install from there.

Drive Imaging

A final way of installing Windows is to install it on one hard disk and then make a copy of that hard disk. This process is called *drive imaging*, and it can be an efficient way to set up many computers quickly. It is typically done with a third-party utility such as Norton Ghost.

It is illegal to use the same copy of Windows on more than one machine. Most companies that employ drive imaging have a site license with Microsoft that permits them to install multiple copies from a single copy, and they have a procedure for entering a unique serial number on each copy post-installation.

Running the Appropriate Setup Utility

Once you have the CDs, boot disks, and/or network shares ready, it's time to start the installation.

Installing Windows 9x

Boot to the startup disk and either put the CD-ROM into the drive or connect to the appropriate network share. The program that performs the 9x installation is called SETUP.EXE, and it's located in the root directory of the Setup CD. Run this program and then follow the prompts that appear onscreen to install Windows.

A duplicate of SETUP.EXE is located in the WIN95, WIN98, or WIN9x folder on the CD. This enables you to copy the entire WIN95, WIN98, or WIN9X folder to a hard disk and install from there. Of all the content on the CD, that folder is the only one that contains files essential for installation.

Once the install is over, or if you have a problem during the installation, there are two files you may want to take a look at: BOOTLOG.TXT and DETLOG.TXT. DETLOG.TXT is created during the install and is a record of all the hardware found in the machine, along with any problems encountered. BOOTLOG.TXT, on the other hand, is created during the system boot phase and records any problems during startup.

Installing Windows NT/2000/XP

Installing Windows NT/2000/XP begins with booting from the Setup CD or running the setup program. Windows 2000/XP have two different setup executables available on the CD: WINNT.EXE is used to start Setup from DOS or Windows 3.x, and WINNT32.EXE is used during an upgrade from an earlier NT-based version or other Windows 32-bit OS.

One major difference between the NT-based Setup and the one for Windows 9x is that you are offered the opportunity to create and delete partitions within Setup. You can specify the type of partition you want, the size, and the filesystem you will be using on it.

Device Driver Configuration

When Windows starts up for the first time, it loads drivers for all devices that it can identify (and for which it has a driver available).

A *driver* is a small program or piece of program code that runs in the background and translates the information going to and from an application and a piece of hardware.

For other devices, it does one of the following:

- It loads a generic driver for that device class, so the device has basic functionality. This is common for monitors, for example.

- It places the device in a class called Other Devices and marks it as having a problem in Device Manager. You must install a third-party driver for the device in order for it to function. This usually happens with Plug and Play (PnP) expansion cards for which Windows doesn't have a driver, for example.

- It ignores the device completely. This happens with non-PnP devices in most cases.

After you install Windows, it's a good idea to check out Device Manager and evaluate how well Windows has used PnP to identify and configure the drivers for your devices. From that point, you can choose to run the Setup utility for a device, update the driver for a device with one you have downloaded from the Internet, or troubleshoot a device to see why Windows is not detecting it (more about this in objective 2.4).

Restoring Data Files

After Windows has been installed, you can restore any data files that were backed up for the PC previously. They may have been copied to a removable disk such as a CD, backed up to a network location, or backed up using Microsoft Backup.

Troubleshooting Setup Problems

The following issues may arise when you're installing Windows.

Hardware Problems

The most common reason for a Windows installation failure is incompatible hardware in the PC. Sometimes hardware that works (somewhat) under an existing installation of Windows halts the Setup process if it's present during Setup.

Make sure that all installed hardware is on the HCL for the OS version (www.microsoft.com /hcl). If you have any noncompatible hardware, remove it from the computer before you retry the installation.

Incompatibility with essential components can sometimes be resolved with a firmware update for the component. Check the manufacturer's website to see whether one is available.

Scandisk Problems

The 9x versions of Windows run Scandisk before the Setup program starts. If your drive is some special type that is incompatible with Scandisk, you can get around it with the /is switch, as in SETUP /IS.

CD Read Errors

If an error appears about not being able to read a certain file, try removing the CD, rotating it a quarter turn, and reinserting it. You can also try cleaning the CD to remove any particles or fingerprints.

Another way to circumvent CD problems is to copy the CD's content to another drive (such as a hard disk), and then run Setup from there.

Exam Essentials

Know how to boot to an installation CD or a network share point.   Understand how to access a CD-ROM from DOS or how to modify the BIOS to allow a bootable CD to start the system. Also, know the basics of how an installation can be done across a network and when a network install is appropriate.

Understand how partitioning and formatting work.   With Windows 9x, this involves understanding how to create and format partitions before starting the install. With Windows NT and 2000, it involves understanding how to create and format partitions during the install.

Understand the hardware requirements of each Windows OS.   Hardware requirements commonly show up on the test. Also, remember which type of tasks each OS was designed for so that you can answer "which OS should you use?" type of questions.

Work through the Setup of each Windows version.   While Setup is automated enough that there are not a lot of things to quiz on, focus on what is happening during Setup, which files are created, and how Setup performs tasks such as hardware detection in each OS.

2.2 Upgrading from Windows 9x/Me, Windows NT 4.0 Workstation, Windows 2000 Professional, and Windows XP

This subdomain looks at the various upgrade paths available within the Windows family of operating systems and examines how Setup is different when you are either upgrading or creating a dual-boot scenario.

Critical Information

An OS upgrade is a process by which the OS is updated to a newer or more powerful version. Upgrades can be preferable to a complete reinstall of the OS because they preserve the user's settings as well as any applications that are currently installed on the older OS. Upgrades can also be a disaster, because older programs or device drivers may not be compatible with the new OS and need to be replaced anyway. Before you decide to do an upgrade, carefully research how the OS change will affect your hardware and software. Once you have decided that you do want to upgrade, the process in Windows is relatively straightforward. Here are the main things to review for the test.

Upgrade Paths Available

The upgrade process checks the current version of your OS and verifies that it can be upgraded. You can upgrade from an older OS version to a newer one, and from a 9x version to an NT-based version, but you cannot go backward in chronology, and you cannot go from NT-based to 9x-based.
   Here are the valid upgrade paths:

- From 95 to: 98, Me, 2000, or XP
- From 98 to: Me, 2000, or XP
- From Me to: 2000 or XP
- From NT 4.0 to: 2000 or XP
- From 2000 to: XP

Selecting the Correct Upgrade Startup Utility

For Windows 9x, the SETUP.EXE file is the utility for both new installs and upgrades. For Windows 2000/XP, WINNT.EXE is the utility for new installs, and WINNT32.EXE is the utility for upgrades from 9x versions to 2000/XP and previous NT-based versions.

Hardware Compatibility and Minimum Requirements

Refer back to Table 8.1 for the requirements for each Windows version. Familiarize yourself with them, because there will likely be questions about the ability to upgrade a system given a certain hardware scenario.

Windows XP runs an Upgrade Wizard that checks hardware compatibility during the upgrade process. It produces a report telling you what problems you might be in store for if you proceed with the upgrade. Some of these problems can be fixed by downloading new drivers from the hardware manufacturer.

If you're in doubt about a piece of hardware, check the Hardware Compatibility List (HCL) at `www.microsoft.com/hcl`.

Verifying Application Compatibility

The Upgrade Wizard in Windows 2000/XP checks the compatibility of all installed applications. For other versions, you must check the application compatibility yourself by visiting the websites for the applications and finding out whether they are specifically supported under the desired OS. A patch or update may be available that will make compatibility possible.

Although it is advantageous to check for compatibility of all applications before upgrading Windows, in reality doing so may not always be practical. You may have to go ahead with the upgrade and then check all applications after the fact, searching for patches and updates to correct any problems you find.

Installing Service Packs and Updates

Having the latest updates is important for any OS, especially in these days of virus infections and security exploits. An *update* is an enhancement or patch that makes the OS work better or closes up a security hole. A *service pack* is a collection of updates that brings the user's system up to the most current level of functionality.

Later versions of Windows include a Windows Update feature that connects to the Internet and runs a wizard that checks for available Windows service packs and patches. In addition, Windows XP has an AutoUpdate Wizard that automatically downloads patches and offers to install them.

Installing Additional Windows Components

During the Setup process for many Windows versions, you can choose to do a Custom install. This allows you to specify which Windows components are installed. For example, on a notebook computer with a small hard disk, you might want to omit extra components like Paint, WordPad, and HyperTerminal. You can also install and remove Windows components later, through the Add/Remove Programs applet in Control Panel.

Exam Essentials

Know which upgrade paths are possible.   Given a particular OS already installed, you should be able to tell which upgrades are possible and which are not.

Know the difference between an upgrade and a fresh install.   Upgrades are installations that examine the existing environment and preserve it as closely as possible in the updated OS. Fresh installs cover up an older install but do not learn from it. Upgrade installs generally preserve existing software, user settings, and other configuration details.

Know the system requirements for each Windows version.   This was a topic under objective 2.1, but it applies here as well. It's best to memorize the specs.

Know how to gather compatibility information.   Be aware of Microsoft's Hardware Compatibility List (HCL) and how to access it.

2.3 Understand Basic System Boot Sequences and Boot Methods

This content area involves examining the key files needed to boot the various Windows versions, the alternative boot modes available, and the processes for creating startup disks and emergency repair disks.

Critical Information

In order to bring an OS up to an operational level, two types of files are required: boot files and system files. Boot files have the job of starting up the computer and preparing the system for the OS. System files then load the OS itself, including its graphic interface and other system components. Boot files are stored in the root of the active partition (generally C:), whereas system files are found in the place where the OS was installed, such as `C:\Windows` or `C:\Winnt`.

Windows 9x Boot Process Essentials

Because Windows 9x is a very different OS than Windows 3.x (which it replaced), most of its configuration is done using different tools than were used in Windows 3.x. Even so, Windows 9x shares a few configuration similarities with its ancestors (Windows 3.x and DOS) for compatibility's sake. The `AUTOEXEC.BAT` and `CONFIG.SYS` files are used to a limited extent by some older programs, but they're not actually needed and are available only for older hardware and software compatibility. In addition, INI files are still used for some Windows programs (generally, older 16-bit apps) to hold configuration settings.

The Windows 9x/NT/2000/XP Registry has taken the place of most INI files. In addition to software extension information, it also contains software configuration information and hardware configuration information. Generally speaking, most of the Windows 9x settings that were previously stored in INI files are now stored in the Registry.

Examining the Windows 9x Boot Process

Let's look at the process you use when you boot the system. When Windows 9x first starts up, it goes through a number of steps before presenting you with a Desktop. The basic elements of a Windows 9x startup are as follows:

1. **System self-checks and enumerates hardware resources.** Each machine has a startup routine called the POST (power on self-test), which is executed by the commands written in the motherboard's BIOS. Newer PnP boards not only check memory and processors during this stage, but also poll the systems for other devices and peripherals.

2. **MBR loads and finds the boot sector.** The master boot record (MBR) is located on the first hard drive and loaded into memory. The MBR finds the bootable partition and searches it for the boot sector of that partition. Information in the boot sector allows the system to locate the root directory of C: and to find and load into memory the IO.SYS file located there.

3. **IO.SYS loads into memory and starts the processor in real mode.** The IO.SYS file performs a number of tasks, each of which is done in *real mode*. Real mode is simply a method of accessing the processor in 16-bit mode. Drivers loaded through the CONFIG.SYS file therefore can continue to function in real mode even after the next step, unless they are replaced by 32-bit Windows drivers. The IO.SYS file performs the following tasks:

   - Provides basic filesystem access to allow the rest of the boot files to be found

   - Accesses the MSDOS.SYS file to obtain boot configuration parameters

   - Loads LOGO.SYS (Windows bitmap display) and DRVSPACE.BIN (compressed drive access) if they are present and needed

   - Loads the Registry file SYSTEM.DAT into memory but does not access it

   - Selects a hardware profile (or allows the user to do so)

   - Processes the commands in the CONFIG.SYS and AUTOEXEC.BAT files if they are present

4. **WIN.COM loads and transfers the processor to protected mode.** The WIN.COM file is automatically executed. This file then loads various drivers as instructed by the Registry. It also examines the SYSTEM.INI and WIN.INI files to obtain additional configuration information. Once the Registry files have been loaded, the processor is transferred into 32-bit protected mode.

5. **Virtual device drivers, the Windows kernel, and the GDI load.** Various 32-bit virtual device drivers load to manage hardware resources, often replacing 16-bit real-mode drivers. The Windows kernel, which controls access to the processor from Windows 9x, is loaded into memory, and once the graphic display interface (GDI) loads to manage screen I/O, the system is ready to accept customers.

6. **The Explorer shell loads, and the user is presented with a Desktop.** The last part of the boot process is the loading of the *shell* program: EXPLORER.EXE. The Explorer is the program

that manages the graphical interface—the toolbar, the Desktop, and the Start menu. Once it loads, network connections are restored and programs in the STARTUP folder are run, all of which are determined by the USER.DAT Registry settings for that user.

Windows 9x Startup Files

We discussed a number of files in the section "Examining the Windows 9x Boot Process." Now we will explain each one further (we've placed an asterisk next to the names of the files that are required in order to boot Windows 9x):

MSDOS.SYS* Primarily handles disk I/O; hence the name *disk operating system (DOS)*. Just like IO.SYS, MSDOS.SYS is loaded into memory at bootup and remains in memory at all times.

EMM386.EXE Provides the OS with a mechanism to see additional memory. The memory space that EMM386.EXE controls has come to be known as *upper memory*, and the spaces occupied by programs in that region are known as *upper memory blocks (UMBs)*.

HIMEM.SYS Used to access upper memory.

IO.SYS* Allows the rest of the OS and its programs to interact directly with the system hardware and the system BIOS. IO.SYS includes hardware drivers for common hardware devices. It has built-in drivers for such things as printer ports, serial or communication ports, floppy drives, hard drives, auxiliary ports, console I/O, and so on.

WIN.INI Sets particular values corresponding to the Windows environment. It's used extensively by 16-bit Windows 3.x applications; it's almost entirely replaced by the Registry for Windows 9x 32-bit apps.

WIN.COM* Initiates the Windows 9x protected-load phase.

SYSTEM.INI Used in DOS and Windows 3.1 to store information specific to running the OS. This and other INI files were used to configure 16-bit DOS and Windows apps.

COMMAND.COM Called the *DOS shell* or the *command interpreter*. It provides the command-line interface the DOS user sees. This is usually, but not always, the C:\> prompt.

CONFIG.SYS Loads device drivers and uses the information from the AUTOEXEC.BAT file to configure the system environment. Memory-management tools and DOS peripheral drivers can be added here.

AUTOEXEC.BAT Used to run particular programs during startup. Also declares variables (such as search paths).

A batch file, named with a .bat extension, is a set of commands that Windows can execute or run. These commands may run utilities, or they may point toward full-blown applications. AUTOEXEC.BAT is a batch file that is automatically executed when the system starts up.

Windows NT/2000/XP Boot Process Essentials

NT-based versions of Windows use completely different startup procedures and different startup files than 9x versions. In this section, we will discuss how Windows 2000 boots and which files are needed to keep it running.

Key Boot Files

Almost all of the files needed to boot Windows 3.x/9x are unnecessary for Windows NT/2000/XP. These versions require only a very few boot files, each of which performs specific tasks:

NTLDR   *Bootstraps* the system. In other words, this file starts the loading of an OS on the computer.

BOOT.INI   Holds information about which OSs are installed on the computer.

BOOTSECT.DOS   In a dual-boot configuration, keeps a copy of the DOS or Windows 9x boot sector so that the Windows 9x environment can be restored and loaded as needed.

NTDETECT.COM   Parses the system for hardware information each time Windows is loaded. This information is then used to create dynamic hardware information in the Registry.

NTBOOTDD.SYS   On a system with a SCSI boot device, recognizes and loads the SCSI interface. On Enhanced IDE (EIDE) systems, this file is not needed and is not even installed.

System Files   Besides the previously listed files, all of which are located in the root of the C: partition on the computer, Windows also needs a number of files from its system directories (generally, \WINNT and WINNT\System32), including the Hardware Abstraction layer (HAL.DLL) and the Windows command file (WIN.COM). Numerous other DLL (dynamic link library) files are also required, but usually the lack or corruption of one of these will produce a noncritical error, whereas the absence of WIN.COM or HAL.DLL will cause the system to be nonfunctional.

The Boot Process

When Windows NT/2000/XP starts, the computer's BIOS performs a number of system checks and then looks for an OS to load. It finds Windows' NTLDR (NT loader) file, which is then read into memory. The NTLDR file (which does not have a file extension, by the way—it is just NTLDR) prepares the system for the boot process and invokes a rudimentary filesystem access that allows it to read the BOOT.INI file in the root of C:. This file is then used to construct a menu from which a user may select an OS. If Windows NT/2000/XP is the only OS installed on the machine, this is a non-issue; but if the system dual-boots, you may choose your OS at this point and boot directly into Windows 9x, Windows 2000, Linux, or whatever. The system waits a predetermined amount of time for a user choice and then loads the default OS. You can configure both the default option and the time in Windows' System properties. Modifications to the menu itself can be made through the BOOT.INI file, which is a text file configurable with any editor.

Once you have chosen to start Windows NT/2000/XP, NTLDR invokes NTDETECT.COM to check the system's hardware and loads NTBOOTDD.SYS if the system uses a SCSI boot device. NTLDR then passes control of the system to WIN.COM, and the graphical phase of startup begins.

During this time, you are presented with a series of screens that show the system's progress during startup; the interface is initiated, and network connections and computer policies (if present) are loaded. Windows 2000 next presents you with a logon screen as discussed earlier, and you can begin to use the system.

If you choose to boot back to a previous OS, NTLDR immediately passes control to BOOTSECT.DOS, and the other files mentioned are not used.

Alternative Boot Modes

Depending on the Windows version, a number of alternative boot modes may be available. These are used almost exclusively for troubleshooting, in situations where Windows will not boot normally. To select an alternative boot mode, turn the computer on and press the F8 key when you see the words *Starting Windows* (roughly at the same time you hear the single beep that tests the speaker). You can also press and release F8 repeatedly as the computer boots, to avoid missing the right moment. Doing so presents you with a list of boot-up choices.

The exact boot modes available depend on the Windows version. Table 8.2 summarizes them, and the following list describes them in more detail:

TABLE 8.2   Alternative Boot Modes by OS

Mode	Description	95	98	Me	NT	2000	XP
Normal	Normal Windows boot	Yes	Yes	Yes	Yes	Yes	Yes
Logged (Bootlog.txt) or Enable Boot Logging	Logs each step of the startup for later review	Yes	Yes	Yes	No	Yes	Yes
Safe Mode	Starts with a minimal set of drivers	Yes	Yes	Yes	No	Yes	Yes
Safe Mode with Network Support	Same as Safe Mode but includes networking	Yes	No	No	No	Yes	Yes
Step-by-Step Confirmation	Steps through the startup line by line	Yes	Yes	Yes	No	No	No
Command Prompt Only	Boots to a DPMI command prompt	Yes	Yes	No	No	No	No

TABLE 8.2   Alternative Boot Modes by OS *(continued)*

Mode	Description	95	98	Me	NT	2000	XP
Safe Mode Command Prompt Only / Safe Mode with Command Prompt	Boots to a command prompt; bypasses the startup files	Yes	Yes	No	No	Yes	Yes
Previous Version of MS-DOS	Boots to an old DOS version if available; otherwise, the same as Normal	Yes	No	No	No	No	No
Enable VGA Mode	Like Normal, but loads the standard VGA video driver	No	No	No	Yes	Yes	Yes
Last Known Good Configuration	Replaces the Registry with the last backed-up version of it that successfully booted	No	No	No	No	Yes	Yes
Directory Services Restore Mode	For domain controllers only; not used for workstations	No	No	No	No	Yes	Yes
Debugging Mode	For programmers' use only; not used for troubleshooting	No	No	No	No	Yes	Yes

Normal   This is the default selection and loads both the graphical interface and all drivers.

Logged (\BOOTLOG.TXT) **or Enable Boot Logging**   If you are having problems starting, this option can help by saving all information about the boot process to a file. You can examine this file later for information that may help you identify the problem. In Windows 9x, it is BOOTLOG.TXT; in 2000/XP it is NTBTLOG.TXT.

Safe Mode   This option starts Windows using only basic files and drivers (mouse, except serial mice, monitor, keyboard, mass storage, base video, default system services, and no network connections). Once in Safe Mode, you can restore files that are missing or fix a configuration error. To exit Safe Mode, restart the computer. If you have fixed the problem, then upon reboot, the computer should operate normally.

Safe Mode With Network Support   This option is the same as Safe Mode, but it tries to load networking components as well.

Step-By-Step Confirmation   If you want to watch the entire boot process or selectively exclude lines from AUTOEXEC.BAT or CONFIG.SYS from the boot process, this option presents you with each option before Startup executes it and asks whether to perform that action.

Command Prompt Only   This option, which is for 9x versions of Windows only, starts Windows without the graphic interface and presents you instead with a DOS-like command-prompt shell. This can be helpful if you are having serious problems with the Windows interface files.

Safe Mode Command Prompt Only / Safe Mode with Command Prompt   This is Windows at its most basic. Only essential drivers are loaded, and there is no GUI.

Enable VGA Mode   This option starts Windows NT/2000/XP using the basic VGA driver but loads the rest of the system as usual. If you install an incorrect video driver or a video driver becomes corrupted, this option allows you to get into the system to fix the problem.

Last Known Good Configuration   This option is useful if you have changed a configuration setting in the Registry, which then causes the system to have serious problems. However, it will not save you from a corrupt file or a deleted-file error.

Debugging Mode   A sort of advanced boot logging, Debugging Mode requires that another machine be hooked up to the computer through a serial port. The debug information is then passed to that machine during the boot process. Technicians rarely use this option because it usually only solves problems involving poorly written applications. It is a great tool for developers, but for technicians, reinstalling and avoiding the offending application is far faster!

Creating and Using a Startup Disk (Windows 9x)

What happens when your Windows computer has a problem so severe that the computer won't boot? Often, if the Registry is corrupt, the Windows interface won't come up—not even in Safe Mode. All versions of Windows 9x come with a utility that allows you to create a disk that can be used to fix Windows. This disk is called the *Windows startup disk*. It contains enough of the Windows startup files to boot the computer from floppy disk, allowing you to perform various diagnostic and repair tasks. The disk contains files and utilities such as FDISK, ATTRIB, CHKDSK, DEBUG, EDIT, FORMAT, RESTART, SCANDISK, and SYS. These files are used to correct basic disk problems as well as file boot problems. However, the Windows 9x emergency disk *cannot* be used to restore a corrupt Registry (apart from copying the USER.DAT and SYSTEM.DAT files from their backup locations).

To create a startup disk, do the following:

1. Select Start ➤ Settings ➤ Control Panel.
2. Select Add/Remove Programs.
3. Select the Startup Disk tab.
4. Insert a blank floppy disk in your A: drive and click the Create Disk icon. Windows 9x starts the process of creating the disk.
5. You are asked to verify that the disk in the A: drive should be overwritten, and then Windows 9x formats the disk and makes it bootable. It also copies numerous utilities to the disk so that you can use them to fix Windows 9x.

6.   When Windows 9x finishes copying files to the disk, remove the disk from the drive, label it "Windows 9x Startup Disk," and put it in a safe place so that you can get to it easily if there is ever a problem.

If you have a problem with your Windows installation and you suspect the disk is the difficulty, you can boot to the startup disk and try to repair the hard disk. Insert the floppy you made into your floppy drive and boot to it. This startup disk creates a small, virtual disk drive (usually labeled D: or something similar) with all the repair utilities installed on it. You can then use these utilities to repair the disk or files. In addition, because you are booted up to a command line, you can copy new files over old, corrupt ones, if necessary.

There are differences between the Windows 95 and Windows 98/Me repair disks. Before you take the exam, create one of each and compare them. For instance, the Windows 98/Me disk has built-in CD support, but partly because of this it has little room for additional utilities you might wish to add.

Windows NT/2000/XP Emergency Repair Disk

The Windows emergency repair disk (ERD) is a special disk you can create in Windows that can be used to repair the Registry as well as startup files. One important difference between the NT-based ERD and the Windows 9x startup disk is that the NT-based ERD contains only information—it is *not* a bootable disk. You must use this disk from a menu within the Setup utility, which means booting using a startup disk set or the NT installation CD itself.

The Windows NT ERD typically contains the following files:

- System Registry hive (`SYSTEM.`)
- Software Registry hive (`SOFTWARE.`)
- Default user profile (`default.`)
- New user profile (`ntuser.da_`) in Windows NT version 4.0 only
- `Setup.log`
- `Autoexec.nt`
- `Config.nt`

You can use these files to restore a Windows NT system to proper operation.

Windows NT 4.0 ERD

To create a Windows NT 4.0 Emergency Repair Disk, you must use the `RDISK` utility. This utility is installed with the default installation of Windows NT and by default is installed to the C: drive in the `WINNT\SYSTEM32` directory. Follow these steps:

1.   Click Start ➢ Run and type **RDISK /S**.
2.   Click the Create Repair Disk button.
3.   RDISK prompts you to insert a disk. Insert a blank 1.44MB floppy disk (or one that is okay to format) and click OK.

4. RDISK formats the disk and copies the configuration files to it.

5. Windows NT presents a screen telling you that this disk contains security-sensitive data and to store it in a safe location.

6. Click OK to finish creating the disk, remove the disk from the drive, label it "Windows NT ERD for <*WORKSTATION NAME*>," and put it in a safe place so that you can get to it easily if there is ever a problem.

Remember that the ERD is unique to each NT machine. Repeat this process at other NT Workstations as necessary.

A crucial part of the Registry is not backed up on the ERD by default: the security information, which includes the users, groups, passwords, and security structure of the local Windows NT Workstation. In order to back up this information, you must add the /S switch (RDISK /S), which adds the following critical security files:

- The Security Accounts Management database (SAM.)
- The Security Registry hive (SECURITY.)

To use an ERD under Windows NT Workstation 4.0, you must first boot the NT computer using either an NT Setup Boot Disk set or the Windows NT CD-ROM. When you get to the screen that asks you to *Press Enter to install Windows NT or press R to repair a damaged installation*, press R. Insert the ERD into your floppy drive when prompted by the Setup program. Once you have started the emergency repair, you have four options:

- Inspect Registry Files
- Inspect Startup Environment
- Verify Windows NT System Files
- Inspect Boot Sector

The option(s) you choose will depend on what you suspect is wrong with your computer, and we will look at this in domain 3.

Windows 2000/XP ERD

The Create Emergency Repair Disk option is part of the Windows Backup program in Windows 2000/XP. This program includes a wizard to help you create a disk to repair your system. Then, as in Windows NT, you can start the machine with either the startup disks or the Setup CD-ROM and use the ERD to restore the system files.

To create an ERD in Windows 2000/XP, use the following steps:

1. Select Start ➢ (All) Programs ➢ Accessories ➢ System Tools ➢ Backup.

2. From the Welcome tab, click Emergency Repair Disk.

3. Backup prompts you to insert a disk. Insert a blank, formatted 1.44MB floppy disk into your floppy disk drive.

4. Select the check box on this screen that will put a copy of the Registry in the C:\WINNT\REPAIR directory (assuming Windows 2000 was installed to C:\WINNT).

5. Click OK to start copying ERD files. Backup displays a progress bar as the files copy.

When you finish installing Windows 2000/XP successfully, information about the setup is stored in the *systemroot*\Repair folder on the system partition. *Do not delete this folder.* It contains the information the ERD requires to restore your system to its original state.

6. When finished, Backup displays a message that the disk was created successfully. Remove the disk, label it as your Windows 2000 or XP ERD, and include the name of the computer it was created for. Put the disk in a safe place so it will be available if your computer has a problem.

To use or test a newly created ERD for Windows 2000/XP, boot to the Windows CD-ROM. When prompted, choose the Repair option by pressing *R*. You can also choose to either run a manual repair (by selecting *M*) or a fast repair (by selecting *F*). During this process, the selected portions of the system are restored from the disk to the setup of Windows. The system restarts automatically when the repair is successfully completed.

Note that the ERD creation process also allows you to update the \WINNT\REPAIR directory on the hard drive. This keeps the same information as the ERD and may be more convenient.

Booting to a System Restore Point

Windows Me/XP come with a System Restore utility that enables even the nontechnical end user to recover from Registry problems or bad installs of applications by restoring a backed-up copy of the Registry and other key system files. This utility can be found on the System Tools menu. See Figure 8.1.

FIGURE 8.1   Selecting a restore point with System Restore

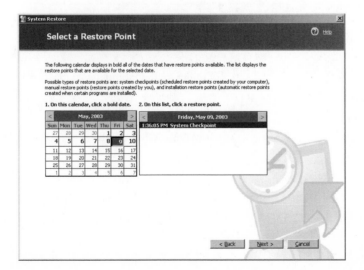

Every day, System Restore creates a restore point. Therefore, you always have at least two weeks of daily restore points to choose from when restoring. You can also manually create restore points at any time—for example, before you install a new application that you are uncertain about. The System Restore interface is simple and self-explanatory; you just follow the prompts to create a restore point or restore the system back to one of your restore points.

Using the Recovery Console

The Recovery Console is a command-line interface for troubleshooting Windows 2000/XP systems. You can use it to repair a damaged Windows installation that will not boot, or to retrieve important files before reformatting.

You can boot to the Recovery Console from the Windows 2000/XP CD-ROM. In the Setup program, choose *R* to Repair, and then *C* for Recovery Console.

If you are planning ahead, you can also install the Recovery Console on your hard disk. If you do this, it appears on the multiboot (BOOT.INI) menu each time you start up. To set this up, run the following command with the Run command, where X: is the CD drive containing the Windows Setup CD:

```
X:\i386\winnt32 /cmdcons
```

Once you get into the Recovery Console, you can use many of the standard command-prompt commands. Type **HELP** and press Enter to see a complete list of the available commands. Then, type a command followed by /? to get help on that specific command.

Table 8.3 lists some of the commands that are unique to the Recovery Console.

TABLE 8.3 Recovery Console Unique Commands

Command	Purpose
Batch	Executes batch commands in a specified text file
Disable	Disables a particular Windows service or driver
Diskpart	A utility for managing partitions, somewhat like FDISK
Enable	Enables a particular Windows service or driver
Fixboot	Rewrites the boot sector
Fixmbr	Repairs the master boot record
Listsys	Lists all available drivers, services, and startup types

Exam Essentials

Know the files necessary to boot Windows 9x and how the boot process works.   Don't get obsessive about the details, such as "How does WIN.COM transfer the processor into Protected Mode?" It doesn't matter. Just know *that it does it.*

Know the files necessary to boot Windows NT/2000/XP and how the boot process works. Remember that Windows NT/2000/XP boot files are nearly identical, so any questions about "What does the BOOT.INI file do in Windows NT?" will have the same answer as "What does the BOOT.INI file do in Windows 2000?"

Understand Safe Mode.   Both Windows 9x and 2000 have Safe Mode. *Windows NT does not have this option.* Know when it is appropriate to enter Safe Mode, how to do this, and what options are available.

Know how to create a startup disk (9x) or an ERD (NT/2000/XP).   Know where to go within Windows to create these utility disks and how to use them. Make sure you know that you must use a different utility to create an ERD with Windows NT 4.0 versus 2000/XP.

Know what the Recovery Console is for.   You should be able to boot into the Recovery Console, and you should know what commands you can execute there and for what purpose.

2.4 Installing/Adding Devices

This objective focuses on making Windows interact nicely with hardware devices. The key to this smooth interaction is having the needed device drivers, so you need to be able to identify good drivers and to acquire them from the device manufacturer when necessary. You must also be able to install them both automatically and manually.

Critical Information

This objective focuses primarily on the procedures for installing device drivers. In many cases, Plug and Play makes driver installation a non-issue, but for those times when intervention is required, a good technician must know what to do.

Managing Hardware

There are three ways to install hardware. Knowing all of these is critical for understanding how Windows works with hardware:

Automatically, during the OS Install   If a piece of hardware is in the computer when you install the OS and is supported by the OS's default driver database, it will be installed and configured automatically during setup.

Automatically, through Detection by Plug and Play If hardware is installed after the installation of the OS, PnP can detect and automatically install the device when you restart the machine. In such a case, you can provide your own drivers, or you can often use standard drivers provided for you. PnP is an industry standard that allows peripheral devices to interact with the OS. The device can report on what it is and what resources it needs, and the OS and device can negotiate particular settings, such as IRQs.

Manually, through the Add/Remove Hardware Icon in Control Panel If your hardware is not detected by PnP, it may be a legacy device. Such components are not designed to work with PnP and must be configured manually. To do this, you generally need to have information on the device's IRQ and DMA settings. You also have to provide drivers or choose the proper driver from the default list.

Plug and Play

Among the most important enhancements debuted by Microsoft with Windows 95 was support for the Plug and Play standard (PnP). This meant that if a device was designed to be PnP, a technician could install the device into the computer and start the machine, and Windows 95 would automatically recognize and configure the device. This was a major advance; but for PnP to work properly, three things had to be true:

- The OS had to be PnP compatible.
- The computer motherboard had to support PnP.
- All devices in the machine had to be PnP compatible.

Unfortunately, at the time Windows 95 came out, many manufacturers were creating their hardware for use in DOS/Windows machines, and DOS did not support PnP; so most pre-1995 computer components were not PnP compliant. As a result, these components—generally referred to as *legacy devices*—often interfered with the PnP environment. Such devices cannot dynamically interact with newer systems. They require manual configuration or must be replaced by newer devices, which don't usually need manual configuration. Due to problems managing legacy hardware under Windows 95, many people soured on PnP technology. Worse, they blamed Windows 95 for their problems, not the old hardware. "It worked fine in DOS" was the standard logic. Nearly a decade later, nearly all PC components are PnP compliant, and configuring computer systems is far easier than it was under DOS.

Windows 9x and 2000/XP work very similarly in dealing with hardware issues. Both rely on PnP and use all three of the methods we've described to install hardware. Windows NT 4.0, on the other hand, does not have PnP support, except for some rudimentary detection capability through the PNPISA utility. As such, NT is a different animal. Because it is not mentioned in the objectives, we'll ignore Windows NT hardware management here, but you should note that it is different.

A number of tools and options let you install, update, and configure your system. We will first look at how you can examine the hardware that is installed on your machine, and then we'll examine how to install a new device.

Device Manager

Device Manager is found on the Hardware tab of the System icon in Control Panel. It gives a graphical view of all the hardware installed in your computer that Windows has detected. (Device Manager is not available in Windows NT.)

Device Manager is used to display all the hardware that Windows knows about and to configure the hardware settings of those devices. If you click the plus sign (+) next to a category of devices, Device Manager will tree out that category and allow you to see the devices in the category, as shown in Figure 8.2.

F I G U R E 8 . 2   Device Manager under Windows XP

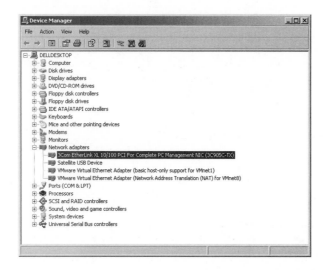

If you then select a device and click the Properties button, you can view the information about that device.

The Driver tab in the Properties box allows you to see the driver name for the device as well as the driver version, if available. (See Figure 8.3.) You can check whether any drivers have been loaded for a device or if drivers specified for a device are not compatible. If you need to load or update a driver, click the Update Driver button. Windows presents a list of drivers to select from or lets you install your own driver from floppy disk or CD-ROM. If you have upgraded to your current version of Windows, you may find that the system continues to use old drivers from the previous OS. A number of updated drivers are available on vendor websites, and these drivers often are far more efficient and stable than the older drivers.

FIGURE 8.3 Examining the device driver settings

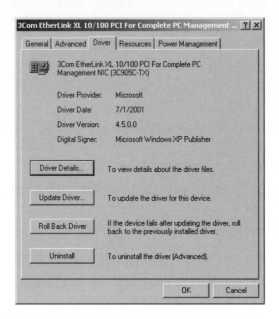

 To add drivers available on the Web, you usually must download the compressed driver files and then expand them onto a floppy disk or into a hard drive folder. At that point, you can run the update and point to the location where you extracted the files.

Most devices also have a Resources tab. From this tab, you can view and configure the system resources the device is using. Most often, the check box next to Use Automatic Settings is checked, meaning Windows PnP has determined the settings for the device and is managing it. However, if the device is not a PnP device and needs to be configured manually, simply uncheck the Use Automatic Settings check box. You can then select the setting (for example, Interrupt Request) and click the Change Setting button to pick the correct setting from a list. When you configure settings manually, Windows lets you know if the setting you have chosen conflicts with another device.

Installing a New Device

Adding new hardware devices is simple under Windows. When you start Windows after installing a new hardware device, it normally detects the new device using PnP and automatically installs the software for it. If it doesn't, you need to run the Add New Hardware Wizard.

INSTALLING A DEVICE USING PLUG AND PLAY

When you install a new device, Windows will probably detect it automatically at startup. Or, in the case of a USB, PC Card, or FireWire device, Windows will detect it immediately when you plug it in. Windows may prompt you for a driver disk; insert the disk it calls for and work through the remainder of the prompts that appear.

If Windows does not automatically notice the new device, you can use the Add New Hardware Wizard from Control Panel to jump-start it. The Add Hardware Wizard works a little differently in each version of Windows, but in all versions it gives you a choice of detecting the device or letting you specify the device. Work through the prompts. If it can't find the new device, see the next section.

INSTALLING A DEVICE MANUALLY

Occasionally, you will find that when you install a new piece of hardware, it is not automatically detected. In this case, one of two things has happened: Either the device is not PnP-capable, or some sort of problem is keeping the device from being recognized. This could range from an interrupt conflict to a malfunction of the hardware itself. If there is an actual problem, you can find that information in domain 3. If the device is not PnP, though, all you need to do is go to Control Panel and run the Add New Hardware (or Add/Remove Hardware) program. This will let you try to force-detect the hardware; and if that does not work, you can manually install the driver and specify the needed resource settings for the device. If you have all the information, this process is easy. If you don't, it can be extremely frustrating.

Before you try to install undetected hardware, be certain to go to the website of the vendor that made the device. Verify that the hardware is supported under the OS you are trying to install it on, and obtain any new drivers that are available. Also check the default IRQ/DMA settings. (Let's hope no one changed them!) Some companies even have configuration programs that allow you to check for the settings on the device and test its functionality.

Signed and Unsigned Drivers

Windows XP makes extensive use of *signed drivers*. A signed driver has been certified to work with a particular version of Windows. When you attempt to install a driver that is unsigned, a warning appears, and you can either cancel the attempt or move past the warning to continue.

You should use signed drivers whenever possible. However, if you have an unsigned driver available and the device will not work otherwise, you can try the unsigned driver. The purpose of signed drivers is to minimize the problems caused by poorly written or inappropriate hardware drivers in earlier Windows versions.

Working with Permissions When Installing

Occasionally, when you're installing software or drivers, you may get a message that says you do not have adequate permissions for doing so. This is more likely under WindowsNT/2000/XP than 9x. To get around this situation, you can:

- Log off the computer and then log on as Administrator.
- Right-click the installation program and choose Run As, and then run it as Administrator.
- Ask your network administrator to assign higher permissions to your account.

Exam Essentials

Know how Windows Plug and Play works.   Understand how the PnP process manages hardware, and also know what its limitations are.

Know how to install and update hardware device drivers.   Practice with Device Manager, and know how to find and add drivers for hardware that is detected but that Windows does not have standard drivers for.

2.5 Optimizing the Operating System

This is a newly added objective, covering some of the ways you can improve a system's performance without adding or upgrading hardware.

Critical Information

There are two major ways to make a computer run better without adding new hardware: improve the efficiency of its memory handling, and improve the efficiency of its file management.

Virtual Memory Management

Virtual memory is a way of using the hard disk to simulate additional RAM so that Windows can use more memory than the system physically has. It works by swapping data into and out of a reserved area on the hard disk from RAM.

All versions of Windows configure virtual memory automatically by default, and in most cases that's the best setting. However, you can sometimes enhance system performance by placing the paging file (the reserved hard disk area) on a certain physical hard disk—for example, one that is very fast, or one that does not compete with Windows program files for usage.

The procedure for accessing virtual memory settings is different among Windows versions:

Windows 95/98/Me   From the System Properties, go to the Performance tab and click Virtual Memory.

Windows 2000   From the System Properties, go to the Advanced tab and click Performance Options. Click the Change button under Virtual Memory.

Windows XP   From the System Properties, go to the Advanced tab and click the Settings button in the Performance section. Go to the Advanced tab in the dialog box that appears, and click the Change button in the Virtual Memory section.

Disk Defragmentation

File fragmentation occurs when a change is made to a file that results in pieces of the file being stored in physically noncontiguous clusters on the disk. This impairs disk performance because the read/write heads must move around gathering up the pieces of the file whenever it is accessed.

To correct fragmentation, you use the Disk Defragmenter utility in Windows. It is found on the System Tools menu, and also on the Tools tab of the drive's Properties box. Figure 8.4 shows it in action.

FIGURE 8.4   Defragmenting a drive

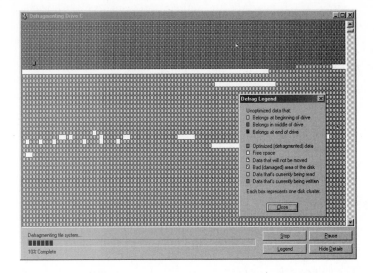

Disk Cleanup

Most versions of Windows include a Disk Cleanup utility that helps clear out unnecessary files. You can run it from the System Tools menu or from the Tools tab of the drive's **Properties** box. It has a list of several categories of file types it can clean up, including temporary files, offline Internet content, and Recycle Bin contents. (See Figure 8.5.)

FIGURE 8.5   Removing unwanted files with Disk Cleanup

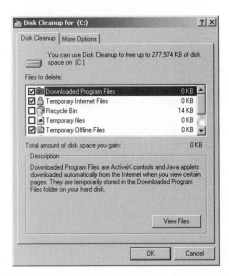

Adjusting System Performance Options

A number of Windows 9x settings can cause minor improvements to performance when they're adjusted optimally. Most of these are accessed from the System Properties dialog box.

Open System Properties, and on the Performance tab you'll find these buttons:

File System   Choose a typical role for the machine: Desktop Computer, Mobile or Docking Station, or Network Server. The Network Server option results in better performance in most cases, even if the computer is not really a server. Also on this tab is a Read-Ahead optimization slider, which controls the buffer size. More is better.

Graphics   You'll find a Hardware Acceleration slider here. Full acceleration offers the best performance, but a lower setting can be useful when you're troubleshooting graphics problems, especially with games.

Exam Essentials

Know how to change virtual memory settings.   The procedure for accessing these settings differs among Windows versions; study it for all versions.

Understand the benefit of defragmenting.   You should know how defragmenting improves system performance and how to run the Disk Defragmenter.

Review Questions

1. What is the RAM requirement for Windows 2000 Professional?

2. Where can you find hardware compatibility information for various Windows versions?

3. What is the correct order for disk preparation for Windows 98?

4. Will FDISK work for NTFS partitions?

5. What line added to the AUTOEXEC.BAT file on a Windows 95 Startup disk loads the real-mode Microsoft CD-ROM driver?

6. What utility on the Windows 2000 CD-ROM enables you to make boot floppies that get the Setup process started on a PC that lacks a bootable CD drive?

7. Which common Windows OS version cannot be upgraded to Windows Me?

8. Which Windows versions do not allow the creation of an ERD?

9. Which file loads first during Windows 2000/XP startup–NTLDR or NTDETECT?

10. Windows NT 4.0 allows only one alternative boot mode; what is it?

Answers to Review Questions

1. Windows 2000 requires 64MB.

2. HCL stands for Hardware Compatibility List, where you can find compatibility information.

3. For Windows 98, the disk must be prepared first by partitioning and then by formatting.

4. No, it is only for FAT and FAT32 partitions.

5. MSCDEX.EXE is placed in AUTOEXEC.BAT to load the real-mode Microsoft CD-ROM driver.

6. MAKEBOOT is the utility that creates a set of Windows 2000 Setup boot floppies.

7. You cannot upgrade an NT version of Windows to a 9x version, regardless of its age.

8. ERDs are only for NT-based versions of Windows. 9x versions can create startup disks via Add/Remove Programs, however.

9. A. NTLDR (NT Loader) is the first of the system files listed here to execute at startup.

10. The only alternative boot mode in NT 4.0 is the ability to boot with a plain VGA driver.

Chapter

9

Domain 3 Diagnosing and Troubleshooting

COMPTIA A+ EXAM OBJECTIVES COVERED IN THIS CHAPTER:

✓ 3.1 Recognize and interpret the meaning of common error codes and startup messages from the boot sequence, and identify steps to correct the problems

✓ 3.2 Recognize when to use common diagnostic utilities and tools. Given a diagnostic scenario involving one of these utilities or tools, select the appropriate steps needed to resolve the problem.

✓ 3.3 Recognize common operational and usability problems and determine how to resolve them

The general theme of the third domain of the A+ Operating System objectives is troubleshooting. Topics range from how to best get information out of users about what problem they are having to how to research or solve some of the more common problems.

Being able to troubleshoot problems—to find out what is wrong with a particular system—is one of the most basic job requirements of a technician. Rarely does a user send a machine in for repair with a note that says, "WIN.COM file is missing." or "The network card driver is corrupt." They just bring in a computer, give a basic description of what is happening ("My computer doesn't work" is a common one), and leave it up to you to decipher what is wrong and fix it. You will soon learn, by the way, that chatting with the user a bit can often turn up valuable information, and we'll cover how to do that as well.

This domain includes three sections. The first deals with the particular problem of troubleshooting the boot process, and the second deals with more general system troubleshooting and diagnostics. The third objective focuses on operational and usability problems and how to resolve them.

3.1 Recognizing and Correcting Boot Sequence Errors

This objective covers some of the more common problems that can appear during startup. We will examine these problems and explain how you can find information about what is causing you trouble.

Critical Information

Normally, if there is a problem with Windows, it becomes apparent during the startup process. This content area looks at problems that either keep the system from starting or cause the startup to be abnormal.

Common Error Messages and Codes

Interpreting the error messages that appear on-screen is the first step in troubleshooting startup problems. Here are some of the more common errors you might see at startup. The exam objectives divide them into some rather arbitrary categories, but we will address them all together:

Invalid Boot Disk   You'll see this error when the disk the system is trying to boot from doesn't have the needed files. One of the most common causes of this error is accidentally leaving a nonbootable floppy in the drive when you reboot. Remove the floppy and try again.

If there is no floppy in the drive, perhaps one of the startup files has been removed from the hard disk. If it's a Windows 9x system, boot from your startup floppy and use the SYS C: command to retransfer the system files to the hard disk. If it's an NT-based system, use the Windows Setup CD in Repair mode.

No Operating System   This error means the computer's BIOS checked all the drives it knew about and couldn't find any disk with a bootable sector. There could be any number of reasons for this error, including the following:

- An operating system wasn't installed.
- The boot sector has been corrupted.
- The boot files have been corrupted or deleted.

If there is a problem with the boot sector, you might try the FIXBOOT command from the Recovery Console (Windows 2000/XP) to repair it. You will probably end up needing to reinstall Windows.

Inaccessible Boot Device   This error can occur if the normal boot device is not available for some reason. For example, perhaps a workstation is set to boot from a network drive that is not currently available. To fix it, make the boot device available again by troubleshooting why the system cannot access it. Perhaps the problem is a loose cable or a physical failure of the drive.

Missing NTLDR   This error is just what it sounds like: NTLDR is missing, so Windows NT, 2000, or XP cannot boot. You can run Windows Setup in Repair mode to fix it, or you can try copying NTLDR from another PC.

Bad or Missing COMMAND.COM   This error occurs on an MS-DOS or Windows 9x system when the COMMAND.COM file is deleted from the root directory of the boot drive or is corrupted. Replace it from another PC, or boot to the startup floppy and use SYS C: to replace it. This error can also occur when you accidentally leave a floppy disk in the PC that was a bootable disk at one time (and hence still has IO.SYS and MSDOS.SYS on it) but has had COMMAND.COM deleted.

WARNING   Remember that the system files for each version of Windows are different. When you're replacing a file, make certain you are using a replacement from the correct OS—and the correct version of that OS. If you have applied a patch or a Service Pack to a system, you need to get the proper files for that Service Pack level.

HIMEM.SYS Not Loaded, or Missing or Corrupt HIMEM.SYS   HIMEM.SYS is the extended memory manager. If it is missing or corrupted, or can't be loaded, Windows can't load. Before you panic, try doing a cold reboot of the system—that is, shut off its power, wait a few seconds, and turn it back on. Sometimes problems with HIMEM.SYS not loading resolve themselves this way. If that doesn't work, replace HIMEM.SYS from another computer or from the Windows Setup CD.

Error in CONFIG.SYS Line XX CONFIG.SYS exists only for backward compatibility with MS-DOS applications, so an error in it is usually not a big deal. This error occurs when the system cannot find a driver or command that is being called from CONFIG.SYS. You can live with the error, or you can edit CONFIG.SYS using Notepad or EDIT to remove the offending line.

Device Referenced in SYSTEM.INI, WIN.INI, Registry Is Not Found This is mostly the same as an error in CONFIG.SYS, except it's an error in one of these other files. SYSTEM.INI and WIN.INI exist only for backward compatibility with Windows 3.x, so errors in them are not critical. You can edit those files with the SYSEDIT utility (from the Run command).

Errors in the Registry, however, can be problematic. If the system boots despite the error, you may be able to disable the offending line through the System Configuration Editor (MSCONFIG from the Run command). That method is preferable to manually editing the Registry with REGEDIT, because it is safer.

Device/Service Has Failed to Start This error means that some device or service referenced in the Registry was not available. It could be as simple as an unplugged device, and it is usually not a critical error that prevents booting. If the device or service is necessary, first check that it is physically operational (for a device) and then try reinstalling its driver.

Windows Protection Error A Windows protection error is a condition that usually happens on either startup or shutdown. Protection errors occur because Windows 9x cannot load or unload a virtual device driver (VxD) properly. Thankfully, this error usually tells which VxD is experiencing the problem, so you can check to see if the specified VxD is missing or corrupt. If it is, you can replace it with a new copy. Often this error occurs when a piece of software is improperly uninstalled or when the uninstall program does not completely remove Registry or INI file references. In such a case, you need to either remove the references to the file to complete the uninstall or replace the file to regain the functionality of the virtual device.

Problems with User-Modified Settings

Sometimes users do things to make their systems not boot anymore, and you need to be aware that the problem might have been user-created. For example, sometimes users delete files that need to remain because they don't know what they are.

When you're troubleshooting, it is important to communicate with the end user and find out what he did immediately before the problem began. It might not have any relationship to the problem, but then again it might.

If you determine that the problem was caused by something the user did, such as install a poorly written application, you can try System Restore (Windows Me/XP only) to return it to its previous condition, or copy the missing file(s) from another PC.

Using the Correct Utilities

This exam objective specifically mentions three utilities you should study: Dr. Watson, a boot disk (which is not a utility but a disk that contains a collection of them), and Event Viewer.

Dr. Watson

Most Windows versions include a utility known as Dr. Watson. This utility intercepts all error conditions and, instead of presenting the user with a cryptic Windows error, displays information that can be used to troubleshoot the problem. In addition, Dr. Watson logs all errors to log files stored in the WINDOWS\DRWATSON directory. Here's the catch—it only works if you keep it running, because you never know when an error is going to occur. You can run it with the Run command by typing **DRWATSON**.

Boot Disk

The startup boot floppy that you create with Windows 95/98/Me contains many useful utilities for troubleshooting system problems and rebuilding a system when required. For example, suppose you cannot boot from the hard disk. You might do the following:

1. Boot from your Windows 9x startup floppy and enable CD support when prompted.

2. Type C: to make the root directory of the hard disk the active drive letter. If you see a C:\> prompt, you know the hard disk is still accessible. If an error appears, you know the hard disk is not accessible.

3. If possible, use the SCANDISK utility to check the hard disk for filesystem errors.

4. Type **FDISK** to start the FDISK utility, and use it to examine the partition information. From this, you can determine whether a valid FAT or FAT32 partition still exists on the hard disk. If it does not, you know the drive has lost everything; if it does, something is preventing it from being seen by the operating system.

5. If you had to recreate the partitions in FDISK, reboot. Then use the FORMAT utility to reformat the hard disk.

6. Use the SYS utility to transfer the boot files for the OS to the hard disk if desired. If you are going to reinstall Windows on it, this step is not necessary.

This is just one example scenario for using a boot disk. Every troubleshooting situation is different and will require different measures.

Event Viewer

Windows NT/2000/XP include an Event Viewer utility that tracks all events on a particular Windows NT/2000/XP computer through log files. Event Viewer is shown in Figure 9.1. Anyone can view events, but you must be an administrator or a member of the Administrators group to modify or clear Event Viewer.

FIGURE 9.1   Windows 2000 Event Viewer

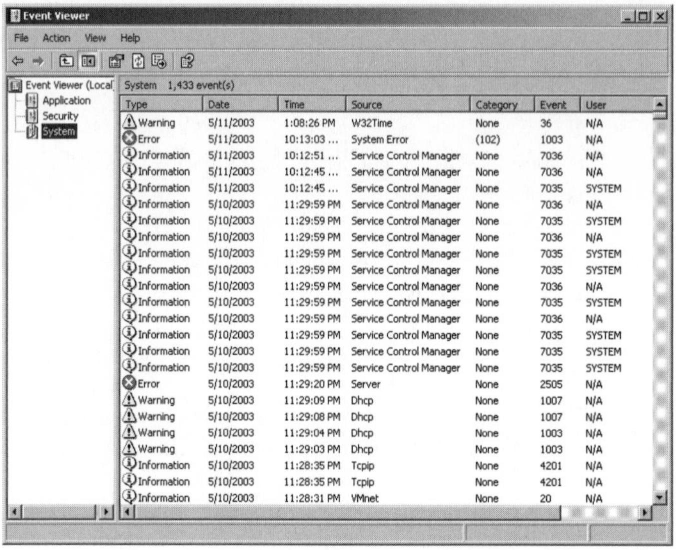

To start Event Viewer, log in as an administrator (or equivalent) and go to Start ➢ Settings ➢ Control Panel ➢ Administrative Tools ➢ Event Viewer. From here you can view the three log files within Event Viewer:

System   Displays alerts that pertain to the operation of Windows. System startup information, problems with NT services, and other general health and status events are recorded here.

Application   Logs server application errors. Any application that is designed to send log information to NT/2000/XP writes its data here. Examples include antivirus programs and database programs, although not all such programs are designed to use the Application log.

Security   Logs security events, such as login successes and failures. It also allows administrators to audit the use of files or printers. By default, security logging is turned off, and this log file will be empty unless security auditing has been explicitly enabled.

These log files can give you a general indication of a Windows computer's health, and it is important that they be available in case of trouble.

There are a couple of possible log problems. One is that the log files can become corrupted. In such a case, you need to delete the log files and let Windows re-create them.

In addition, the Event Viewer log files can fill up, in which case the log cannot add new information. There are two solutions to this problem. The first is to enable *circular logging*, which allows the system to delete old events as new ones are added. In most cases, this solution works well, but valuable troubleshooting information can be lost.

The other solution is to back up and clean out the log files occasionally. Doing so allows you to keep a record of all events, but it requires more work. To do this, use Event Viewer to save each of the log files, and then choose Clear All Events from the Log menu. This erases all events in the current log file, allowing you to see new events more easily when they occur. Another option, of course, is to increase the size of the logs, which can also be done through Event Viewer.

Failure to Start the GUI

Occasionally, the Windows GUI won't appear. The system hangs just before the GUI appears. Or, in the case of NT versions, the Blue Screen of Death (BSOD)—not a technical term, by the way—appears. (The BSOD is another way of describing the blue-screen error condition that occurs when Windows NT/2000/XP fails to boot properly or quits unexpectedly.) In Windows 9x, instead of a BSOD, you get a black screen (usually with a blinking cursor in the upper-left corner) that indicates a problem.

Because the device drivers for the various pieces of hardware are installed at this stage, if your Windows GUI fails to start properly, more than likely the problem is related to a misconfigured driver or misconfigured hardware. Try booting Windows in Safe Mode to bypass this problem. Alternatively, some of the files necessary for the GUI may be having problems, and you may need to replace WIN.COM or other system files from the \WINDOWS or \WINNT directory.

Exam Essentials

Know how to identify common startup problems and recover from startup errors.   This includes knowing which files are needed to boot Windows 9x, NT, and 2000, as well as what steps should be taken to bring back these files.

Know which system files can be modified and what they do.   These include AUTOEXEC.BAT and CONFIG.SYS, INI files, and the NT/2000/XP BOOT.INI file. Know how to use a text editor to modify these files.

Know how to deal with Windows error messages.   Understand how Dr. Watson works in shutting down and controlling problems and how Event Viewer and other files record information useful for troubleshooting.

3.2 Using Common Diagnostic Utilities and Tools

This objective tests your knowledge of the utilities that come with Windows. It also includes coverage of the various Windows startup modes, although this seems odd because they are also covered under objective 3.1 and are not really utilities. Finally, it covers customer interaction skills such as how to elicit problem symptoms from customers.

Critical Information

The key to studying this objective is not necessarily to have in-depth knowledge of each of the areas, but to be able to apply critical thinking toward a problem and use your familiarity with the list of tools available to select the proper tool. For example, the test will not ask you about the minute details of MSD in terms of keystrokes, but you should know what MSD is and be able to say, in a given situation, whether MSD would help you solve the problem.

Startup Disks

Recall from Chapter 8 that Windows 9x can create startup floppy disks that contain boot files and a collection of utility programs for troubleshooting and repairing a system when Windows will not start. This is possible in Windows 9x because these versions are built on a DOS foundation—they have a DPMI (DOS protected mode interface). This isn't possible in NT versions of Windows because there is no command-line underpinning.

The files required for a Windows 9x startup disk are IO.SYS, MSDOS.SYS, and COMMAND.COM. The first two must reside in the first data cluster on the disk, so if you ever make a boot disk manually, you must place these system files on the disk with the SYS command rather than copying them there.

The startup disks created in Windows 98/Me include CD-ROM support. That is, they include a variety of generic CD drives that each attempt to load from CONFIG.SYS when you boot from the disk. One of them will work (or so the theory goes). Then MSCDEX.EXE will load from AUTOEXEC.BAT, and you will have real-mode CD-ROM drive support from the command prompt.

Startup Modes

When Windows won't start properly, it is sometimes due to a driver or some piece of software that's not loading correctly. To fix problems of this nature, you should first try to boot Windows in *Safe Mode*. In Safe Mode, Windows loads a minimal set of drivers (including a VGA-only video driver) so that you can disable an offending driver to keep it from loading—and from failing again.

To start Windows in Safe Mode, press the F8 key when you see the Starting Windows display during Windows bootup. Doing so brings up a menu that allows you to start Windows in Safe Mode. Once you've booted in Safe Mode, you can uninstall any driver you suspect is causing a Windows boot problem or reinstall the driver if you suspect it is corrupted. Upon reboot, the system should go back to normal operation (non–Safe Mode).

 A *corrupt* driver is one in which the software files for the driver have been damaged. This can be caused by a disk error, by a virus, or by standard "act of God" problems such as power outages.

Both Windows 9x and Windows 2000 offer Safe Mode. Windows NT does not. You can also use the F8 menu in 9x or 2000 to select other boot options, such as logging all messages to a log file during boot, booting to a command prompt, or starting Windows in Safe Mode with network support. The Windows 2000 options include those in the following list. Windows 9x offers similar options, but with differences based on the version:

Safe Mode   Starts Windows 2000 using only basic files and drivers (mouse, except serial mice; monitor; keyboard; mass storage; base video; default system services; and no network connections). Once you're in Safe Mode, you can restore files that are missing or fix a configuration error.

Safe Mode with Networking   Same as Safe Mode, but tries to load networking components as well.

Safe Mode with Command Prompt   Similar to Safe Mode, but doesn't load the Windows GUI. Presents the user with a Windows 2000 command-prompt interface.

Step-by-Step Mode   Similar to normal booting, except it asks you for a Yes/No answer to each step of the process. This mode is useful for excluding a certain item that you suspect is causing a problem.

For the test, know what all of the Safe Mode options are and which problems Safe Mode can (and can't) allow you to correct.

Diagnostic Resources

When you are stumped by a computer problem, where do you turn? The exam objectives specify that you should know about the following resources:

User/Installation Manuals   Consult the manuals that came with the hardware and software.

Internet/Web Resources   Consult the websites of the companies that make the hardware and software. Updates and patches are often available for download, or the websites may be knowledgebases of troubleshooting information.

Training Materials   If you have taken a class pertaining to the hardware or software, consult the materials you received for that class.

Diagnostic Tools and Utilities

A big part of being a successful technician is knowing what tools are appropriate to correct which problems. The exam objectives specifically mention familiarity with these tools:

Task Manager   Lets you shut down nonresponsive applications selectively in all Windows versions. In Windows 2000/XP, it does much more, allowing you to see which processes and applications are using the most system resources. To display Task Manager, press Ctrl+Alt+Delete. It appears immediately in Windows 9x; in Windows 2000/XP, you must click the Task Manager button to display it after pressing Ctrl+Alt+Delete. Use Task Manager whenever the system seems bogged down by an unresponsive application.

Dr. Watson   Covered under objective 3.1; enables detailed logging of errors. Use it whenever you think an error is likely to occur (for example, when you're trying to reproduce an error).

Boot Disk with CD-ROM Support   This is not really a utility, but just a reminder that the Windows 9x startup disks contain utilities you can use for troubleshooting. Use one when the system will not boot to Windows (even in Safe Mode).

Event Viewer   Also covered under objective 3.1; it enables you to see what's been going on behind the scenes in Windows NT/2000/XP. Use Event Viewer when you want to gather information about a system or hardware problem.

Device Manager   Another utility that has already been covered in this book in greater detail (see objective 2.4). Device Manager shows you what hardware is installed and lets you check its status. Use this when a device is not functioning and you are trying to figure out why.

WinMSD   Another name for System Information, the same utility you can select from the System Tools menu. (Running it at the Run command with `WINMSD` is an alternative.) WinMSD provides comprehensive information about the system's resource usage, hardware, and software environments. Use it when you need to gather information about the system.

MSD   The MS-DOS version of System Information. It shows resource allocation, memory usage, and more. Running on today's fast computers, however, it may show incorrect information because it was designed for much slower PCs with much less RAM and smaller hard disks.

Recovery CD   Some computers that come with Windows preinstalled do not come with a full version of Microsoft Windows; instead they come with a Recovery CD that can be used to return the PC to its original factory configuration. The important thing to know about these Recovery CDs is that they wipe out all user data and applications. Use one only when you cannot restore system functionality in any less-drastic way.

CONFIGSAFE   A third-party utility for backing up system configuration data. For information about it, see www.imaginelan.com. It is odd that the A+ exam objectives mention it, because generally they do not mention other third-party utilities.

Dealing with Customers

Talking to the user is an important first step in the troubleshooting process. Your first contact with a computer that has a problem is usually through the customer, either directly or by way of a work order that contains the user's complaint. Often, the complaint is something straightforward, such as "There's a disk stuck in the floppy drive." At other times, the problem is complex, and the customer does not mention everything that has been going wrong.

Eliciting Problem Symptoms from Customers

The act of diagnosis starts with the art of customer relations. Go to the customer with an attitude of trust: Believe what the customer is saying. At the same time, go to the customer with an attitude of hidden skepticism, meaning *don't* believe that the customer has told you everything. This attitude of hidden skepticism is not the same as distrust, but just remember that what you hear isn't always the whole story, and customers may inadvertently forget to give some crucial detail.

For example, a customer may complain that his CD-ROM drive doesn't work. What he fails to mention is that it has never worked and that he installed it himself. On examining the machine, you realize that he mounted it with screws that are too long and that these prevent the tray from ejecting properly.

Having Customers Reproduce Errors as Part of the Diagnostic Process

The most important part of this step is to have the customer show you what the problem is. The best method I've seen of doing this is to ask them, "Show me what 'not working' looks like." That way, you see the conditions and methods under which the problem occurs. The problem may be a simple matter of an improper method. The user may be doing an operation incorrectly or doing the process in the wrong order. During this step, you have the opportunity to observe how the problem occurs, so pay attention.

Identifying Recent Changes to the Computer Environment

The user can give you vital information. The most important question is, "What changed?" Problems don't usually come out of nowhere. Was a new piece of hardware or software added? Did the user drop some equipment? Was there a power outage or a storm? These are the types of questions you can ask a user in trying to find out what is different.

If nothing changed, at least outwardly, then what was going on at the time of failure? Can the problem be reproduced? Can the problem be worked around? The point here is to ask as many questions as you need to in order to pinpoint the trouble.

Using the Information

Once the problem or problems have been clearly identified, your next step is to isolate possible causes. If the problem cannot be clearly identified, then further tests will be necessary. A common technique for hardware and software problems alike is to strip the system down to bare-bones basics. In a hardware situation, this could mean removing all interface cards except those absolutely required for the system to operate. In a software situation, this may mean booting up with the CONFIG.SYS and AUTOEXEC.BAT files disabled, or disabling elements within Device Manager.

Generally, then, you can gradually rebuild the system toward the point where the trouble started. When you reintroduce a component and the problem reappears, you know that component is the one causing the problem.

Let me make one last point in this brief introduction to troubleshooting: You should document your work. If the process of elimination or the process of questioning the user goes beyond two or three crucial elements, start writing them down. Nothing is more infuriating than knowing you did something to make the system work but not being able to remember what it was.

Exam Essentials

Know how to create and use a startup disk.   Refer back to Chapter 8 as needed for specifics. You should be able to make a startup disk, boot from it, and access its utilities.

Understand how Safe Mode works in Windows 9x and 2000.   Knowing when to use Safe Mode can help you recover from numerous problems, primarily driver troubles. Understand the differences between the various Safe Mode options and when each is appropriate.

Identify the appropriate utility for a situation.   Given a troubleshooting scenario, you should be able to tell which utility would most likely help you identify the problem, and why it is appropriate.

Know how to deal with customers.   The ability to talk to—and listen to—customers is critical to your success as a technician. Learn how to ask questions tactfully. "Why would you do something so stupid?" will not reveal the information you need.

Know where to find answers.   Understand how Help, FAQs, and other support options can assist you in finding answers.

3.2 Recognizing and Resolving Common Operational and Usability Problems

This objective deals with specific problems, including printing, system errors, network connection problems, and viruses. Given a particular error, you should know what types of troubleshooting procedures are likely to help narrow down and solve the problem.

Critical Information

This objective breaks down its topics into three main sections: printing problems, other common problems, and viruses. We will look at them that way in the following review materials as well.

Troubleshooting Printing

Printers are one of the most important things to become proficient with, because printer problems are generally mission-critical for users. A number of things can go wrong with printers, many of which have nothing to do with software or configuration.

Troubleshooting Windows-Specific Printing Problems

A number of different printer-related issues can cause a PC to require service. Some of the general problem areas include the following:

Printer Hardware Problems   Sometimes you have a problem with physical printer hardware—something is broken, a paper jam occurs, and so on. This is not something that is covered in the A+ OS exam, because hardware issues are covered in the Core Hardware exam.

"Out of" Errors   It is sad to say, but these are by far the most common printer problems. Paper, toner, or ink supplies are depleted, and the printer therefore does not produce as hoped. Again, this is not covered in the A+ OS exam.

Problems with PC or Cable Hardware   It is also possible that the computer's printer port is malfunctioning or that the printer cable is either disconnected or damaged. In such a case, you need to either replace or reattach the cable or check out the PC's printer port. Again, though, this is not information for the A+ OS test.

If none of these seems to be the problem, then you need to start looking for OS issues—and these issues *are* covered during the A+ OS exam. Following are a number of problems that may come up.

Incorrect/Incompatible Driver for Print

The print driver is the crucial software for configuring—and therefore for troubleshooting— printer problems. Each printer has a particular set of features and implements them through its own specific driver. Because of this, in order to function properly, a printer must be matched with its proper driver. Incorrect drivers may be designed for a completely different printer or may be outdated software.

If the driver that is installed for a printer is not even close, print jobs sent to the printer normally come out as nothing more than a garbled mess of odd characters. If the driver is close, but not exact, only certain elements—such as color or particular fonts—may be a problem. In either case, the solution is to obtain and install an updated driver, using the Advanced tab of the printer's Properties page, as shown in Figure 9.2.

FIGURE 9.2   Printer Properties Advanced tab showing the New Driver button

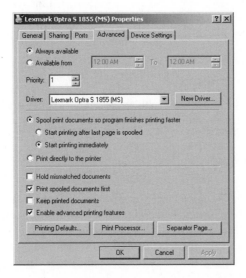

Another common source of printer driver errors is corruption of the driver. If a printer driver does not appear to be properly processing information, and you have verified that the driver is the proper version, you can delete the printer from the Printer Settings window and reinstall it.

A quick way to test the printer functionality is to use the Print Test Page option. This option is presented as the last step when you're setting up a new printer in Windows. Always select this option when you're setting up a new printer so you can test its functionality. To print a test page for a printer that's already set up, look for the option on the printer's Properties menu.

After the test page has been sent to the printer, the computer will ask if it printed correctly. For the first few times, you'll probably want to answer No and use the Troubleshooting Wizard that appears; but after you have troubleshot a few printer problems, you may prefer to answer Yes and bypass the wizard, which is rather simplistic.

Print Spool Is Stalled

One of the most important features of the screen shown in Figure 9-2 is the middle section, containing the spool settings. This section allows you to configure whether Windows spools print jobs. For some printers there may be a Spool Settings button that opens these options in a separate dialog box instead of this section.

If print jobs are spooled, every time you click Print in a program, the job is printed to a spool directory (usually a subdirectory of the C:\WINDOWS\SPOOL directory) by a program called SPOOL32.EXE. Then the job is sent to the printer in the background while you continue to work. From the Advanced tab shown in Figure 9.2, you can choose either Spool Print Documents so Program Finishes Printing Faster or Print Directly to the Printer. Choose the appropriate option and click OK. Once you have made changes to a printer, click OK on the Properties page to save them.

Incorrect Parameter

Each printer driver may have any of a number of additional settings, and depending on how these are configured, any number of problems may occur. For the A+ exam, remember that you are not expected to know how to set the particular properties for a printer. There are just too many of them! This is the sort of thing that experience will teach you, but that you won't be tested on.

Other Common Problems

This chapter has talked about startup problems, printer problems, and system errors. Now it is time for the grab bag of troubleshooting information. These are additional trouble areas you need to know about for the test.

General Protection Faults

A General Protection Fault (GPF) is probably the most common and most frustrating error. A GPF happens in Windows when a program accesses memory that another program is using or when a program accesses a memory address that doesn't exist. Generally, GPFs are the result of sloppy programming. A simple reboot usually clears the memory. If GPFs keep occurring, check to see which software is causing them. Then find out if the manufacturer of the software has a patch to prevent it from failing. If not, you may want to consider another software package.

Windows Protection Error

A Windows protection error typically occurs because Windows 9x could not load or unload a virtual device driver properly. The error message usually reports which VxD is causing the problem, so you can check to see if the specified VxD is missing or corrupt and replace it with a new copy from the original application disk.

Illegal Operation

Occasionally, a program quits for no apparent reason and presents you with a window that says *This program has performed an illegal operation and will be shut down. If the problem persists, contact the program vendor.* An illegal operation error usually means that a program was forced to quit because it did something Windows didn't like. It then displays this error window. The name of the program that has been shut down appears at the top of the window. Use the Details button to view the details of the error. Details include which module experienced the problem, the memory location being accessed at the time, and the registers and flags of the processor at the time of the error.

Illegal operations can happen due to nothing more than a glitch and often do not reappear. Some illegal operations, however, are chronic, and in this case it is likely that some sort of hardware or software incompatibility (or conflict) is the problem. Also, this is the error that Windows NT/2000/XP reports when DOS applications try to access hardware directly, which is not allowed on those systems. In such a case, you cannot run these programs on NT/2000, and you'll need to find a Windows 9x machine or buy an NT/2000/XP version of the software.

Invalid Working Directory

Some Windows programs are extremely processing-intensive. These programs require an area on the hard disk to store their temporary files while they work. This area is commonly known as a *working directory*; its location is usually specified during that program's installation and can be accessed by examining the properties of the application's shortcut icon, as shown in Figure 9.3. If that directory changes after installation, or if the working directory is deleted, Windows will report an error that says something such as *Invalid working directory*. The solution is to either reinstall the program with the correct parameters for the working directory or create the directory the program is trying to point to.

FIGURE 9.3   A working directory

Some programs use a unique directory as their working directory, whereas others do not specify any working directory at all and instead just use the system default (normally TEMP). In NT-based versions of Windows, you may find that permissions restrictions on the filesystem cause a user to not have access to the directory an application tries to write temporary information to. Because the permissions of the application are an extension of the permissions of the logged-on user, this situation can also produce this error.

System Lockup

It is obvious when a system lockup occurs—the system stops responding to commands and stops processing completely. System lockups can occur when a critical system file is corrupted or when an application issues an instruction that the OS interprets as a STOP error—a dangerous system event. Often, lockups occur because two applications have attempted to access the same critical resource simultaneously. Although system lockups were common in Windows 3.x and happened occasionally in Windows 9x, they are rare in NT versions of Windows.

The remedy for a system lockup is to reboot. However, if the lockups are persistent, the machine may have a serious hardware-related problem or need to have its software reinstalled to repair corrupt files.

Option (Sound Card, Modem, or Input Device) Will Not Function

When you are using Windows, you are constantly interacting with some piece of hardware. Each piece of hardware has a Windows driver that must be loaded in order for Windows to be able to use it. In addition, the hardware has to be installed and functioning properly. If the device driver is not installed properly or the hardware is misconfigured, the device won't function properly. Common reasons for hardware to not work include:

Hardware Is Nonfunctional   Replace the device.

Hardware Is Not Properly Connected to the Computer   Check connections or reseat the device in its slot or port.

Device Is Not Detected by Plug and Play   This can be a symptom of any of a number of problems. The connection port the device is using may be disabled. A printer on LPT1 won't be detected if LPT1 is disabled. Also, the device itself may not be PnP-compliant. In such a case, you have to install it by specifying all drivers and resource settings.

Resource Conflicts   In newer machines, most devices are PCI, and the PCI architecture allows resource sharing between PCI devices using a resource pool idea. Older ISA devices do not have this option, and if two devices try to use the same interrupt or I/O address, one or possibly both of them will be unusable. This is probably the most common reason for problems with hardware in older machines.

Be ready for problems like this on the test, where you will be asked how to diagnose problems with Windows and hardware access. Problems installing or configuring new hardware are among the most common reasons for a machine to be sent in for service.

Application Will Not Start or Load

Once an application is successfully installed, you may run across a problem getting it to start properly. This problem can come from any number of sources, including an improper installation, software conflict, or system instability. If your application was installed incorrectly, the files required to properly run the program may not be present, and the program can't function without them. If a shared file that's used by other programs is installed, it could be a different version than what should be installed that causes conflicts with other programs. Finally, if one program fails, it can cause memory problems that destabilize the system and cause other programs to crash. The solution to these problems is to reinstall the offending application, first making sure that all programs are closed.

 One of the primary improvements of the 32-bit architecture is the ability to isolate applications from each other and from the OS. This makes it less likely that the failure of one application will affect the entire system.

Cannot Log On to Network (NIC Not Functioning)

If your computer is hooked to a network (and most computers today are), problems that prevent the PC from accessing the network are frequent. In most cases, the problem can be attributed to the following:

Malfunctioning Network Interface Card   If you have checked everything and you can't get the card to initialize, it may be bad. Replace it, or try it in another machine.

Improperly Installed or Configured Network Software   If you do not have the proper combination of driver/protocol/client, then you won't be able to access network resources. For a scenario in which the NIC appears to not be functioning, the problem is usually that the NIC driver is incorrect. It is also possible that the NIC driver has been configured improperly—perhaps it is set to 100Mbps and is on a 10Mbps network. The Advanced tab for the NIC displays any of these settings that are available, as shown in Figure 9.4.

FIGURE 9.4   The Advanced Properties window for a NIC

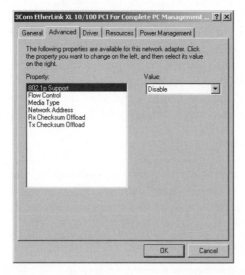

Corrupt Network Software   As always, the files could be bad. Before you try much else, reinstall the drivers for the NIC.

The biggest indicator in Windows that some component of the network software is nonfunctional is that you can't log on to the network or access any network service. You may not even see the Network Neighborhood on the Desktop. To fix this problem, you must first fix the underlying hardware problem (if one exists), and then properly install or configure the network software.

TSR (Terminate and Stay Resident) Programs

In the days of DOS, there was no easy way to run a utility program in the background while you ran an application. Because necessity is the mother of invention, programmers came up with Terminate and Stay Resident (TSR) programs. These programs are loaded from the AUTOEXEC.BAT file and stay resident in memory until called for by some key combination. Unfortunately, although that approach works for DOS, Windows 95 has its own method for using background utilities. If any DOS TSR programs are in memory when Windows 9x is running, they can interfere with the proper operation of Windows programs. Before you install Windows 9x, make sure that any DOS TSRs are disabled in the AUTOEXEC.BAT file. Whereas Windows 9x doesn't like TSRs, Windows NT/2000/XP will not run them at all. TSRs have been replaced in NT/2000/XP by services, which are far more stable and efficient.

Applications Won't Install

We've all experienced this frustration: You are trying to install the coolest new program and, for whatever reason, it just won't install properly. It may give you one of the previously mentioned errors or a cryptic installation error. If a software program won't install and it gives you an error such as a GPF or illegal operation error, use the solutions for those errors first. If the error that occurs during the install is unique to the application being installed, check the application manufacturer's website for an explanation or update. These errors generally occur when you're trying to install over an application that already exists or when you're trying to replace a file that already exists but that another application has in use.

When you're installing an application, it is extremely important that you quit all running programs before installing so that the installer can replace any files it needs to. Also, some programs are written specifically for Windows 98 or Windows NT and will not run on any other OS. Make sure that the hardware and OS on which you are installing the application are supported.

Network Connection

If the machine will not attach to the network, but you are certain that the NIC is functional and properly configured, it is very possible that the network resource you are attempting to find is having problems or that the network itself is down. In this case, you should contact the network administrator to see if there are problems. We'll cover other network-related configuration settings in domain 4.

Viruses and Virus Types

Most computer problems come in one of two sorts: accidents (hardware goes bad or software corrupts) or self-inflicted wounds (user deletes files or changes something). There is one other option, though. For reasons entirely their own, some people with strong computer knowledge use that knowledge to create programs called *viruses* that can damage your computer software—and potentially even your hardware.

What They Are

A computer *virus* is a program that replicates itself to other computers, usually causing the computers to behave abnormally. Generally speaking, a virus's main function is to reproduce. A virus attaches itself to files on a hard disk and modifies the files. When these files are accessed by a program, the virus can *infect* the program with its own code. The program may then, in turn, replicate the virus code to other files and other programs. In this manner, a virus can infect an entire computer.

There are two categories of viruses: benign and malicious. Benign viruses don't do much besides replicate themselves and exist. They may cause the occasional problem, but it is usually an unintentional side effect. Malicious viruses, on the other hand, are designed to destroy things.

Sources

Most viruses and other malicious problems are passed on through the opening and use of executable files, such as SETUP.EXE. Installing applications acquired from the Internet can also be dangerous to the health of a machine, and the growth of the Internet has made the problem of keeping viruses under wraps far more difficult than it previously was. Download and use only content direct from vendor sites or respected mirror sites, and try to get users to do the same.

In addition, one of the most common sources of viruses in recent years has been e-mail. Virus authors seem to especially enjoy writing viruses for Microsoft's Outlook software, often using Visual Basic scripts (VBS files) to do their dirty work.

When an infected file is transferred to another computer (via disk or modem download), the process begins on the other computer. Because of the ease and speed of virus transmission in the age of the Internet, viruses can run rampant if left unchecked. For this reason, antivirus programs are crucial for every computer user's system. They check files and programs for any program code that shouldn't be there and either eradicate it or prevent the virus from replicating. An antivirus program is generally run in the background on a computer and examines all the file activity on that computer. When it detects a suspicious activity, it notifies the user of a potential problem and asks what to do about it. Some antivirus programs can also make intelligent decisions about what to do. The process of installing an antivirus program on a computer is known as *inoculating* the computer against a virus.

How to Determine Their Presence

Wouldn't it be nice if Microsoft included an antivirus program with its operating systems? It did, but only with MS-DOS. MS-DOS comes with antivirus software that lets you detect viruses on your computer as well as clean any infected files. This software is called Microsoft Anti-Virus, and it has been included with DOS since version 6.0. The same program contains files to allow it to work with Windows.

Although Windows 9x/NT/2000/XP do not come with antivirus software, these programs are available from a number of third-party vendors. The better ones can scan for viruses in both files and e-mail and can be updated regularly from the Internet or through product updates. It is recommended that you update any virus software regularly—generally, monthly.

Know how to use install, use, and update antivirus programs, as well as how to check for viruses on a system you suspect is infected. Remember, though, that because these are third-party programs, you will not need to know specifics for the exam—just general concepts.

WARNING Because its job is to prevent programs from modifying your system's configuration or files, antivirus software can cause problems during application installations. You should generally disable any antivirus software while installing a new application—after scanning the install files for problems, of course!

Exam Essentials

Know how the printing process works and how to troubleshoot problems. Printing is well-represented on the exam, and you should be very familiar with how print spooling, print drivers, and printer ports work.

Know how to solve configuration and corruption errors within Windows. For the test, this means being familiar with the common error messages and knowing which class of error they represent. There is only so much troubleshooting you can do in a test question, so the problems and answers are generally straightforward.

Understand viruses and virus protection. Know how to spot the signs of a virus and how to scan a system for viruses. Also know how to install antivirus software.

Review Questions

1. If you accidentally left a nonbootable floppy disk in a PC and then rebooted it, which error message would you be likely to see?

2. How can a Windows 98 startup floppy be used to help fix system problems?

3. Which of these is a common problem involving Event Viewer?

   A. Running it creates a General Protection Fault.

   B. The Event Log becomes full.

   C. It interferes with system performance.

   D. Circular logging prevents old events from being deleted.

4. What is a VxD?

5. Which of these is *not* a required file for a bootable floppy?

   A. CONFIG.SYS

   B. IO.SYS

   C. MSDOS.SYS

   D. COMMAND.COM

6. Which of these steps through startup one step at a time, with user confirmation between each step?

   A. Safe Mode

   B. Safe Mode with Command Prompt

   C. Safe Mode with Networking

   D. None of the above

7. In Windows XP, to open Task Manager, you must press Ctrl+Alt+Delete and then do what?

8. WinMSD is the name of the executable file for which common Windows utility?

9. Which type of error occurs when a program accesses memory that another program is using?

10. In which ways can a system can be infected with a virus?

Answers to Review Questions

1. If the boot disk does not contain the needed startup files, as a nonbootable floppy would not, the *Invalid Boot Disk* error appears.

2. A Windows 9x startup floppy boots to a command prompt. From there, you choose which utilities to run to troubleshoot or repair.

3. B. The Event Log can fill up. Enabling circular logging allows Event Viewer to delete old events so that new ones can be added.

4. VxD files are virtual device drivers.

5. A. `CONFIG.SYS` is optional; the other three are required for booting.

6. D. Step-by-step confirmation is a separate mode from any of the Safe Modes.

7. Click the Task Manager button. In Windows 9x, however, you do not have to do anything.

8. System Information and WinMSD are the same thing.

9. A General Protection Fault (GPF) is usually the result of sloppy programming, and can result from a program accessing another program's memory space or accessing a memory address that does not exist.

10. Viruses can enter a system in a variety of ways, including via the opening of an e-mail attachment containing a virus, by booting a floppy disk infected with a virus, or through running a program infected with a virus.

Chapter

10

Domain 4 Networks

COMPTIA A+ EXAM OBJECTIVES COVERED IN THIS CHAPTER:

- ✓ 4.1 Identify the networking capabilities of Windows. Given configuration parameters, configure the operating system to connect to a network.

- ✓ 4.2 Identify the basic Internet protocols and terminologies. Identify procedures for establishing Internet connectivity. In a given scenario, configure the operating system to connect to and use Internet resources.

In preparing for a career as a computer technician, you may have already done a great deal of work putting together computers, troubleshooting hardware, and installing Windows and various software. If you are like most PC techs, the networking questions are probably the part of the A+ test you are most concerned about. Many companies draw a distinct line between PC techs and network techs—and for good reason. Both jobs require a high level of knowledge, and it is best to specialize to some extent.

In the modern computing environment, though, it is simply not possible for a tech to ignore networks. In troubleshooting and repairing computers, your concern with networking should focus on two very broad categories:

- Being able to troubleshoot a customer's connection to a LAN or dial-up connection

- Being able to effectively use your local network or the Internet to gain access to needed software and information

The first of these requires that you know how to install and configure networking components and how to set up any shared resources that a particular computer needs to share with the network. The second looks at how you can use that connection to access a shared drive or information on the Internet.

Over the course of this chapter, we will examine the most critical aspects of networking—more specifically, of Microsoft networking, which is what the test covers. This information is relatively straightforward, and the A+ networking domain breaks it down into two simple parts: how to get a machine on the network (objective 4.1) and how to set up and use an Internet connection (objective 4.2).

4.1 Configuring the Networking Capabilities of Windows

Networking is a mixture of hardware and software. The Core Hardware exam tests your knowledge of the hardware part, and objective 4.1 in the OS Technologies exam tests your knowledge of the software part.

Critical Information

For this objective, you need to know how to configure network client options in Windows, how to select and install the needed protocols, how to use basic command-line networking utilities, and how to share resources.

Network Components

In order for a PC to communicate with another PC, the most basic criterion is that some sort of network-capable hardware be installed. This can be one of any of a number of things—modem, network interface card (NIC), infrared port, and so on. The key point is that the OS itself can't do anything without help from the hardware.

Once you have a network connection device, that device needs to be configured for use by the OS. This requires the introduction of three software elements—adapter, client, and protocol—and allows for an optional fourth—service. Let's take a brief look at each:

 The terms *adapter* and *client* also have hardware meanings. *Adapter* is a synonym for a circuit board in some cases, for example, and *client* is a synonym for an entire computer that participates in a network. In this objective, however, we are using the terms in a purely software sense, referring to specific drivers in Windows that help networking occur.

Adapter   The *adapter* is the device driver for your network interface card or other networking device. Windows may automatically detect popular NICs and install the needed adapter files, or you may need to run the Setup utility that came with the NIC to install the adapter.

Client   The *client* is software that allows your machine to talk to servers on the network. Each server vendor uses a different way of designing its network access, though; so if a computer needs to get to both a Novell and a Microsoft network, the computer must have two pieces of client software installed, one for each type of server. The two most popular clients (and the two that come with most versions of Windows) are Client for Microsoft Networks and Client for Netware Networks.

Protocol   Once the client service and the adapter are installed, you have cleared a path for communication from your machine to the network servers. The *protocol* is the computer language you use to facilitate communication between the machines. If you want to talk to someone, you have to speak a common language. Computers are no different. The most popular protocol in use today—and the only one used on the Internet—is TCP/IP. Other protocols that you may occasionally encounter include IPX/SPX-compatible (for Netware networks) and NetBEUI (for small networks that do not include routers).

Service   A *service* is an optional component that gives a bit back to the network that gives it so much. Services add functionality to the network by providing resources or doing tasks for other computers. The most common service is File and Printer Sharing for Microsoft Networks.

Choosing a Network Type and Client

When you connect a computer to a network, you must decide on the networking technology—that is, which brand of client software you will use. The two main choices are Microsoft and Novell.

If you are setting up a client/server network (discussed in Chapter 6), the client software you install on the individual client PCs depends on your choice of server software. If the server is running Novell Netware, for example, you'll install Client for Netware Networks in Windows. If the server is running Microsoft Windows Server, you'll install Client for Microsoft Networks.

If you are setting up a peer-to-peer network, you'll install the Client for Microsoft Networks on all the client PCs, because it is built into Windows and requires no additional third-party software.

The Client for Microsoft Networks installs by default when you first install an adapter.

The Client for Microsoft Networks is probably already installed. To check, open the Properties dialog box for networking in Windows 9x, or for an individual adapter in Windows 2000/XP, and look for a client on the list that appears.

If you need to add a client in Windows 9x, follow these steps:

1. Open the Network Properties box and click Add on the Configuration tab.
2. Click Client, and then click Add.
3. Select the manufacturer name (Microsoft) and then choose the client from the list.
4. Click OK.

In Windows 2000/XP, Client for Microsoft Networks is always automatically installed. To add Client Service for Netware, do the following:

1. From Control Panel, open Network Connections in Windows XP, or Network and Dial-up Connections in Windows 2000.
2. Right-click the adapter and click Properties.
3. Click Install, click Client, and then click Add.
4. Choose Client Services For NetWare, and then click OK.

Once you have installed a client, a login screen for that network type appears each time you start the machine. This screen allows you to enter a network username and password that give you access to resources on that type of server.

Choosing a Protocol

In order for two people to communicate, they must speak the same language, and the same is true with computers. There are several protocols you should be familiar with: IPX/SPX (NWLink), NetBEUI, AppleTalk, and TCP/IP. TCP/IP is the most common, and also the most complex in terms of what you need to know for the exam, so we will save it for last.

Protocols are installed basically the same way as clients (as described in the preceding section). View the network properties in Windows 9x or the properties for a specific network connection in Windows NT/2000/XP; then click Add, select Protocols, and browse for the one you want.

NWLINK/IPX/SPX

The Internetwork Packet eXchange/Sequenced Packet eXchange (IPX/SPX) protocol was adopted by Novell as the primary protocol for the NetWare server family. In order to connect Microsoft machines to older NetWare servers, the client had to use the IPX/SPX protocol— or its Microsoft equivalent, NWLink.

Now that NetWare is also going to a TCP/IP-based architecture, NWLink is quickly being made obsolete, but it is still installed by default whenever the Client for NetWare Networks or Client Service for NetWare is installed. If the NetWare server uses IP only, you need to add TCP/IP and remove the unneeded NWLink. If, on the other hand, the network runs on NWLink, setup is easy: Install the protocol through the network properties, and then set the network number to whatever value the network administrator specifies.

About the only configuration problems possible with NWLink are an incorrect network number or the wrong frame type. The network number is a way of grouping machines logically on a network. Machines with different network numbers cannot see one another. The frame type is best thought of as a protocol dialect for NWLink. If two machines are running NWLink to communicate, they both must be using the same frame type.

NETBEUI

The NetBEUI protocol is insufficient on so many levels that discussing its faults is too big a job for this chapter. It is an extremely fast protocol for allowing a few computers on a single network to communicate, but due to the fact that it is not routable, it doesn't scale well, which doomed it as networks grew and started to interconnect.

The death knell of NetBEUI wasn't a problem, because TCP/IP and other protocols were ready to take over. The one thing that has continued to cause confusion and trouble, though, is that NetBEUI was tied to another Microsoft protocol called NetBIOS, which has been far more difficult to replace.

NetBEUI and NetBIOS are obviously similar-looking terms, and unfortunately, a certain amount of confusion surrounds them. Briefly, *NetBEUI* is a transport protocol. It is responsible for the way data is transmitted between two computers. It is not routable and is rarely used in modern computing. *NetBIOS* is a name-resolution system. It allows a computer to search for another computer on the network by its Microsoft computer name. It must be operational on every Microsoft-based network up to Windows 2000, or Microsoft OS-based machines cannot be able to communicate properly. The NetBIOS naming process can work with NWLink or TCP/IP, so NetBEUI is not required for it to function. You will hear more about how NetBIOS works in the next section.

APPLETALK

This protocol is used for Apple Macintosh networks. When a PC participates as a client in such a network, the AppleTalk protocol must be installed in Windows. It does not come with Windows; you get it from Apple. It installs like any other protocol.

TCP/IP

Developed in the late 1960s by the Department of Defense, and originally known as the DOD protocol, TCP/IP stands for Transmission Control Protocol/Internet Protocol. TCP and IP are actually just two of the many different protocols that make up the TCP/IP protocol suite.

This protocol is the standard communication language for the Internet and for Microsoft's Windows Active Directory. Unix and Macintosh can use TCP/IP, as can NetWare and all Windows OSs. In most environments, this is the only protocol you need.

Understanding TCP/IP Addressing

An IP address consists of four numbers from 1 to 254, strung together by periods like this: 192.168.3.7. These numbers must be within this range because each is an 8-digit binary number, and binary 11111111 equals 255. The top number (255) is reserved, so that leaves a range of 1 to 254. Each computer's IP address must be unique on the network.

Within an IP address are two separate addresses: the *network address* and the *host address*. The network address is the first part; it is like an area code. It's the unique identifier of the network segment on which the PC resides. The host address is the unique identifier of the PC within that segment.

Unlike with area codes, however, the divider line between the network and host addresses is fluid. The exact dividing point depends on the *subnet mask*. A subnet mask of 255.255.0.0, for example, indicates that the dividing point is after the first two numbers. A subnet mask of 255.255.255.0 indicates that the dividing point is after the third number.

A particular network segment passes local traffic freely among all the connected nodes it includes, but for traffic to go to a different segment, it has to pass through a specific out port called a *gateway*. The gateway has its own IP address. Sometimes when you're configuring a network IP address you will be asked to enter a default gateway. Your network administrator should provide this address.

Assigning and Resolving IP Addresses

There are two ways to manage TCP/IP. The manual way involves going to each machine and entering an IP address. This is called *static addressing*.

Another possibility is to use the Dynamic Host Configuration Protocol (DHCP). If your network is using DHCP, all you have to do is install TCP/IP and reboot. A special server called a *DHCP server* will then provide your machine with all the values it needs when it starts up again. The DHCP server gives leases to the IP addresses that the server manages and the clients must periodically renew their leases.

Finally, if your network does not contain a DHCP server, Windows will automatically assign an IP address to each PC within a specified reserved range beginning with 169.254. This is called Automatic Private IP Addressing (APIPA).

IP addresses are not the only way of referring to a network address, however. Another way is to use domain names, which is how the Internet does it. A domain name consists of text, so it's easier to remember than an IP address. For example, `Microsoft.com` is a domain name. Special servers called Domain Name System (DNS) servers handle the translation between IP addresses and domain names. See objective 4.2 later in this chapter for more information.

TCP/IP Utilities

Several utilities in Windows can help you determine a PC's TCP/IP status and IP address. They are summarized in Table 10.1. You can run them with the Run command or at a command prompt.

TABLE 10.1   TCP/IP Utilities

Utility	Function
WINIPCFG	A graphical utility in Windows 9x that allows you to get information about your IP configuration. Also allows you to release a DHCP lease and request a new one. See Figure 10.1.
IPCONFIG	Does the same thing as WINIPCFG but for Windows NT/2000/XP. A command-line utility rather than a graphical utility.
PING	Allows you to test connectivity with another host by typing **ping** and the name or IP address of the machine you are trying to communicate with—for instance, **ping www.sybex.com** or **ping 192.168.1.250**.
TRACERT	Trace route utility that lets you watch the path information takes while getting from your machine to another one. Whereas PING just tells you if the path is possible, TRACERT shows you the path.
NSLOOKUP	Looks up the IP addresses of domain names, and also reports the local PC's IP address.

Using these utilities is pretty straightforward. You should work with each of them—and know what their options are—before you take the test. Remember that both WINIPCFG (shown in Figure 10.1) and IPCONFIG are essentially read-only utilities. Their only configuration option is to allow you to release or renew DHCP leases (if you are using DHCP). PING and TRACERT are troubleshooting tools.

FIGURE 10.1   The Windows IP Configuration utility

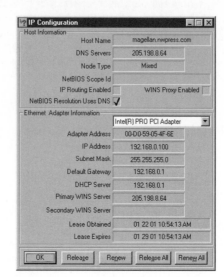

Sharing Resources

You can set up Windows 9x/NT/2000/XP to share files and printers with other users on the network. This sort of networking, in which users share each other's resources, is an example of the peer-to-peer network type discussed earlier, where each computer acts as both a client and a server.

In order to share, the machine must already have a working client configuration. This is a must, because file and printer sharing is possible only if the proper adapter, client, and protocol are already set up. Once they are in place, you need to enable file and printer sharing and then specify which resources you wish to share.

Simply enabling file and printer sharing does not make any folders or printers available on the network. You must specifically share any directory or printer that you want to make available on the network. We will look at the issues with both of these steps.

Setting Up Sharing

The first step in sharing resources is installing the File and Printer Sharing service in Windows if it is not already installed. On Windows 9x, you do this by clicking the File And Print Sharing button on the Network Properties tab. You can choose to enable either file or printer sharing (or both). In Windows 2000/XP, sharing is enabled by default when networking is installed, and this is reflected by the presence of File And Printer Sharing For Microsoft Networks in the Local Area Connection Properties page.

Besides enabling sharing, Windows 2000/XP also creates a number of default shares: printers, scheduled tasks, and a hidden administrative-only share of the root of each drive. Hidden drives in NT-based Windows versions are designated by a $ at the end of the share name. Therefore, the admin share of the C: drive would be C$ and of D: would be D$.

Sharing Folders

Any folder can be shared (including the root of the C: drive). When you share a folder, the person you share it with can see not only the folder you've shared but also any folders inside that folder. Therefore, you should be certain that all subfolders under a share are intended to be shared as well. If they are not, move them out of the share path.

Once you have decided what to share, right-click the folder that is the start of the share and choose Sharing from the menu that pops up. This option brings up the Properties window of that folder with the Sharing tab in front. You can also access the Sharing tab (Figure 10.2) by right-clicking a folder, choosing Properties, and clicking the tab.

FIGURE 10.2   The Sharing tab of the Properties window

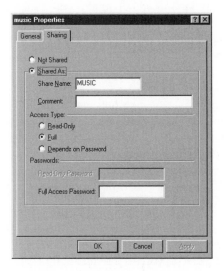

To enable the share, click the Shared As radio button. Two previously grayed-out fields become visible. The first field is Share Name. The name you enter here will be used to access this folder; it should be something that accurately represents what you are sharing. The second field allows you to enter a description of the share as a comment that helps identify the contents of the share to users. The share name is required, and the comment is optional.

Remember that if the share name is more than eight characters long, many older OSs, such as DOS, will not be able to access it properly. That and other file-naming/file-recognition issues between Windows' long filenames and DOS could easily come up in a test question.

WINDOWS 9X SHARE SECURITY

Finally, you can specify the access rights and password(s) for the share. Two different security schemes are available: Share Level and User Level. Share Level security is the default selection.

There are three options for Windows 9x access rights when you're using the share-level security scheme. Click the radio button next to the option you want to use:

Read-Only   Anyone accessing the share can only open and read the files inside the folder and any subfolders. You must specify a password that users can use to access the share in read-only mode.

Full   Everyone accessing the share has the ability to do anything to the files in the folder as well as any subfolders, including delete those files. You must specify a password that the users can use to access this share.

Depends On Password   Probably the best option of the three. Users can use one password to access the share in read-only mode and a different password to access it in full-access mode. You can give everyone the read-only password so that they can view the files, and give the full-access password only to users who need to modify the files. Note, though, that this option uses only one password for each security level and does not require a username.

By default, a new share is a full-control share. This means anyone on the network can come in and view, modify, or even delete the files in the share. Often this arrangement is a bit too dangerous, so you should probably use a Read Only or Depends On Password security setting.

The second security scheme option, User Level, requires that you have another machine available to provide a user/password database for the Windows 9x machine to draw from. Because 9x does not have a user database, it cannot authenticate users on its own, but it can be configured to authenticate through a Windows NT Workstation, Windows 2000 Professional, or NT/2000/NetWare server.

If you choose user-level security, you need to manually select the users or groups of users whom you want to have access to the folder and then also set the level of access you want them to have.

WINDOWS 2000/XP SECURITY

In Windows 2000/XP, sharing is enabled the same way as in Windows 9x. Shares can also be created in much the same way (right-click the folder that is the start of the share and choose Sharing from the menu that pops up).

> Don't confuse sharing options (on the Sharing tab) with the NTFS Security options (on the Security tab). NTFS permissions affect local sharing as well as network sharing and are present only on drives that use NTFS.

Depending on the filesystem you are using, your sharing options may include the following:

Share Level   NT/2000/XP can also use share-level security, but its definition of *share level*, oddly, is far closer to Windows 9x's user-level security. With share-level security, Windows NT/2000/XP sets user/password security at the level of the shared folder, exactly as Windows 9x does. All files and folders under the share have the same access permissions through the share. Drives formatted with FAT or FAT32 can use only this level. This is handled on the Sharing tab for the folder's properties.

File Level   If the NT/2000/XP drive is formatted with NTFS, you have the option of setting files directly on the folder or specific files, rather than setting them on the share. This may seem like a small distinction, but it is actually a tremendous difference. Using file-level security, you can ensure that files always have the same level of access for a particular user, regardless of which share they come through. File-level security even protects files if the user logs on to the machine itself, something share-level protection cannot do. This is handled on the Security tab of the folder's properties.

> There is no equivalent of Windows 9x's share-level security in Windows NT/2000.

Accessing a Shared Resource

You also need to know how to get to files shared on other machines. To access shared folders and printers, we'll turn to the Network Neighborhood (or My Network Places) icon. When you double-click this icon, you can browse the network for resources.

You can double-click any computer to see the resources it hosts. Once you have found the share you require, using a shared folder is just like using any other folder on your computer, with one or two exceptions: First, the folder exists on the network, so you have to be connected to the network to use it. Also, for some programs to work properly, you must map a local drive letter to the network folder.

UNC PATHS AND DRIVE MAPPING

This brings up a distinction you should be familiar with. Windows (and other systems) uses a standardized method called the *Universal Naming Convention* (*UNC*) to reference resources on the network. A UNC path provides an easy and exact reference format. UNC paths come in the form `\\`*machinename*`\`*share*`\`*path*`\`, so a directory called `JAN2000` under a share called `Reports` on a machine called `MYPC` would be expressed as `\\MYPC\Reports\JAN2000`. Typing this at a Run prompt will take you directly to that directory (if you have permission to access it).

Although using UNC paths works well in most cases, there is another option for using network shares—drive mapping. Mapping a drive involves associating a UNC path to an alphabetical shortcut. Doing so makes it simpler and faster to access a resource regularly. For instance, by mapping \Myserver\Reports to R:, a user can access the JAN2000 directory by typing **R:\JAN2000**, rather than having to use the entire path. In addition, mapped drives are listed in the Explorer, meaning the user does not have to remember the path to access them. One important distinction is that the drive letter *cannot* be mapped directly to the \Myserver\Reports\JAN2000 directory. Drive mappings go only to the share level, and any further levels must be appended onto the drive letter. To map a drive, you reach the share by browsing to it, and then right-click the share to get to the Map Network Drive option. You must then pick a drive letter (one that is not being used) and click OK to map the drive.

Drive mappings are often done through login (or logon) scripts if the machine is on a network, using the command-line NET utility. These scripts allow the network administrator to set up network resources for users, making them even more convenient to use. To map a drive, you need to type **NET USE R: \Myserver\Reports**. As mentioned earlier, some programs work only if they are able to access files using a drive letter. Older DOS programs, for instance, are notorious for this. Most newer programs can use either option without problems.

Now that you can see all the resources the computer is hosting, you can map a drive letter to a resource by right-clicking the folder (REPORTS in this case) and choosing Map Network Drive. Doing so causes the screen shown in Figure 10.3 to appear. Remember that most Windows applications can use UNC paths and don't need drive mappings, but even some newer applications still require a drive letter.

FIGURE 10.3   The Map Network Drive dialog box

Sharing Print Services

Sharing printers is similar to sharing folders. First, you must have the printer correctly set up to print on the machine that will be the print server. Second, print sharing must be enabled in My Network Places.

Once you've done this, follow these steps:

1. Right-click a printer in the Printers folder and click Sharing. The Printer Properties page appears with the Sharing tab selected to allow you to share the printer.

2. Click Shared As and specify a name for the share. The name defaults to a truncated version of the name you gave the printer when you installed it. The name you give this share (called the *share name*) should be something that everyone will recognize when they see it on the network and that accurately describes the printer. Good names are things like "Classroom printer" and "3rd floor conference room printer." Note that you can use long names and spaces, as long as DOS or older 16-bit Windows applications do not need the printer.

WARNING   If older applications will be printing, you need to use a share name of eight or fewer characters, with no spaces.

3. In addition to specifying the name of the printer share, you can also enter a comment that describes the printer accurately.

4. To finish sharing the printer, click OK. If there is a password needed for the printer, Windows prompts you for the password. Type it in the box that appears and click OK, and the share will be active.

The Printers folder now has a hand under it, indicating that it is shared.

Exam Essentials

Know how to install and configure network components.   This includes Windows 9x/2000/XP, as well as Windows NT 4.0. Also, know the available components for each OS and how they work together.

Understand how to share resources on Windows 9x/NT/2000/XP.   You should be familiar with how the share-level and user-lever security schemes work on 9x and how share and file permissions interact on Windows NT/2000.

Be able to access network resources using a Windows client.   Be able to get to network resources using Network Neighborhood (My Network Places in 2000/XP), or the NET command.

4.2 Understanding Basic Internet Protocols, Terminology, and Configuration

While many of the other content areas branch out widely in their coverage, domain 4.2 is extremely focused. This is, to be quite frank, an Internet-only zone. This objective tests your knowledge of Internet protocols and terminologies, connectivity technologies, and installing and configuring web browsers (mostly Internet Explorer).

Critical Information

In this section we will look at the following concepts:

- Internet concepts and terminology
- Ways to connect to the Internet
- Installing and using Internet applications

Internet Concepts and Terminology

There are some common terms and concepts every technician must understand about the Internet. First, the Internet is really just a bunch of private networks connected together using public telephone lines. These private networks are the access points to the Internet and are run by companies called *Internet Service Providers (ISPs)*. They will sell you a connection to the Internet for a monthly service charge (like your cable bill or phone bill). Your computer talks to the ISP using public phone lines, or even using broadband technologies such as cable or wireless.

There probably won't be any "What is an ISP?" questions on the test, because most of the exam centers on practical knowledge rather than vocabulary. Even so, you should be familiar with the following.

Web Browsers

A *browser* is software that allows you to view web pages from the Internet. The two browsers with the largest market share are Netscape Navigator and Microsoft Internet Explorer (IE), shown in Figure 10.4. Both work equally well for browsing the Internet. Microsoft includes its browser, IE, with all versions of Windows except the original Windows 95, whereas Netscape Navigator, which is free, must be downloaded separately.

FIGURE 10.4   The Internet Explorer browser

Because Internet Explorer is installed by default (and is, according to Microsoft, "integral" to the OS), you don't need to worry about installing/uninstalling it. However, if you are looking for a newer version of IE, you can go to Microsoft's website, `www.microsoft.com/windows/ie`. Netscape Navigator is not installed by default, so to obtain—or upgrade—it, you should go to `www.netscape.com`. Once you are there, select the version you want and specify the type of machine you will be using it on. You can then download and install the software, just like any other application.

Web pages are typically written in a programming language called Hypertext Markup Language (HTML). An HTML document is a plain-text document containing embedded tags. A *tag* is a code enclosed in angle brackets, like this: <p>. Although a web page may contain complex programming such as Java applets, the core of most pages is an HTML document, in which those other codes are embedded.

The protocols involved in web browsing include the following:

HTTP   Hypertext Transfer Protocol, the main protocol for the Web. Does not provide security.

HTTPS   Secure HTTP, a method of securing the transfer of web data by encrypting it.

SSL   Secure Socket Layers, a method of securing the transfer of web data by using a different, secure socket (port number) than regular HTTP.

FTP

The File Transfer Protocol (FTP) is available to you either through the command-line FTP client, a third-party graphical FTP client, or through your browser. Most people are so accustomed to using FTP through a browser or a utility such as CuteFTP or WS_FTP that they forget command-prompt FTP access is available. For example, to access the Microsoft FTP site through the command prompt, open a prompt and type **FTP ftp.microsoft.com**. The site will respond with a request for your e-mail address, and you will then be given access. You can use standard DOS navigation commands to move between directories, and you can retrieve or send files using the GET *<filename>* or PUT *<filename>* command. When you are finished with your session, type **QUIT**.

Internet Explorer also supports FTP. To go to Microsoft's website, you can type in **http://www.microsoft.com**, and you will be taken to a web page. If you change the first part of the name to `ftp://`, though, the system knows to look for an FTP resource instead. Typing **ftp://ftp.microsoft.com** will also take you to the Microsoft website, and you can then use all the standard Explorer GUI file-management techniques, just as you would if you were connecting to any other network drive.

Because Microsoft's FTP site is a public site, it allows you to use a special anonymous account that provides access. If you go to a site where that account has been disabled, you will need to provide another username and password, which should be provided by the site's administrator, or you will not be allowed into the site. In addition, most FTP sites allow visitors only to download data, so PUT commands generally will be rejected unless you have a real (nonanonymous) account on the server.

E-mail

Another common use of the Internet is to send and receive electronic mail. E-mail allows you to quickly and inexpensively transfer messages to other people. To send and receive e-mail, you need to have only two things: an e-mail account and an e-mail client. A company can provide the account, or it can be associated with your ISP account. Either way, you have an address that looks like *username@domain.com.*

The last part of this address (after the @) identifies the domain name of the company or ISP that provides your e-mail account. The part before the @ is your username. A username must be unique on each domain. Two Bill the Bard users on a single network, for instance, might be billthebard@domain.com and billthebard1@domain.com.

Among the protocols associated with e-mail are *Post Office Protocol (POP)* and *Simple Mail Transport Protocol (SMTP)*, which are types of e-mail servers. A POP server is a machine on the Internet that accepts and stores Internet e-mail and allows you to retrieve that mail when you are online. An SMTP server accepts mail you want to send and forwards it to the proper user. In order to send and receive mail, you need both.

An alternative to POP is *Internet Mail Application Protocol (IMAP)*, which works better for situations where the user is accessing e-mail from various locations via a web interface.

 Once you have the settings configured, you need to install an e-mail client or use the built-in client included with Windows 98 and higher. That client is called Outlook Express, and it's a good, basic e-mail application.

Telnet

Telnet is a rather old technology; it is used to simulate a point-to-point terminal connection between computers, much like the old-style Bulletin Board System (BBS) type. Telnet can be done through a web browser by preceding the URL with `telnet://` rather than the usual `http://`, or at a command prompt with the `Telnet` command.

Types of Internet Connections

Until recently, most people connected to the Internet via slow dial-up modem connections. However, that is changing rapidly now that faster, broadband technologies are becoming widely available. For the exam, you should be able to name the major Internet connection methods, differentiate among them, and offer a professional opinion as to the correct technology to use in a given situation.

Dial-Up Networking (Modem and ISDN)

Dial-up connections such as connections via modem require you to use dial-up networking (DUN) to establish the connection. DUN is built into Windows.

DUN coordinates between the modem and the software to create a connection through Point-to-Point Protocol (PPP) or an earlier variant called Serial Line Internet Protocol (SLIP). A modem sends and receives data at up to 56Kbps over ordinary telephone lines.

 Ordinary telephone lines are sometimes called POTS (Plain Old Telephone Service).

Although modems are the most common DUN device, an ISDN terminal adapter may also be used for a DUN connection. Integrated Services Digital Network (ISDN) is a special type of all-digital phone line that allows two data lines to operate simultaneously, plus a voice line, so you can connect to the Internet at up to 112Kbps while talking on the telephone at the same time. ISDN lines are rather expensive, and the speed gain is modest, so ISDN is not very popular.

Digital Services Line (DSL)

DSL uses regular telephone lines, but it takes advantage of unused portions of the line to send digital data at high speeds. It is an always-on connection that does not require dial-up, and it can achieve speeds of 1Mbps or more.

There are two varieties: Asynchronous (ADSL) and Synchronous (SDSL). Asynchronous carries uploads slower than downloads; SDSL is the same speed in both directions. ADSL is cheaper and more common in residential installations. The main drawback to DSL is that it is not available in all areas.

Cable

Cable Internet uses the cable TV line (digital cable areas only) to send and receive Internet data. Unlike the other technologies discussed so far in this section, cable Internet has nothing to do with the telephone line or phone company. Its speed is roughly equivalent to that of DSL (around 1Mbps). Cable is an always-on connection that does not require dial-up.

Satellite

Satellite Internet provides broadband access in areas that are not served by cable or DSL providers. Although it's more expensive and slower than either of those options (generally around 500Kbps), it may be some users' only choice.

There are two types of satellite: one way and two way. One-way satellite uses the satellite for downloading but uses a regular modem for uploading. It is a dial-up connection. Two-way satellite uses the satellite for both, and does not require a telephone line. It is an always-on connection.

Wireless

Wireless Internet service uses the same system that wireless telephone service uses. This type of Internet service is used with most Internet-enabled PDAs. Its primary advantage is its mobility; you aren't tied to a specific location but can move around freely anywhere within the service area. The disadvantages are that it can be slower and more expensive than other broadband services.

LAN

Large companies typically get a full-time broadband T1 or T3 line that connects to the Internet, and then share that connection with all employees via the company's LAN. The computer sees this as a network connection to the Internet—and indeed, that's what it is. The speed is usually very good—1Mbps or more—and the cost per user is low in a large organization, and gets lower the more users you have.

Installing and Configuring Browsers

By *browsers*, this objective is really referring to Internet Explorer. Test-takers need to know how to change certain options in IE. The topics in the objective are by no means a complete list of settings a good technician should know how to change, but we'll stick to the published ones in the following discussion.

Configuring Security Options

Web browsing is a compromise between staying safe from malicious scripts and applets and being able to fully enjoy the content. Different users have different ideas of the perfect balance.

For example, some web pages contain scripts, such as JavaScript, that perform functions HTML alone can't handle. The trouble is, sometimes such scripts and applets contain viruses. For maximum security, some users prefer to disable their support. To do so, follow these steps:

1. Choose Tools ➢ Internet Options and click the Security tab.
2. Click the Custom button. The Security Settings dialog box opens.
3. Click Enable or Disable for the various types of scripts and applets. For example, to change the script options, scroll down to the Scripting section.
4. When you're finished, click OK.

Configuring Proxy Settings

A proxy server sits between a user and the Internet at large. It caches frequently used pages for faster access to them, provides some security from hackers, and has other benefits as well. Some ISPs require users to use a proxy server, or at least highly recommend it.

To turn on/off proxy server usage:

1. Choose Tools ➢ Internet Options and click the Connections tab.
2. Click the LAN Settings button.
3. Mark or clear the Use A Proxy Server For Your LAN check box.
4. Click OK.

Firewall Protection under Windows XP

Windows XP has built-in firewall capability. To enable or disable it, do the following:

1. Choose Start ➢ Connect To ➢ Show All Connections.
2. Right-click the icon for the Internet connection and choose Properties.
3. Mark or clear the check box under Internet Connection Firewall.
4. Click OK.

Exam Essentials

Understand the functions for which the Internet is commonly used, and know about the software used in those functions.   Be able to configure and use e-mail, FTP, and HTTP. This includes knowing about available software and how to install and set options on that software.

Understand how to install and use Windows' dial-up networking.   Be able to install dial-up networking and configure a connection to an ISP.

Know the features and advantages of Internet connection methods.   Make sure you understand and can differentiate among cable, DSL, ISDN, dial-up, wireless, and satellite.

Be able to change Internet Explorer settings.   Be familiar with security, privacy, and proxy server settings.

Review Questions

1. What is the driver called that makes Windows see the network interface card?

2. What driver runs the Windows connection to a specific type of network, such as Microsoft or Netware?

3. TCP/IP and NetBEUI are examples of what type of protocol?

4. Which protocol is the dominant protocol on the Internet?

5. Why is the NetBEUI protocol unsuitable for large networks?

6. What type of server dynamically assigns IP addresses on a network to PCs that request them?

7. What type of server translates between domain names and IP addresses?

8. What utility shows you the complete path from one network location to another, including all the routing hops?

9. Which Internet protocol is used for sending e-mail?

10. Which of these is a dial-up Internet connection method?

    A. ISDN

    B. ADSL

    C. Cable

    D. Two-way satellite

Answers to Review Questions

1. The adapter is the NIC, and the driver that runs it is also called the adapter.

2. The driver that runs the Windows connection to a network is called the client. Examples include Client for Microsoft Networks and Client for Netware Networks.

3. Both of these are communications protocols.

4. The Internet runs primarily on TCP/IP.

5. NetBEUI is a nonroutable protocol and therefore is not scalable for larger networks.

6. A DHCP server provides IP addressing services.

7. A DNS server converts domain names to IP addresses that have been assigned to them.

8. TRACERT is short for trace route, which is an apt description of what it does.

9. SMTP is the protocol used for an outgoing e-mail server.

10. A. ISDN, although digital, is a dial-up connection. The others are all always-on.

Glossary

Note: each glossary definition is followed by the CompTIA objective number where the term was explained. An *H* indicates the term came from the Hardware chapters, and an *OS* indicates it was discussed in the Operating System chapters.

Accelerated Graphics Port (AGP) A bus developed to meet the need for increased graphics performance. (H 4.3)

active terminator A terminator that uses a voltage regulator to perform the termination, resulting in superior termination. (H 1.7)

adapter A term used to describe both the NIC itself and the software that is used to communicate with it. (OS 4.1)

address bus The bus that connects the RAM to the CPU. (H 4.3)

ADSL (Asynchronous DSL) A type of DSL wherein the maximum upload and download speeds are different. (H 6.3)

antistatic wrist strap Also called an ESD strap. A specially designed device used to bleed electrical charges away safely. It uses a 1-megaohm resistor to bleed the charge away slowly. Attaching this device to a grounding mat protects the computer system's components from accidental damage. A wire wrapped around your wrist will not work correctly and could electrocute you! There is only one situation in which you should not wear an ESD strap: If you wear one while working on the inside of a monitor, you increase your chances of getting a lethal shock. (H 1.2, 3.2)

API (Application Programming Interface) A set of standards to help the programmers writing applications and the hardware designers of video cards and other hardware develop products that work together. (H 1.10)

application Software that is added to an operating system to give it enhanced functionality, such as a word processor or a game. (OS 2.4)

AT commands The commands sent to the modem by the communications program to initialize it. These commands tell it such things as how many rings to wait before answering, how long to wait after the last keystroke was detected before disconnecting, and at what speed to communicate. Each AT command does something different. The letters AT by themselves ask the modem if it's ready to receive commands. (H 2.1)

ATAPI (ATA Packet Interface) An interface that allows other non–hard-disk devices (such as tape drives and CD-ROMs) to be attached to an ATA interface and coexist with hard disks. (H 1.6)

attribute An option set on a file that identifies it as part of a particular class of files or changes it in some way. (OS 1.4)

batch file A file used to run a series of commands. (OS 2.3)

beep code A series of beeps from the PC speaker that indicate the nature of a problem that is preventing the PC from booting normally. (H 2.1)

BIOS chip A special memory chip that contains the BIOS software that tells the processor how to interact with the hardware in the computer. (H 1.1)

BNC (Bayonet Neil Connector, or British Naval Connector)   A connector type used on coaxial cables, as with cable TV or 10Base2 networking. (H 6.1)

boot disk   A disk used to troubleshoot or install an operating system. (OS 2.1)

boot files   Files used to start a computer and prepare it for use by the operating system. (OS 2.3)

browser   Software used to access the World Wide Web, the Internet's graphical interface. (OS 4.2)

bus   A set of signal pathways that allows information and signals to travel between components inside or outside of a computer. There are three types of buses inside a computer: the external bus, the address bus, and the data bus. (H 4.3)

cache memory   A storage area for frequently used data and instructions. (H 1.1)

capacitor   An electronic component that stores an electrical charge. (H 3.2)

circular logging   A log file option that deletes old information as the Event Viewer log file reaches its capacity, thereby preventing the log from becoming filled. (OS 3.1)

client   Software that allows a machine to communicate with a particular type of network. (OS 4.1)

CMD   The utility that opens a command prompt window under NT versions of Windows. (OS 1.3)

CMOS battery   A battery that provides power to the portion of the BIOS that stores CMOS settings. A PC must retain certain settings when it's turned off and its power cord is unplugged. (H 1.1)

CMOS (Complementary Metallic Oxide Semiconductor) chip   A chip used to retain system settings when the PC is turned off or unplugged. (H 4.4)

coaxial cable   A type of cable consisting of a metal core surrounded by insulation. Typically uses a BNC connector. (H 6.1)

COMMAND   The utility that opens a command-prompt window under 9x versions of Windows. (OS 1.3)

command interpreter   A program that supplies a command prompt that users can interact with. For example, COMMAND.COM serves this function under MS-DOS and Windows 9x. (OS 2.3)

command prompt   A command-line interface, such as in MS-DOS or in a command-prompt window opened through Windows. (OS 1.3)

COMMAND.COM   The command interpreter under MS-DOS and Windows 9x, necessary for command line input. (OS 1.2)

DC power supply (DCPS)   A power supply that converts house current into three voltages used by a printer: +5VDC and −5VDC for the logic circuitry and +24VDC for the paper-transport motors. This component also runs the fan that cools the printer's internal components. (H 5.1)

DDR SDRAM (Double Data Rate SDRAM)   A type of RAM that runs at twice the speed of the system bus. (H 4.2)

defragment   To rearrange the storage clusters on a disk so that as many files as possible are stored contiguously, thus improving performance. (OS 1.5, 2.5)

Degauss   To disrupt a magnetic field in a monitor that is making the picture distort. (H 2.1)

demineralized water   Water that has had minerals and contaminants removed to prevent damage to computer components. (H 3.1)

denatured isopropyl alcohol   The most common cleaning component found in any repair facility. You can use denatured alcohol to clean most components of a PC. It's commonly used to clean electrical connections. (H 3.1)

Device Manager   The utility used in Windows 95 and higher to report detailed information about the computer's devices and their resource usage. (H 1.4)

dial-up   An Internet or other network connection that requires connection, usually via telephone lines. (H 6.3)

direct memory access (DMA)   A method used by peripherals to place data in memory without utilizing CPU resources. (H 1.4)

Direct Rambus   A memory bus that transfers data at 800MHz over a 16-bit memory bus. Direct Rambus memory modules (often called RIMMs), like DDR SDRAM, can transfer data on both the rising and falling edges of a clock cycle, resulting in an ultra-high memory transfer rate (800MHz) and a high bandwidth of up to 1.6GBps. (H 4.2)

docking station   A box containing ports (and sometimes drive bays) that add capabilities to a notebook computer whenever it is connected (docked) to the box. These capabilities might include extra keyboard and mouse ports, USB ports, extra serial or parallel ports, a SCSI adapter, an extra IDE adapter, and so on. (H 1.3)

Dr. Watson   A program that intercepts errors and reports on them. (OS 3.1)

DRAM (Dynamic RAM)   A type of RAM that loses its data rapidly if it is not constantly electrically refreshed. (H 4.2)

driver   Software used to access a particular piece of hardware. (OS 2.1)

DSL (Digital Subscriber Line)   A technology that uses regular telephone lines to carry high-speed Internet. (H 6.3)

Dual Inline Memory Module (DIMM)   A double-sided RAM circuit board used in modern systems. DIMMs typically are 168-pin and 64-bit. (H 4.2)

ECP (Enhanced Communication Port)   A printer or parallel port setting that allows bidirectional communications and can be used with newer ink-jet and laser printers, scanners, and other peripheral devices. (H 4.4)

EDO (Extended Data Out)   An older type of DRAM that requires refreshing less frequently than regular FPM RAM, resulting in improved performance. (H 4.2)

EEPROM (Electrically Erasable Programmable Read-Only Memory)   The type of ROM chip that can be flash-updated with software. (H 1.10)

electrostatic discharge (ESD)   An exchange of electrons that happens when two objects of dissimilar charge come in contact with one another, thereby standardizing the electrostatic charge between them. This charge can, and often does, damage electronic components. (H 3.2)

EPP (Enhanced Parallel Port)   A printer or parallel port setting that allows bidirectional communications and tat can be used with newer ink-jet and laser printers. (H 4.4)

ERD (emergency repair disk)   A floppy containing data that can help the Windows NT/2000/XP Setup utility to repair a Windows installation more successfully. (OS 2.3)

expansion bus   A bus that connects I/O ports and expansion slots to the motherboard chipset. The expansion bus allows the computer to be expanded using a modular approach. When you need to add something to the computer, you plug specially made circuit boards into the expansion slots on the expansion bus. The devices on these circuit boards are then able to communicate with the CPU and are part of the computer. (H 4.3)

extended memory   RAM above the 1MB mark in a PC. (OS 1.1)

extension   A set of characters appended to a filename that define how the file should be handled by the operating system. (OS 1.4)

external command   A command that is an executable file, such as FORMAT or FDISK. (OS 1.3)

external data bus   The bus that carries data from the CPU to the chipset on the motherboard. (H 4.3)

external modem   A modem that is contained in a separate box connected to your computer by a cable. It does not require resource assignment because it uses the resources assigned to the port to which it connects. (H 1.8)

external speed   The speed at which the CPU communicates with the motherboard. (H 4.1)

fiber optic cable   A type of cable consisting of thin flexible glass fiber surrounded by a rubberized outer coating. Uses an ST or SC connector. (H 6.1)

filesystem   The organizational scheme that governs how files are stored and retrieved from a disk. Examples include FAT16, FAT32, NTFS 4.0, and NTFS 5.0. (OS 1.1, 1.4)

flash update   Special software provided by the motherboard manufacturer to replace or change the capabilities of the BIOS. (H 1.10)

form factor   The size and shape of a component. For example, AT and ATX are two form factors for motherboards. (H 4.3)

format   To prepare a disk for use in a specific operating system by creating the allocation units that will be used for storage. (OS 1.4)

formatter board   A circuit board that takes the information a printer receives from the computer and turns it into commands for the various components in the printer. (H 5.2)

FPM (Fast Page Mode RAM)   An older type of DRAM that measures its speed in nanoseconds of delay. Typical of SIMMs. (H 4.2)

FTP (File Transfer Protocol)   A protocol used to transfer data across the Internet. (OS 4.2)

ghosting   Light images of previously printed pages that you can see on the current page. (H 5.2)

GPF (General Protection Fault)   An error caused when a Windows program accesses memory that another program is using. (OS 3.3)

HCL (Hardware Compatibility List)   A list of all hardware that has been verified to work with a particular operating system. (OS 2.1)

High-Voltage Power Supply (HVPS)   A power supply that provides high-voltage, low-current power to both the charging and transfer corona assemblies in laser and page printers. (H 5.2)

HIMEM.SYS   The extended memory-management utility, required for Windows 9x. (OS 1.2)

hubs   Devices used to link several computers together. They repeat any signal that comes in on one port and copy it to the other ports (a process that is also called broadcasting). (H 6.2)

HVD (High-Voltage Differential)   An improved SCSI technology resulting in very high maximum distances but incompatible with SE and LVD systems. (H 1.7)

image smudging   A problem that occurs when toner is not properly fused to the paper. You can smudge the printed text or graphics by wiping a finger across the page. (H 5.2)

inoculation   The process of protecting a machine from viruses. (OS 3.3)

internal command   A command that is built into the command interpreter (COMMAND.COM) and does not exist as an executable file outside of it, such as DEL or DIR. (OS 1.3)

internal modem   A modem consisting of an expansion card that fits into the PC. It requires a resource assignment, which may come either from Plug and Play or from manual configuration. (H 1.8)

internal speed   The speed at which a CPU processes data inside its registers. (H 4.1)

interrupt request (IRQ) lines   Signals used by peripherals to interrupt or stop the CPU and demand attention. (H 1.4)

IPCONFIG and WINIPCFG   Utilities used to display Windows TCP/IP configuration information. (OS 4.1)

ISA (Industry Standard Architecture)   An old, nearly obsolete type of expansion slot in a motherboard. (H 1.9)

ISDN (Integrated Services Digital Network)   A digital type of phone line that can support two simultaneous 60Kbps data channels and one voice channel. (H 6.3)

ISP (Internet Service Provider)   A company that provides access to the Internet. (OS 4.2)

jumpers and DIP switches   Means of configuring various hardware options on the motherboard. (H 1.1)

L1 cache   The front-side cache holding data waiting to enter the CPU. (H 4.1)

L2 cache   The back-side cache holding data that has exited from the CPU. (H 4.1)

LBA (Logical Block Addressing)   A means of translating the locations on a hard disk into memory addresses the PC can understand, so that a larger hard disk can be addressed by the PC. (H 1.9)

legacy device   A device that is based on old technology and is not Plug-and-Play compatible, such as a non-PnP circuit board, an ISA board, or a device that connects to a COM port. (H 1.9, OS 2.4)

logical drive   An area of space within a partition mapped for use by the operating system and identified by a drive letter, such as C: or D:. (OS 1.4)

LVD (Low-Voltage Differential)   An improved SCSI technology resulting in higher maximum distances than SE. LVD is compatible with SE but reverts to the SE performance level when combined with it on a chain. (H 1.7)

master   An IDE drive responsible for managing data transfers for itself and the slave drive. (H 1.6)

memory address   The named hexadecimal address of a particular location in memory. The operating system uses memory addresses to keep track of what data is stored in what physical location with memory banks.

memory management   The methods used by the operating system to manage the transfer of information from storage on the hard disk to a place in RAM. (OS 1.1)

memory slots   Slots that hold the memory chips. (H 1.1)

MSD.EXE   A utility that can display information about the computer's memory, I/O ports, IRQs being used, and many other PC resources. (H 1.4)

MSDS (Material Safety Data Sheet)   A document that explains the best way to handle and dispose of a potentially environmentally hazardous chemical or piece of equipment. (H 3.3)

network interface card (NIC)   A computer peripheral card that allows the PC to communicate with a network. The NIC provides the physical interface between the computer and cabling. It prepares data, sends data, and controls the flow of data. It can also receive and translate data into bytes for the CPU to understand. (H 6.2, OS 4.1)

notification area   An alternative term for the System Tray, the area in the bottom-right corner of the Windows screen where the clock resides, along with icons for programs running in the background. (OS 1.1)

NTLDR   The bootstrap or startup file for NT-based Windows versions. It starts the loading of the operating system. (OS 1.2)

operating system   Software that takes charge of the computer in order to manage disk and file management, device access, memory management, input/output, and the user interface. (OS 1.1)

page description language   A language that describes a whole page being printed by sending commands that describe the text as well as the margins and other settings. (H 5.1)

paging file   The file used for virtual memory swapping on the hard disk. Also called the swap file. (OS 1.1)

paper transport assembly   The part of a printer responsible for moving the paper through the printer. It consists of a motor and several rubberized rollers that each perform a different function. (H 5.1)

parallel cable   A cable that carries data multiple bits at a time in a given direction. (H 1.5)

partition   A logical division of a physical hard disk, used to create separate drive letters. Also refers to the act of creating partitions. (OS 1.4)

passive terminator   A terminator that uses resistors to perform the termination. (H 1.7)

PC Card device   A small card, about the size of a thick credit card, that plugs into the side of a notebook PC and adds capabilities to it. Also called a PCMCIA device. The modern standard for such devices is called CardBus. (H 1.3)

PCI (Peripheral Connect Interface)   The modern standard for general-purpose expansion devices in a PC. (H 1.9)

Peripheral Component Interconnect (PCI)   An interconnection system that supports both 64-bit and 32-bit data paths, so it can be used in both 486 and Pentium-based systems. In addition, it is processor independent. The bus communicates with a special bridge circuit that communicates with both the CPU and the bus. (H 4.3)

Plug and Play   The technology that enables a PC and an operating system to automatically recognize certain types of hardware, including most peripheral devices. It installs the needed drivers for the hardware without user intervention. (H 1.8, OS 2.4)

port replicator   Roughly the same as a docking station, except it tends to be smaller and does not contain drive bays. (H 1.3)

POST (power on self-test)   A diagnostic program that runs when you turn on the computer. (H 2.1)

POST card   A circuit board that monitors the PC's boot process and displays a numeric code indicating the part of the boot process being executed. (H 2.1)

PPP (Point-to-Point Protocol)   A protocol used to allow computers to communicate over analog (standard telephone) lines. (OS 4.2)

printer controller circuitry   A large circuit board that converts signals from the computer into signals for the various assemblies in a laser printer. (H 5.1)

printer driver   A software component that allows an application to interface with the hardware of a printer. (H 5.2)

processor slot   A slot that permits the attachment of the CPU to the motherboard, allowing the CPU to use the other components of the system. (H 1.1)

protocol   A computer language. Examples of protocols are NetBEUI, IPX/SPX, and TCP/IP. (OS 4.1)

proxy server   A server that acts as an intermediary between a PC and the Internet, caching frequently used information and providing some security. (OS 4.2)

RAID (Redundant Array of Inexpensive Drives)   Methods of making several physical disks work together to create a single volume that has properties not possible on a single physical drive. (H 1.6)

Real mode   Sixteen-bit hardware access. (OS 2.3)

Registry   The hierarchical configuration database in Windows 9x/NT/2000, containing Windows initialization settings. It includes information about both the computer and the users on the system. For Windows 9x, it's contained in USER.DAT and SYSTEM.DAT. For Windows NT/2000/XP, it's contained in SAM, SECURITY, SYSTEM, SOFTWARE, and DEFAULT, plus NTUSER.DAT. (OS 1.2, 1.5)

resource conflict   A problem caused by two or more devices trying to use the same resource. (H 1.4)

ring   A topology in which each computer connects to two other computers, creating a unidirectional path where messages move in a circle from workstation to workstation. Each entity participating in the ring reads a message, then regenerates it, and hands it to its neighbor on a different network cable. (H 6.2)

riser board   A circuit board that connects to the motherboard and provides expansion slots (ISA, PCI), so the expansion boards can sit parallel to the motherboard. Common on NLX (low-profile or slimline) systems. (H 4.3)

RJ-11   A connector used to connect a two-pair wire to a receiving jack. The most common example of the RJ-11 connector is a standard telephone cord. (H 1.5)

RJ-45   The connector type used with UTP or STP cable for a 10/100BaseT network. The RJ-45 connector is the industry standard for Ethernet or Fast Ethernet networking. This four-pair connector allows a short network cable, known as a patch cable, to attach the computer to the wall jack. (H 1.5, 6.1)

routers   Highly intelligent devices that connect multiple network types and determine the best path for sending data. They can route packets across multiple networks and use routing tables to store network addresses to determine the best destination. (H 6.2)

Safe mode   A method of running Windows using a minimal set of system drivers. (OS 2.3)

SCSI-1   Small computer systems interface (SCSI) that supports data throughput up to 5Mbps. (H 1.7)

SCSI-2   The standard type of SCSI. Supports data throughput up to 10Mbps, with an 8-bit (narrow) or 16-bit (wide) bus width. (H 1.7)

SCSI-3   Also called Ultra SCSI. Supports data throughput up to 80Mbps with an 8-bit (narrow), 16-bit (wide bus) The wide bus supports speeds up to 160Mbps. (H 1.7)

SDSL (Synchronous DSL)   A type of DSL wherein the maximum upload and download speeds are the same. (H 6.3)

SE (Single-Ended)   The standard type of SCSI (including SCSI-1 and SCSI-2). (H 1.7)

serial cable   A cable that carries data one bit at a time in each direction. (H 1.5)

service   Software that allows a PC to receive and respond to requests from the network. (OS 4.1)

service information sources   Service manuals that can be used for troubleshooting. These manuals can come in several forms, such as booklets, readme files on the CD-ROM or floppy disks, and the manufacturer's website. In most cases, the most up-to-date information is on the website. (H 2.2)

Service Pack   A collection of updates to an operating system or application that bring it up to a certain update level. (OS 2.2)

sharing   The process of making a resource available for use by other PCs through a network. (OS 4.1)

signed driver   A driver that has been certified to work under a specific Windows version and has not been changed since is creation. (OS 2.4)

Single Inline Memory Module (SIMM)   An easily removable circuit board that contains RAM chips. SIMMs are either 8-bit, 30-pin or 32-bit, 72-pin. (H 4.2)

slave   A drive that shares a channel with the master and does not manage data transfers. It is totally reliant on the master drive for communication. (H 1.6)

social troubleshooting   The process of troubleshooting a problem by talking with end-users. (H 2.2)

SPP (Standard Printer Port)   A printer or parallel port setting that allows bidirectional communications and that can be used with older ink-jet and laser printers. (H 4.4)

SRAM (Static RAM)   A type of RAM that does not require constant electrical refreshing. (H 4.2)

stand-off   A spacer between the motherboard and the case floor, made of brass or plastic. (H 1.2)

star   A topology that branches each network device off a central hub, making it very easy to add a new workstation. If any workstation goes down, it does not affect the entire network. (H 6.2)

startup disk   A bootable disk (usually floppy) that contains startup files and utilities for troubleshooting and repair. It can be used to bring up a command prompt and access system utilities for MS-DOS or Windows 9x. (OS 2.3, 3.2)

STP (shielded twisted pair)   A type of cable consisting of two or more pairs of twisted wires that carry data with electrical pulses, surrounded by a metal mesh casing for EMI shielding. (H 6.1)

switches   Like hubs, devices used to link several computers together. Switches differ from hubs in a few important ways. As hubs do, switches repeat signals to the ports, with one exception: Rather than send network traffic to all ports, switches have enough intelligence to send the traffic directly to the port the packet was intended for. This reduces the work done by the OSI layers below the Network layer. (H 6.2)

Synchronous DRAM (SDRAM)   DRAM that is synchronized to the speed of the systems in which it is used (PC66 SDRAM runs at 66MHz, PC100 runs at 100MHz, PC133 runs at 133MHz, and so on). Synchronizing the speed of the systems prevents the address bus from having to wait for the memory because of different clock speeds. (H 4.2)

system board   The spine of the computer, also called the motherboard. This component is made of green or brown fiberglass and is placed in the bottom or side of the case. (H 1.1)

system files   Files used to load the operating system, including its graphic interface and other system components. (OS 2.3)

terminal adapter   A device that helps connect to a broadband digital Internet service. In functionality it is like an external modems, but unlike a modem it is pure digital, with no conversion to or from analog. (H 1.8)

terminator   A device placed at each end of a chain of devices. It tells the controller that there are no other devices on the chain by creating an electrical short. (H 1.7)

toner cartridge   The printer component that holds the toner. Toner is a black, carbon substance mixed with polyester resins and iron oxide. In most cases, the toner cartridge contains a medium called the developer, the print drum, and a cleaning blade. (H 5.1)

transfer corona assembly   A laser-printer assembly that is charged with a high-voltage electrical charge and that carries toner from the photosensitive drum onto the paper. When the laser writes the images on the photosensitive drum, the toner sticks to the exposed areas. The transfer corona assembly charges the paper, which pulls the toner from the photosensitive drum. (H 5.1)

troubleshooting   The process of determining what is wrong with a machine and then taking steps to solve the problem. (OS 3.1)

TSR (Terminate and Stay Resident) program   A program that loads into memory but is not active unless needed. (OS 3.3)

UltraDMA   An operating mode for IDE hard disks that conforms to the ATA-4 standard and higher, allowing high-speed data access (33MBps to 100MBps). (H 1.6)

update   A newer version of a piece of software. Upgrades generally have new features and must be purchased, but updates are usually free and are provided to fix problems or improve performance. (OS 2.4)

upgrade   An installation of a newer or more feature-rich version of existing software that preserves existing settings. (OS 2.2)

Upgrade Wizard   A utility in the Setup program for Windows 2000/XP that examines the current Windows installation and determines whether there will be any hardware or software compatibility problems in upgrading. (OS 2.2)

USB (Universal Serial Bus)   A high-speed, hot-pluggable serial interface used for connecting external peripherals to a PC. USB is the fastest growing interface type at this time. The flexibility of the device architecture provides manufacturers with a high-speed chainable port system that is easy to configure. USB devices can be chained with the use of hubs, allowing up to 32 devices to be connected to one port. The transfer rate is also very good, with a maximum throughput of 4Mbps. (H 1.5, 1.8)

UTP (unshielded twisted pair)   A type of cable consisting of two or more pairs of twisted wires that carry data with electrical pulses. Does not have EMI shielding. (H 6.1)

virtual machine   A separate computing space created by an operating system to run an application separate from the rest of the system. (OS 1.1)

virtual memory   An area of the hard disk set aside for simulating additional RAM by swapping data into and out of the real RAM. (OS 1.1)

virus   A self-replicating program that "infects" files on a computer. Viruses can be harmless, or they can be extremely destructive. (OS 3.3)

voltage regulator module (VRM)   A device on a motherboard that can adjust the voltage provided to the CPU, to accommodate different CPUs. (H 4.1)

VxD   A Windows virtual device driver. (OS 3.1)

wildcard   A character that stands for other characters. An asterisk (*) stands for any number of characters; a question mark (?) stands for any single character. (OS 1.3)

Windows component   A part of the operating system that can be individually installed or uninstalled. (OS 2.1)

working directory   The place where an application stores files it creates during the course of its operation. This is the application's "cubicle." (OS 3.3)

Index

Project Management Skills for all Levels

Project Management JumpStart™
By Kim Heldman
ISBN: 0-7821-4214-1
US $24.99

Project *Management JumpStart* gives you the solid grounding you need to approach a career in project management with confidence.

◆ The basic skills of a successful project manager

◆ Creating project schedules and determining project budgets

◆ Winning the support of department managers

◆ Monitoring project progress, resources, and budgets

◆ Communication and negotiation skills

PMP®: Project Management Professional Study Guide
By Kim Heldman
ISBN: 0-7821-4106-4
US $59.99

Whether you're looking to advance your career as a project manager or simply strengthen your business skills foundation, the highly respected PMP certification from the Project Management Institute is the credential you need to succeed in today's competitive marketplace.

◆ More comprehensive than any other PMP exam prep package

◆ In-depth coverage of all official PMP exam objectives

◆ Project management case studies included to provide real-world insights

PMP: Project Management Professional Workbook
By Claudia Baca and Patti Jansen
ISBN: 0-7821-4240-0
US $34.99

Here's the one-of-a-kind book that will give you hands-on experience as you prepare for the PMP exam. This Sybex Workbook provides:

◆ Clear introductions that put the exercises in context and explain the importance of key project management skills

◆ Dozens of exercises designed by two veteran project managers to correlate directly with PMP objectives

◆ Cross-references to Sybex's PMP Study Guide for additional instructional content

SYBEX®

www.sybex.com

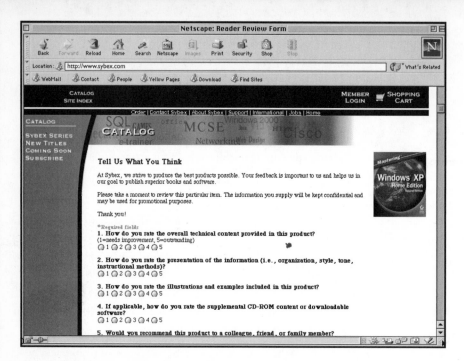